Let My People Go

Immense restraint has been shown in South Africa by the African people in the face of continuous provocation, a restraint largely due to the influence of Albert Luthuli, whose greatness was acknowledged by the award of the Nobel Peace Prize.

Grandson of a Zulu chief, he became a schoolmaster, local chief, and finally President of the pan-African organisation, the African National Congress. His stand on public affairs led to imprisonment on several occasions.

A Christian whose religion has had a profound effect on his activities, Albert Luthuli once said, "I am in Congress precisely because I am a Christian."

ALBERT LUTHULI

Let My People Go

AN AUTOBIOGRAPHY

Introduction by
Charles Hooper

Collins
FOUNT PAPERBACKS

First published 1962
First issued in Fontana Books 1963
First issued in Fontana Paperbacks 1982
Thirteenth impression April 1987

Copyright © Albert Luthuli 1962

Made and printed in Great Britain by
William Collins Sons & Co. Ltd, Glasgow

This book was prepared for publication
by Charles and Sheila Hooper

The front and back cover photographs are
reproduced by courtesy of *Drum Magazine*

To Mother Africa, so long in fetters;
To all who love her and strive to set her free;
And to two noble women of Africa:
Mtonya, my late mother, and Nokukhanya, my wife,
To whom, under God, I am most deeply indebted.

CONTENTS

ILLUSTRATIONS

INTRODUCTION BY CHARLES HOOPER

It is not easy to discern who at this moment might speak with full authority for South Africa's ten million Africans. Africans have always been denied the right to signify their choice by voting on the country's affairs. White rulers have throughout our history fostered all signs of hostility and jealousy between Africans, though they have never so blatantly and ruthlessly as at present divided in order to rule. Furthermore, no African organisation has successfully penetrated all sections of African society. It is to this day just conceivable that there are, on white farms and in remote reserves, Africans who have never heard of Chief Luthuli—or, for that matter, of Dr. Verwoerd.

Nevertheless, there has so far been at least one African organisation—the now banned African National Congress—with some claim to being comprehensive: the best claim, at least. The Pan-African Congress, which for a while commanded world attention as the result of police shootings at Sharpeville, was, at the time of its suppression in 1960, of recent origin; and it appears to have had only a small following drawn exclusively from a few cities and towns. When it was forced—on the surface, anyway—into premature retirement, it had conducted no political campaign to a successful conclusion, and it had thrown up no leaders seasoned in the conflict. It had yet to prove itself.

The African National Congress, on the other hand, had for many years been the largest anti-apartheid, anti-supremacist organisation in the country. It could claim a following drawn from city, town and country, from peasants and professionals, from chiefs and labourers, from the mature and from the young. It could claim experience. It could claim to have achieved, latterly, effective liaison with groups other than African—with Indians, Europeans and (on occasion) Coloured people—all of whom regarded it as the spearhead of resistance. It could not, unfortunately for South Africa, claim to have fashioned the machinery necessary for running itself in a country so large, and in face of persistent Government and police interference, obstruction and persecution.

Unchallenged at the head of the African National Congress,

for the roughest and most heartbreaking ten years in South African political life hitherto, stood Albert John Luthuli. Placed there by the vote of his own Congress, and accepted by organisations of other races willing to co-operate, the ex-chief deposed by Dr. Verwoerd became head of something more than a mission reserve. He became, his stature and influence growing yearly, leader of the real opposition, embracing South Africans of all complexion. As far as there is, or ever has been, an embodiment both of the African people and of the multi-racial resistance to apartheid and supremacy, it is to be found in Chief Luthuli.

The impact which the Chief makes at first encounter is difficult to analyse. One is aware of an impact; but no quality, unless it be that of charming and generous warmth, stands out. His character, his temperament, his qualities and his stature reveal themselves discursively, and only as they unfold does one begin to grasp the striking wholeness of the man, his coherence and his integrity. A mind is at work; but never merely academically, never without imagination. Imagination is at work; but never without restraint and discipline, never engaged in fantasy, and never at the expense of truth. Restraint and discipline are there; but they issue neither in inflexibility nor in untoward austerity. No quality stands out by itself, each balances the others, and all go to the making of a man at whose centre is greatness of heart.

On one occasion Chief Luthuli and his wife visited us briefly—a small, purely domestic occasion—at a seaside cottage. The African tenants on that property and on adjacent lands, illiterate and pitiful people for the most part, got word that a chief was there, though few had ever seen one in their lives. They gathered outside and then asked permission to enter in order to pay their respects. Chief Luthuli received them. Until then we had known the leader of the resistance. Now we watched a man who knew the woes of landless squatters. He discovered each of them as an individual; he inquired after children and absent relations; and he gave them, quite unconsciously, a glimpse of dignity and composure, of some glory departed. They went away comforted: some with tears in their eyes, but nevertheless comforted.

It was not the occasion. It was the stature of the man they had met. Somehow, within his person, Chief Luthuli reconciles a multitude of men—peasant, townsman and squatter, scholar and student, chief and subject, greybeard and angry young man, men of the new Africa and men of the old.

A year after this minor incident one of the squatters whom the Chief had met was evicted by white landowners. He had been born on the property, but white conquest had turned all Africans there into squatters. His eviction, in the context of South African laws, at once made it illegal for this man and his family to be *anywhere*: squatting elsewhere was unlawful, and neither reserve nor city would have him. Even out on the road, where he found himself with his wife, children, pots and pans, he was liable to arrest for vagrancy. There was no legal answer, nowhere to go.

When we told the Chief this story he remembered the man, even remembered that he was an epileptic. He must have heard many similar hard-luck stories—the country abounds in them; yet he flinched as he listened; and his first reaction was not to the intolerable injustice of the "case", but to the plight of the man and his children. There was anger over the perverse cruelty of Nationalist laws and over the white landowners' failure to envisage the consequences of their actions in human terms; but anger came after compassion. Nor was the compassion mere sentiment: the Chief immediately set about trying to do something to help the homeless epileptic whom he had met only once, a year earlier.

Compassion is a part of Chief Luthuli's habitual way of looking at people. Its obverse is a large sense of comedy, an unquenchable delight in people. Yet, for all the ease of his rich, joyous laughter, and his quick pity, there is a detachment about people too: not from them, but about them, whether friend or foe. It is as though something in him holds aloof, subject neither to the sudden partisanships of the emotions, nor to bitterness and resentment. About the policy, the act of cruelty, or the vicious law, he is ruthless and can be formidably angry; but he refuses to assault the personalities of the men behind these things.

It may be that it is this detachment, coupled with his gifts of imagination, which accounts for Chief Luthuli's extraordinary power of entering the minds and emotions of other people. He is capable of understanding the Afrikaner dilemma with far greater clarity than most of their English-speaking fellow-whites; and the quaint, backward-looking Englishry of Natal is more explicable to Luthuli than it is to Dr. Verwoerd. His imagination falters only when the mental state of his opponents enters the world of shadow: "I can understand and disagree with the man who says, 'I want five farms.' But I cannot grasp what is in his mind when he says, 'I would rather murder or be shot than surrender *one* of them.'"

Yet Chief Luthuli's perception of the maladies which ail South Africans of various race does not deflect him. For instance, the fact that white South Africans see in the idea of universal adult suffrage a terrifying threat evokes in him the desire to reassure them; but he continues, with a kind of serene assurance, to demand universal adult suffrage regardless of race.

The Chief's assurance has about it something paradoxical. It is far removed from the ruthless political bigotry of his more notable opponents and their adherents. It is the assurance of a man who, now in his sixties, is still exploring, who is still open to humane and reasoned argument, and who thinks it no indignity to learn from the shrewd wisdom of peasants and the insights of the young. He will come in and say, "There, now! A worker I met at the bus stop has just told me something I never knew about soil-erosion!" Or, "Think twice, Ismail. Don't dismiss that white fellow's argument too lightly, just because he was angry." I think the paradox is this: the assurance is so deeply grounded in intellectual humility that it is not possible to distinguish one from the other. Neither quality would be there but for the other. Assurance without arrogance, and the humility of a man who cannot be humiliated: this is a rare combination. "Nationalistic laws seek to degrade us. We do not consent. They degrade the men who frame them. They injure us—that is something different."

Assurance and humility stand the Chief and his country in good stead, as do other of his qualities: resilience, youthfulness of spirit, undauntable courage, wisdom, tolerance, charity, a zest for living, patience. If there is one quality, usually associated with leadership, which he lacks, it is ambition. There is behind him no struggle for power, and within him no determination to rule in person.

But above all, perhaps, Chief Luthuli is a great patriot, the greatest in a country not altogether devoid of true patriotism. Few whites can even glimpse this. To white South Africa (with exceptions—eminent names such as Jan Hofmeyer, Alan Paton and Margaret Ballinger come easily to mind, but there are others) patriotism has come to mean allegiance to a white group waited on by black helots. When Luthuli speaks, one is aware of his profound concern for South Africans, invariably men of all races, of his appreciation of the teeming cities, the farms, the crowded reserves and the look of the land, and of his love for Mother Africa and her troubled peoples.

The Verwoerd Government's reply to the challenge of this man has been to remove him. His third ban, a five-year one, is not half run. He lives in a politically indifferent area, to which the ban confines him. Policemen knock on his door at odd hours: "Where is Luthuli?" They dog him wherever he goes, tap his telephone, open his mail, inspect his visitors.

The orator's voice is silenced. When he was banned in 1959, the Chief was part of the way through a tour of a nature quite unprecedented in South Africa. His modest account of it, towards the end of this book, gives little hint of its true significance. For the first time, whites were crowding to hear what an African leader had to say, a few Nationalists among them; and some were coming away with a new faith in South Africa, new doubts about the course followed for so long by successive White governments, and a maimed belief in the African bogey. Naturally it became imperative for the Nationalists to silence him. He is, for their purposes, quite the most unfortunate embodiment of African aspirations which the African people could have found— an incorruptible, fearless and altogether unfrightening crusader.

Today the mood is changing. The negotiations are over. Dr. Verwoerd proclaims the Afrikaner republic with the country on what the newspapers call a "war-footing". In one of their aims— whether conscious or not, there is no knowing—the Nationalists have succeeded. The sanest men are bound; and out of South Africa's complexity the ruling minority have wrought a situation in which black and white are at last lining up in tense opposition. Formerly the white determination was to ride the patient beast; now there is a mounting desire to fight him. Not all matadors survive.

For Africans the choice narrows down rapidly to servitude or death. That is what the "war-footing" proclaims. The army has been described by a Cabinet Minister as an instrument only secondarily designed to protect South Africa's frontiers; its primary function is "to shoot down the black masses".

In face of this sort of threat, and deprived of their leaders by one means and another, what will the African people do? For how long will they continue to be approachable? Chief Luthuli's influence, despite his banishment, is still strong. He still represents the African wish to bring about a newly ordered South Africa peacefully, without bloodshed or unnecessary dislocation. The offer is still open.

But every week brings change. The African people are now confronted finally by the inflexible refusal of the Government to compromise—the outcome of the Commonwealth Prime Ministers' Conference demonstrated this at home as nothing else has. They are confronted by an impossible choice: voluntary subjection or enforced subjection. They are confronted by the flat, toneless denial of every single thing which Chief Luthuli demands in the name of his people.

If this situation is allowed to continue unabated—and it shows no sign of abating—how long will it be before the Union's African people are seeking a new embodiment of new wishes? How long before, out of the depths, they cry, "If the man of peace does not prevail, give us the men of blood"?

PREFACE

This book is the outcome, after long hesitation on my part, of the urging of a number of my friends. It is true that in the last thirty years I have been increasingly identified with the movement of resistance against oppression by white supremacy in South Africa, until now I find myself at its head. Nevertheless, I regard my life as one among many, and my role in the resistance as one among many. If I have anything to say, it is not because of any particular distinction, but because I am identified with those who love South Africa, and will resist with them the attempt to smash a noble land with base and ignoble doctrines, and sub-human practices.

Among the many friends who have encouraged me to write this book—and had they not implanted the idea, it would not have been written—it fell to Charles and Sheila Hooper to deliver the final blow to my reluctance. When they approached me for material for a biography which they intended to write, I asked them to undertake what has probably proved a far harder task. I asked them to become my amanuenses. They willingly agreed to this, and they have persisted with it in spite of the fact that my unforeseen five months in detention protracted the term of their labour.

Our manner of writing was this. Each of the Hoopers made independent records as I dictated to them what I had to say. Out of these records they compiled a first draft of the book, arranged—I fear it was not thus dictated—chronologically. To this draft I added my afterthoughts, occasional corrections, and this preface.

I record here my gratitude and indebtedness to them both. Before I met them I had heard of them, in connection with the upheavals over passes for African women in the Zeerust district. I met them long before the possibility of this book was broached, and out of our first meeting there has grown up a deep and abiding friendship, born of a common outlook in facing the tragedy threatening our common homeland, and a common belief in the relevance of the Christian faith to our problems and needs, however complex.

15

It may be noticed that names, which might have been expected in a book of this type, do not appear. The reason for this is not churlishness on my part, or lack of the desire to give honour where it is due. But the roll of men and women who fight valiantly in the cause of freedom and justice is a long one; and in a book addressed to readers outside as well as in South Africa, it has been necessary at times to deal briefly with matters predominantly domestic in their interest. If I have done injustice to any, I ask pardon, and I point out that this book is in part dedicated to them. But the last impression I wish to create is that their role is minor, while mine is major. Indeed, the reverse is true. As I look back I accuse myself of having contributed too little.

May God's Will, holy and perfect, be done in South Africa, the dearly loved land whose children we all are.

1. *The home of my fathers*

At about the time when the Battle of Waterloo brought to an end the turbulent and disruptive career of the Emperor Napoleon, a man of similar ambition came to power in far-off and little-known Zululand. In a brief twelve-year reign, Shaka, undoubtedly the greatest of the Zulu kings, welded a number of bickering clans into a strong united nation.

Shaka achieved the feat of creating the Zulu nation by methods which were sometimes ruthless. All the same, his occasional ruthlessness was minor in comparison with that of modern dictators, and it was seldom, if ever, as calculated and sub-human as theirs.

Shaka has been much maligned by white South African historians. His outlook was that of his day, and when that is taken into account, and when all that can be said to his discredit has been said, this king of legendary physique emerges as a brilliant general, and a ruler of great courage, intelligence and ability. Without the moral support of any precedent, he had the strength to withstand (and on occasion to expose) the power exerted over his people by wizards. His reorganisation of his army was enough to make it in his time the mightiest military force in Africa.

Nevertheless, Shaka did violate some of the customs of his people, and this was his undoing. In particular, he over-used his army, allowing his soldiers little time for the normal pursuits of peace. As the years passed, his ambitions got the better of him. That he could be despotic was probably no great matter, but his people expected their king to temper this with benevolence. Shaka's rule grew harsher. Finally, he estranged himself from his people by setting up as an unqualified dictator. For a time his subjects submitted to arbitrary rule as loyally as they could. In the end, however, Shaka went the way of most tyrants. Even his army appears to have connived at his assassination by his half-brother, Dingane. The extent to which he had forfeited the allegiance of his subjects is seen in that no murmur was raised against his assassins. Shaka died unmourned by the nation which he had raised out of obscurity.

Dingane succeeded him, inheriting a kingdom which extended from Swaziland to the Transkei, and from the Drakensberg range to the Indian Ocean.

Within this realm, far to the south of the royal capital and fifty miles beyond the Tugela river, a small party of English traders had been admitted in the time of Shaka. They formed a tiny settlement in the neighbourhood of what is now Durban. For the moment they were allowed to remain there by permission of the Zulu monarch, a community in whose fortunes neither the Zulus nor the white government at the Cape were notably interested.

Europe was recovering from Napoleon. The Cape was pre-occupied with the beginnings of the Trek and with frontier wars against the amaXhosa. Zululand was recovering from the later years of Shaka. Nobody at that time can have had any idea of what the coming of the whites to Natal was going to mean by way both of gain and of loss. Still hidden in the future lay both the rape of Zululand and the impact of Western enlightenment.

For a time after Dingane's accession the white settlement consisted as in Shaka's time of a handful of traders, hunters and adventurers. The first appearance of a more benign element occurred in 1835. In that year the Church followed Trade—for the time being the Flag hung back.

In January 1835 a British Naval Commander, Captain Allen Francis Gardiner, arrived in Natal. He had abandoned his career to come to work among the Zulus as a missionary pioneer. He was received by Dingane, and attempted to explain his strange mission to the Zulu monarch and his advisers. In the end he was told that the Zulus had no desire to learn his doctrine, but that he would be welcome to stay among them if he would teach them how to use the barrel-loading musket. Gardiner declined. Nevertheless, he was ultimately made *induna*, or headman, of Durban, which at that time the Zulus regarded as an outlying kraal. Then, in return for services in this capacity, he was given permission to found the first mission station[1] north of the Tugela river.

In the meantime, independently, the American Board of Commissioners for Foreign Missions sent their first three men into the area. In the middle of January 1836 they arrived at Dingane's capital, where they were received "with the utmost kindness and attention". They formed a high opinion of the people. "We think," one of them wrote home, "the Zoolahs have two most remarkable traits of character for a heathen community, honesty and chastity. . . . So far as safety is concerned, with what I know of the Zoolahs, I would sooner trust a

[1] It was called kwaNginani—"Lo, I am with you."

18

sister or wife alone, for days and nights, than in my own country."
Later in the year one of them, the Rev. George Champion, began
work at kwaNginani. The other two, Dr. Newton Adams and
the Rev. Aldin Grout, gave their attention, for the time being, to
those Zulus (about 3000) who had collected in the neighbourhood
of the white settlement farther south.

Some time after this Grout left his work near Durban and,
after failing to gain a foothold deep in Zululand, settled near the
Umvoti river. Here he built his mission station, on a site today
known as Groutville or, more officially, the Umvoti Mission
Reserve.

Groutville is my home, and the home of my fathers.

From the time he began his labours here across the Umvoti,
Grout's missionary work began to show results. Before long it
was obvious that Groutville was turning into a developing
Christian community. One of the reasons for this was the intimacy of the relationship between missionary and people—an
intimacy which has lamentably fallen away in more recent
years.

The number of converts was initially small. But because the
Christian life was being lived *in the midst* of the people, they
had the chance to inspect and assess it over an indefinite period.
An increasing number came to accept the truth of Christianity
as time went on, while even those who did not accept it could
see a part of its value and respect it. The attitude of the neighbouring chiefs was benign. They saw and allowed the development of this new society among their people.

The revolution which Christianity brought into the lives of
converts was profound, as can perhaps be imagined. Conversion
meant an entirely new way of life, a new outlook, a new set of
beliefs—the creation, almost, of a new kind of people. They were
still Zulus to the backbone—that remained unchanged except
for a few irrelevant externals. But they were Christian Zulus,
not heathen Zulus, and conversion affected their lives to the
core.

The standard of early converts was high. A few members of
the original Groutville Christian community did revert to
heathen ways, the main reason being their desire to contract
customary unions. But on the whole it would seem that the early
converts lived closer to the tenets of their faith than many of
their descendants do now.

If this is true it has possibly come about because missionaries
have too easily become "supervisors of Native work", no longer
identified enough with their people. Moreover, that missionaries
are not usually representative of whites, and closer contact with

most whites who claim to be Christians has brought disillusionment.[2]

But the worst impediment to the spread of Christianity and the maintenance of early standards nowadays is not even the fact that many white Christians are unwilling to practise what they profess. It is the recent glorification of the past, and the cry by the present Government (with legislation to match) that Africans should "develop along their own lines". That, indeed, corrupts Christian standards. The effort currently being made to pour us back into the mould of nineteenth-century African tribalism is detrimental to our advancement and to Christianity.

Augmented by a number of fugitives from the rule of a few anti-Christian chiefs farther north, the community grew, and with this growth came the need to have somebody in charge of secular affairs. In theory—Zulu theory, anyway—the local chief was in charge. In practice he tolerantly left the new community with its Christian ethos largely to its own devices, until Grout went to him and asked him to appoint a chieftain over Groutville.

Since the first man thus appointed was ill-attuned to the needs and customs of the new community, the arrangement came to an early end. The experiment was instructive, all the same, for when Grout asked for a new appointment to be made, the chief this time recommended a Groutville Christian for the office.

Among the few people who had shared Grout's ups and downs was one man who had probably joined up with him soon after his arrival in Natal. This man, Ntaba Luthuli, was my grandfather, and it was he who became Groutville's second head. I know little about him but, according to Church records, he and his wife, Titisi, were Grout's first two converts to Christianity. Both were zealous Christians whom, as the founders of the Luthuli Christian line, I deeply honour.

One of the few anecdotes which I recall about him suggests that on relations between Church and State he was basically sound. Being a deacon (elder) of the Groutville congregation, he was asked, at a time of war between the Zulus and the British, to pray for the success of the Queen's forces. The prayer stuck in

---

[2] It is interesting, in passing, to notice how clearly the three pioneer American Board missionaries foresaw the danger. Writing in 1836, they said: The present is a favourable moment. . . . Seize it now when it can be done, and dig deep and lay the foundations well, before the ten thousand evil influences, arising from the increase of whites here, shall poison the minds of chief and people, and retard the work for many, many years.

Ntaba's throat. "O God," he prayed eventually, "protect the victims of whoever is the aggressor in this war!"

Partly (no doubt) because of his gifts of diplomacy, Ntaba remained at the head of Groutville affairs until his death. First his cousin, and then later my uncle, Martin, succeeded to the office. The interesting thing about Martin's appointment is that it was, contrary to older Zulu custom, the occasion of a definite popular choice by the community. There was another candidate for the office, and the choice between the two was made by election in a democratic manner. I might add that, although four out of Groutville's seven chiefs have been Luthulis, my family has never laid claim to any hereditary rights. The people of Groutville have found democratic methods effective and satisfactory. They have used these processes not only to elect chiefs but on two occasions to replace them when their rule was felt to be not in the community's interest. This has the advantage that the tribe need never chafe under harsh rule, the standard of rule must be reasonably high, chiefs need not fear the more traditional elimination by assassination or revolt, and the people understand the process fully.

In the time of Martin Luthuli's chieftainship the Groutville community became more clearly established. Relationships between the Reserve and the Colonial Administration became more fully defined, land boundaries were marked, and independence from surrounding non-Christian communities was accepted. The *abasemakholweni* (converts) were a people in their own right, a small settlement of peasant farmers eking out a modest existence on the soil. The authorities of the time accepted such mission settlements as examples to be encouraged. Recently, however, the attitude has altered. In some areas their line of development has been reversed by the Government. Whatever motive inspires the Nationalist desire to return to the primitive, it is certain that they knowingly and deliberately destroy missionary influence in a heartbreaking way. Perhaps that *is* their motive.

In 1921 Josiah Mqebu succeeded Martin Luthuli as chief; and in 1935 I was elected to follow Josiah.

2. *A Christian upbringing*

My father, John Luthuli, was the second son of Ntaba, and thus the younger brother of Martin. Since he died when I was about six months old, I have no recollections of him at all.

My mother, Mtonya, upon whom fell the main burden of my upbringing, spent a part of her childhood in the Royal Kraal of King Cetewayo, a descendant of Dingane, in Zululand. It came about in this way. In the Zululand of the last century there existed a custom whereby important members of the tribe would, in paying their respects to the king, offer him the custody of children. (The nearest European parallel to this which I know of was the practice of "adopting" pages into courts of medieval Europe.) My mother's mother was a child transferred from her own family to Cetewayo's court in this manner. For all practical purposes she became thenceforward a part of the royal house, enjoying the status of a king's daughter.

In the course of time Cetewayo gave her in marriage to a man whom he desired to honour, Mnqiwu Gumede, and my mother was a child of this marriage. When she was past childbearing my grandmother was given leave, in accordance with accepted custom, to return to her home—that is, the royal court. Her younger daughter, Mtonya, went with her to minister to her needs.

But the old lady seemed to have been of a restless and adventurous disposition. She found her life circumscribed, and court routine dull. She resolved to leave Zululand and, bringing my mother with her, she crossed into Natal and settled in Groutville with her husband's cousins. Had her flight been discovered before she crossed the Tugela, she might well have paid with her life.

Before her marriage to my father in Groutville, Mtonya became a Christian and lived for a while within the mission precincts. There she learned to read, and to her life's end she was a fluent, devoted and assiduous reader of the Bible in the vernacular. Curiously, she never learned to write nor to decipher longhand script.

Some time after their marriage my father left Natal with a group of young Europeans from neighbouring New Guelderland and went to Rhodesia. This was the time of the Matabele Rebellion—as it is called—and my father went to serve in some

22

capacity with the Rhodesian forces. I can do no more than speculate about the attractions which this venture held for him—probably he was young and curious, and felt like a change.

When hostilities ended he stayed on, attached to a Seventh Day Adventist mission near Bulawayo as an evangelist and interpreter. At this stage my mother, who in the meanwhile had suffered the death of one of her two sons, took the remaining son, Alfred, and dutifully went up into the unknown to join my father. I was born a while later on Rhodesian soil. My father died not long after my birth, and his mortal remains lie buried at Solusi Mission, about thirty miles from Bulawayo.

I cannot be precise about the date of my birth, but I calculate that I was born in the year 1898, and certainly before 1900. My recollections of early years spent in Rhodesia are few and vague. I can remember the cemetery where my father lies buried, and I recall my brother Alfred's marriage and the building of his home.

Two incidents, however, stand out with sharp clarity, and they both concern discipline. On one occasion my mother sent me on an errand. I dallied by the way, and she came upon me playing happily with twigs and stones in the sand. (My mother, I should explain, came of Qwabe stock, a clan renowned for its strict discipline.) I had what was probably my first taste of Qwabe discipline that day, and I can remember at this moment the feel of the leathering my mother gave me with one of my twigs. Not going when sent ceased abruptly to be one of my habits.

My mother dealt decisively with another of my infringements of her code. It seems that I contracted the habit of hanging around the home of my playmates—some of them little white boys—when they were being fed, and of cadging part of their food. Unknown to me, my mother came to hear of this. She made no immediate mention of it.

One evening I came to the end of what had seemed an ordinary meal of sweet-potatoes.

"Thank you, Mother," I said, "I am satisfied. The food was good." I began to sidle away.

"No, my boy, no." My mother recalled me and placed before me a fresh helping of food. "You are far from satisfied. You are a hungry child. You are not properly fed at home, your mother neglects you and you have to beg from the neighbours. Eat now!"

My mother came and stood over me while I addressed myself of necessity to more sweet-potatoes. I ate my way into them falteringly. Each hesitation was rewarded by a light flick from a cane, and only when I was ready to choke over another mouthful did the lesson end. I got the point.

The Seventh Day Adventists wanted to begin missionary activities in Natal. They asked my brother to return in order to act as their interpreter. Round about 1908 or 1909, in consequence, we left Rhodesia and returned to what was soon to become the Union of South Africa. We paid a short visit to Groutville and then left for the Vryheid district of Northern Natal. Here we stayed on the farm of a white adherent of the Seventh Day Adventists. My brother took up his duties. I tended the mission mules—there were no schooling facilities.

It was my mother who rescued me from my intimacy with mules. She decided that I needed education and sent me back home to Groutville to get it.

Here I became a member of the household of my uncle, Martin, who was by this time the chief of Groutville. As can be imagined, I did not see much of him. His life was taken up by the affairs of the community. He had a constant stream of visitors, but of course their comings and goings took place well beyond my horizons—the courtesies demanded that when adults came, children disappeared. And the village deliberations, which were conducted in the traditional Zulu manner in the open, were not any affair of a child.

Nevertheless, my uncle did not ignore my existence. I recall with a glow how he assigned to me the special task of preparing his fire each evening, and how he said to me once: "Son, I have not been cold since you came!"

Sometimes the cleavage between village affairs and those of the household disappeared. One incident, indelibly engraved on my memory, brought the trials of chieftainship into the house with a rush. A furious woman entered, hotly pursued by her husband. My uncle and an adviser found themselves in the middle of a "civil case" before they knew it had begun.

"She has deserted me!" shouted the man, throwing overboard all pretence at manners. "Look at her! There she stands in the very clothes I have provided!"

This was the last straw for the deserting woman. She stripped herself completely naked, rolled her clothing into a bundle, and threw it at the man. To cap it all, my uncle and his *induna* bolted from the scene like terrified horses. It was a revelation to us children—that a woman could make a chief run.

Had the household been a European one, I should probably have been lonely, since my cousins, Martin's daughters, were all grown up. But, as is frequent in African society, my uncle and aunt were the guardians and caretakers of various children and relatives, and I had company enough, particularly that of a girl-cousin, Charlotte. It was a secure and happy household, and the

24

moving spirit in purely domestic affairs was naturally my aunt. She was a woman of deep piety, very prominent in church affairs. In her dealings with the children of the house she did not distinguish in one detail between her own children and the children of relatives, either in discipline or in care. Largely because of her influence, the home was conducted as a Christian home should be. Although there was no formal religious teaching at home— this was dealt with in church—family prayers in the evening were as invariable as supper.

The children took their part in the routine work of the household. This was not irksome, and there was no great labour in it. Apart from making my uncle's fire each evening, I was allotted such tasks as fetching water—for in Groutville the traditional Zulu distinction between male and female work tended to disappear. Over the weekends I did a certain amount of weeding in the lands, and herding.

All the time, unconsciously, I was busy absorbing the Christian ethos of home, and church congregation, and the social ethos of the community. As in earlier times, it was still (as it is today) a mixed community of heathens and Christians, of relatively well-educated people, and people with no literacy at all. Looking back, I realise that I was aware at the time of the distinction between Christian and non-Christian. But a fortunate feature of Groutville life was the fact that distinction did not mean discrimination. Somehow, we did not imbibe with our faith the sense that "Christians are better". In spite of great differences of education and outlook, Groutville has managed to throw up no élite cut off from the ordinary life of the village.[1]

During this early phase of my life in Groutville my mother and my brother and his family came home permanently. They severed their connection with the Adventists and returned to the Congregational Church as in former years. On the family site which had been occupied by Ntaba, a new house was built. I left the home of my Uncle Martin, and for the rest of the time until I went away to boarding-school I lived in the care of my mother.

Being a child, I did not then realise the extent to which my mother laboured to ensure my education. I saw her then as an extremely industrious woman. She was diligent about her small fields—a very successful vegetable gardener. In addition to her

[1] I think this is greatly to the credit of Groutville as far as education is concerned. In this field it has produced a distinguished little group—a university lecturer, an eminent editor, the first African head of a training institution with a staff of mixed race, and the first Zulu woman graduate.

work on her fields, the lack of ready cash and the lack of capital to work the whole of the land, forced her to walk regularly five or six miles to Stanger, the nearest European settlement, in order to earn a few shillings washing clothes—a far cry from the royal household of King Cetewayo. When she had earned what she could, she returned to her garden. Over the years, although my uncle helped now and again, the sweat of her brow provided nine-tenths of my education.

Since one of my brothers died before my birth, and the other was grown up and married, I was virtually an only child. Yet my mother's discipline did not waver any more than her devotion did—a thing for which I am deeply thankful, because without discipline I suppose I might easily have turned out a spoilt mother's boy.

In 1914, having reached Standard 4 in the Groutville school, I continued my education at the Ohlange Institute—a boarding-school. This school had been founded by Dr. Dube, and at the time when I went to Ohlange he was its principal.

As it happened, I was there for only two terms, so I cannot say that the school made any particular impression on me. War-time conditions, which brought a shortage of food to Africans, made life somewhat rough-and-tumble after the disciplined courtesy of Groutville. I remember that it was risky to close one's eyes during the grace before meals—the food might disappear before one opened them. The monitors who brought food from the kitchen generally needed guarding.

I remember how Dr. Dube dealt with complaints from the boys about the quality and quantity of the food. "Well, boys," he said, "times are hard. Would you like me to return your fees[2] and then you can look after yourselves?" The boys regarded the principal's dilemma and left it at that.

At the end of the year, having passed my examinations, I was transferred (my uncle had intended this all along) to a Methodist institution at Edendale, near Pietermaritzburg. It was at Edendale, I think, that I began to wake up and look about me.

That is to say, I woke up and looked about after I had run the gauntlet of initiation. I had already encountered this at Ohlange, but there I was relatively protected by the number of Groutville boys already at the school. At Edendale, initiation could be unpleasant and disconcerting. I well remember, for instance, my astonishment when a menacing group of older boys surrounded me and insisted that I should be thrashed—because (so they said) I was too forward in answering questions in class.

[2] £3 per term.

26

Oddly enough, I have forgotten whether they carried out their threat or not.

The main novelty of life at Edendale was that for the first time I was taught by white teachers. (There was one African teacher on the staff.) Looking back from the present, I realise that it may seem odd that we were not particularly conscious that they *were* Europeans. From our point of view in those days they belonged to the genus *Teacher*, and our discussion of them followed the usual lines: "How far can you go with him? Is she easy to lead up the garden path? Is he harsh? Is she even-tempered?" It did not occur to us to explain their idiosyncrasies by the colour of their skins. The behaviour of Europeans did not interest us: the behaviour of teachers absorbed us. We respected justice, sympathy and understanding, and resented caprice.

One relief which Edendale brought was the end of corporal punishment. Except on one occasion, when I was among the "victims".

In my first year there I was involved in a strike, an unusual one for those days in that it was not about food. An indifferent disciplinarian on the staff had a way of punishing boys by causing them to carry stones from the river to the school. Eventually the boys objected for the good reason that their parents could not afford to replace clothes damaged in this process. The principal came down, when the matter reached him, on the side of authority.

The boys were angry. They boycotted the classroom and talked quite seriously of leaving the school altogether. Then the "strikers" were called in to interview the principal one by one. Each boy leaving his office was taken to one or the other of two classrooms—the sheep were being separated from the goats.

When my turn came (far down the queue, for I was among the youngest) I found that the principal was being assisted by an African clergyman, the Rev. Msimanga. The principal opened with a question:

"Are you willing to carry stones, Albert? Yes or no?"

"No, sir."

"Do you really know what you're doing?"

"Yes, sir."

"You're being misled, you know, by the older boys."

"No, sir."

The principal turned to Mr. Msimanga:

"You'd better take this boy home with you and pump this out of him."

When Mr. Msimanga failed to change my mind, I was sent off to join the other goats. Then the goats learned that the sheep

27

had succumbed to argument, and for a while there was confusion, until we decided to give in also. But one boy, Mavuso, stood out. When the question was put to us again, Mavuso replied, "No, I will not carry stones. I will not!"

"Mavuso," said the principal, "you leave these premises right away. Do you understand—right away!"

"Yes, sir."

Mavuso went off to pack. Then the sheep were let loose among the goats. They asserted indignantly that they had *not* agreed to carry stones. After heated argument we all reached a common decision: "If Mavuso goes, we all go!"

We went to join Mavuso in packing. The principal was attracted to the scene by the clatter of our few possessions being hurled into boxes.

"What's all this packing?" he demanded.

There was no reply.

"Very well. I would rather have an empty institution than boys who won't obey me."

Watching covertly for signs of some reaction, we finished our packing in silence and left. There was no reaction. We were rather disappointed. The principal simply stood and watched us leave in a body.

We headed for Pietermaritzburg. On the way we stopped short, realising suddenly the hazards which governed our lives outside the institution. In Pietermaritzburg there would be a curfew. The police, no doubt, would arrest us—the principal might have telephoned them. There was a particular tone in the talk of the older boys which made me aware, for the first time in my life, of the feeling which Africans share about the police.

We slept that night in the open veld, and made our way into the town next day in small groups.

We were allowed to return in the end, provided our guardians accompanied us. To my uncle fell the doubtful privilege of taking me back. To him also fell the task of administering to me the public thrashing which all the strikers got.

I recall one further brush with authority at Edendale. Externally it was of minor importance, but the effects within me were lasting. It occurred towards the end of my time as scholar there. I abused my position as a prefect by conniving at what amounted (in a schoolboyish way) to the theft of food by other boys. The head teacher, Dr. Harold Jowatt,[3] detected me in this. He ignored the other boys, who were not prefects, and dealt with me.

Dr. Jowatt pointed out that my action was a breach of trust.

[3] Later a Director of Education in Rhodesia.

28

In my heart I agreed with every word he said, and I can remember no occasion in my whole life when I was so thoroughly ashamed. My admiration for Dr. Jowatt was not impaired, especially as the incident ended there for both of us.

Still in Edendale, I went on a two-year Teachers' Course. A good deal of emphasis was placed, here, on personal responsibility, and the developing of active adult leadership. The prevailing atmosphere was thoroughly healthy, our teachers were diligent and dedicated, learning was grounded in religion, and the institution had, on the whole, a maturing effect. I was happy there and enjoyed my time at Edendale thoroughly. Furthermore, I acquired a regard for the teaching profession, imbibed from the high standards of my teachers, which has never left me. I learned to love teaching.

I am angered by the Nationalist gibe nowadays that such schools as this one, or Adams College, or St. Peter's, Rosettenville, turned out "Black Englishmen". It was no more necessary for the pupils to become Black Englishmen than it was for the teachers to become White Africans. Two cultures met, and both Africans and Europeans were affected by the meeting. Both profited, and both survived enriched. At Edendale, at Adams, and informally at other times, I have been taught by European mentors. I am aware of a profound gratitude for what I have learned. I remain an African. I think as an African, I speak as an African, I act as an African, and as an African I worship the God whose children we all are. I do not see why it should be otherwise.

At the conclusion of my training I went to teach at a place called Blaauwbosch in the Natal uplands. I was appointed principal of an Intermediate[4] school. This was not very impressive —I was also the entire staff.

It was while I was there that my religion received the jog that it needed. Up to this time I had more or less drifted along. At Edendale I had done no more than take my part in school worship. I had done nothing about being confirmed. In fact, I was a Christian by accident of upbringing rather than by conscious choice.

But at Blaauwbosch I came under the influence of an old and very conscientious African minister, the Rev. Mtembu, and he raised the issues which I had taken for granted. I had also the good fortune to be lodged with the family of an evangelist of the Methodist Church, named Xaba, the devout and peaceful atmosphere of whose home echoed that of my own.

[4] Standards 5 and 6.

I do not pretend to pinpoint any moment of "conversion", but I know that without the dutiful attention of Mr. Mtembu I might quite easily have drifted away from my earlier teaching. As it turned out, I was roused. There was no local Congregational Church. But since there was a working understanding between the Congregationalists and the Methodists, I was confirmed in the Methodist Church, in which I subsequently became a lay preacher.

While I was at Blaauwbosch I had my first encounter with Dr. C. T. Loram, Natal's first Chief Inspector for Native Education. He came to my school with the district Inspector, and the two of them spent the morning examining records and my teaching and the grounds. In the afternoon I was called in to confer about the school. All went well to begin with—and then he came to the contentious subject of "Manual work".[5] Dr. Loram was an enthusiast about work of this type. I had a greater interest in moulding the pupils' minds. But, even if we had held the same views about manual work, there was no equipment with which to teach these crafts.

Dr. Loram opened the attack.

"There's just one thing, Luthuli. You're a teacher. You're supposed to be a leader in your community. But the garden at this school is a shameful sight!"

"Sir," I replied, "I've tried to make some improvements since I've been here. The plain fact is that I've got no equipment. This place is sandy. It can't be worked without implements. I have to ask the pupils to bring them from their homes, where they can ill be spared."

"What? I don't see *that* in your log book."

"No, sir. It did not occur to me to put it in."

"Well, then," Dr. Loram asked, "what do you do with pupils who don't bring tools? How do you occupy them?"

"Some cut grass. Others have to spend the time doing nothing."

"Have you started grass-work in this school?"

"A little," I said, "but not much."

"Why not much?"

"Sir, as you are aware, one does not pick the grass that grows by the roadside and weave it into baskets. Most of the proper material has to come from the coastal area. How is it to get there?"

"Huh, Luthuli!" said Dr. Loram. "There's a lot of Government time stolen in this school!"

There was not, but I forbore to say it. After a while the con-

[5] This means gardening, weeding, laying stone paths, weaving, etc.

versation mellowed, and finally Dr. Loram asked me if I had anything to say.

"Yes, sir. There is one thing."

"Well—?"

"I can't say I'm very pleased by your visit."

"You're not *what*?"

"On the subject of manual work," I went on, "you regard me as an evasive liar. I can see it—you accept nothing that I say."

"Oh, no, no, Luthuli, you mustn't take my remarks that way. You know, I've graded you well. After all, just suppose I'd come here and praised your work—it would have spoiled you as a young teacher. Now, tell me," said the doctor, pointing at neat lines of children marching out of school, "how do you manage to get your pupils to keep their lines so well?"

At about this time the Education Department opened a Higher Teachers' Training Course at Adams College. When I had been at Blaauwbosch for two years, the Department notified me that I had been recommended for a bursary (for which I had not applied) which would see me through this course. I took it as a gift from the Almighty. I also suspected the hand of Dr. Loram behind the recommendation. I left Blaauwbosch, little imagining that I would be spending the next fifteen years of my life at Adams.

3. *Life at Adams College*

Three distinct departments, each with its own head, came under the supervision of the Principal of Adams College—a High School, a Training College for Teachers, and an Industrial School. For the next two years I lived uneventfully and busily as a student in the Training College, settling down to the vocation which seemed to have chosen me. The careers open to Africans, then as now, were extremely few—except for manual labour. Besides teaching, very little was open to us beyond the Church, and clerical posts with lawyers and (in the third grade only) in the Civil Service. In these circumstances it is not surprising that I had done very little about picking a career, and I took it for granted that I would spend my days quietly as a teacher. I must add that, even had I lived in a country where the colour-bar does not impose so restricted a range of careers, teaching would probably have been my choice—either that or law.

I was fascinated by the horizons which my own education opened up, and eager to be instrumental in helping to educate others. The riches of the land and the material opulence of the cities were not for Africans. All the more, then, did we regard education as a thirsty wayfarer yearns for a water-hole.

At the end of my student year I was faced with a hard choice. Dr. Loram offered me a bursary which would see me through the University College of Fort Hare. To this day I have no doubt that I chose rightly, but I regretted terribly having had to decline. My reply to his offer needed little pondering.

"I'm grateful for the offer, Dr. Loram, extremely grateful. But my mother has been labouring all these years to ensure my education. Now she's old. For the last two years I've been able to do nothing to help her. I must go out to teach again, so that I can release her from work in her old age."

I did not, however, go out to teach. I stayed on to teach at Adams. Adams was then leading the way in the experiment of using Africans to train African teachers. With one other African teacher I was appointed to the staff at Adams. The subjects in which I specialised were Zulu and Music, and some years later School Organisation was added. Besides these, there was much general teaching. At the end of my time at Adams, thirteen years later, I had become Supervisor of teachers in training at outlying schools. Throughout these years one job, which I enjoyed immensely, persisted—I was College Choirmaster. It did indeed appear that I was settling in to a teacher's life.

When I first joined the staff at Adams, African education in Natal was undergoing a drastic revision. The revolutionary at the helm was Dr. Loram, newly appointed as Natal's first Chief Inspector of Native Education. Previous to his appointment, African education had followed conventional lines. Except in the matter of language, there was not much difference between black and white education, and both conformed to the general pattern evolved in Europe.

Now came Dr. Loram, a vigorous product of the craze for "practical" education which was then in vogue. His driving intention seems to have been, in all good faith, to equip African children for the lives white South Africa decreed they would have to live. Since they had been cast for the role of hewers of wood and drawers of water, their education must equip them to hew wood and draw water. I doubt whether Dr. Loram was aware of how cramped a future he was (by implication) predicting for us. In fact, I imagine that he assumed uncritically that we shall for ever be what most of white South Africa says we are, and he set out to make us contented in our mental shackles. He had, I do not doubt, the best of intentions.

The result of his efforts was that the Three Rs became luxury subjects almost at once, and a disproportion of time was awarded to manual work and menial crafts. Utility was the thing. Standards of attainment in Arithmetic, Mathematics and English went downhill at a gallop.

Fortunately Dr. Loram did not stay in his position for long, though it took longer to repair the damage than to inflict it. He did, however, stay long enough to coin the phrase "develop along their own lines" which has become one of the war-cries of apartheid. Whether the Nationalists learned anything from Dr. Loram's educational theory or not, there is some similarity.

For Dr. Loram it can be said that his rash adventure was an experiment in keeping with fashions then current elsewhere, especially in America. Though not judicious, it was a sign of life. Against the present policy of the Nationalists it must be pointed out that they have resuscitated and intensified an approach already tried and abandoned.

It now seems ironical that at the time I broke a lance in defiance of Dr. Loram's revisions. In the *African Teachers' Journal* I expressed support of the extension of the vernacular in our schools (Mother Tongue Instruction), though I did not agree with the emphasis on manual subjects. *Ilanga laseNatal*, a newspaper edited by Dr. Dube and published in Zulu, took me severely to task, and there is no doubt that the African community was very strongly opposed to Dr. Loram's reforms.

I learned a lesson, seeing clearly for the first time the danger of giving such matters purely academic consideration, and of being an enthusiast in the realm of theory. To me, at that moment, and in spite of my disagreement over some things, Dr. Loram seemed to represent progressive trends in education. The Zulu community, more wisely, knew that he was cutting off the air supply. Like most young teachers at the time, I did not take into account the political and social context. I was aware of an educational situation, I was engrossed with equipping myself to be of some use in it, and failed to reckon with the setting in which Dr. Loram was going to work.

Life at Adams College contrived to insulate us in some measure from what was happening in South Africa. It was not that restraints were put on us. Rather, in some ways Adams was a world of its own in which we were too busy with our profession to pay more than passing attention to what happened elsewhere.

It was an extremely busy world. For the first five or six years the urge to master my profession kept me fully occupied in the interludes of a very heavy schedule. When I could spare time I fitted in haphazard reading—religion, sociology, political philosophy. I must confess that I still have a large gap in my political education: I have read none of the Marxist classics, and now it would be illegal (in South Africa) to do this.

In 1928 secretaryship of the African Teachers' Association was added to my voluntary and routine activities, and in 1933 I became president of the same body. Probably the main preoccupation of the Association was not teaching but pay—not surprising, since we were paid something like £60 a year. This work, involving as it did negotiations with the authorities, gave me some training in arts which have since become redundant. South African authorities no longer receive deputations, and they do not discuss their decisions with those affected by them.

As secretary of the Association I had some practice in organisation too, and during these years we made our first application of the boycott method. We boycotted Dr. Loram's Winter Schools on the ground that the money spent on them would be better used to raise our wages.

But we did concern ourselves—and more wholeheartedly—with more than money. While I was secretary of the Association it became increasingly clear to me that if we were to devote our major attention to conditions of employment and pay we should end up in chronic disgruntlement.

With this, among other things, in mind, I took the initiative in founding the Zulu Language and Cultural Society as an auxiliary to the Teachers' Association. I believed then, as I do now, that an authentic, comprehensive South African culture will grow in its own way. This will not be determined by cultural societies, but they may influence it. It seems to me that African teachers ought to play some part in the process.

We were thoroughly aware of the meeting of cultures, African and European, and of the disorganisation of both—especially the African—as a result. We did not have the desire of the Nationalists that we should return to the primitive. But we have had an intense wish to preserve what is valuable in our heritage while discarding the inappropriate and outmoded. Our people were ill-equipped to withstand the impact of a twentieth-century industrial society. Our task seemed to consist of relating the past coherently to the present and the future.

The Zulu Language and Cultural Society throve satisfactorily until some time after I had left the teaching profession. Then it accepted a government grant, lost its independence, became involved in the Native Affairs Department and Zulu Royal House politics, went into decline, and (after withdrawal by the teachers) collapsed.

Beyond playing an occasional game of tennis for exercise, I took no part in sport while at Adams. None the less, the streak of fierce fanaticism which is looked for in presidents of African National Congresses showed itself in one way even then—I became a compulsive football fan. To this day I am carried away helplessly by the excitement of a soccer match, and I confess that when I watch matches between white South Africans and visiting teams, I invariably want the foreigners to win. So do other Africans.

Leaving Adams wrenched me from this addiction, as my political ban does now. All the same, over twenty-five years I have played what part I could in organising African and inter-racial sport, to the extent, for instance, that I was made the first secretary of the South African Football Association.

I think that what had attracted me as much as the game has been the opportunity to meet all sorts of people, from the loftiest to the most disreputable. I well remember how on one occasion after a football match, I found myself the only sober man in a car which was being driven at breakneck speed. To take my mind off my own imminent death, I confined myself to restraining a companion from simply opening the door and stepping out on to a road moving backwards at sixty miles an hour—in order to relieve himself!

One of the great benefits of Adams was that it brought those of us who stayed there over a number of years into contact with many people. I am not aware that I could have been dominated by a stereotyped set of ideas—it could probably be said that I have spent a lifetime modifying my views in the attempt to fit them to the realities as I have been able to understand them. My ambitions are, I think, modest—they scarcely go beyond the desire to serve God and my neighbour, both at full stretch. But contact with people is the very breath of life to me.

At Adams the privilege of meeting people extended beyond students and staff. Perhaps because it was an American foundation, it attracted numbers of visitors, men who preached in the College Chapel or who addressed us at meetings, who were open to challenge and discussion, and who brought in with them a breath of the larger world.

Although I can thank no one person for exerting a decisive influence on me, I must set down here my gratitude to the many (most of them unwitting) who have deepened my understanding.

Among my colleagues I recall the pleasure and stimulus of friendship with Professor Matthews. He was not a professor then. He came to head the High School soon after I joined the staff of the Training College, and he built up his department of Adams in an impressive way. Certainly neither of us young African academes had the faintest suspicion that we should meet one day in Johannesburg to stand trial together for High Treason—Professor Matthews to be hauled from his study at Fort Hare University College, and I from my mission allotment. Still less could I foresee that at the end of an honourably and distinguished career, the professor would resign within two years of retirement, forfeiting about £7000 in gratuities rather than submit to the travesty of the Separate Universities Act.

Still among my colleagues I recall with affection the head of the Industrial School, Dr. Breuckner. I did not find him an arresting preacher, but one sentence which he spoke has lived with me until today: "You must give a charitable interpretation to every man's actions," he told us, "until you can prove that such an interpretation is unsound." I have tried to adhere to this in my meetings with people.

One of my strangest encounters—subsequently it has become a bewildering one—with a colleague was by interchange with a man named de Villiers: an Afrikaner who, because of the "modernist" views which he held, was not accepted into the ministry of the Dutch Reformed Church. Mr. de Villiers seemed closer to the Africans on the staff than most white teachers. Certainly he associated with us more freely and more often than did most of his white fellows. Not only did he often join us in

36

our common room—a mild brand of apartheid prevailed at Adams—but he engaged us in lengthy discussions in our private rooms.

More than any one person, this man helped me to forestall intolerance of whites in general and of Afrikaners in particular. Although at this time the existence of oppression was seldom in the forefront of my mind, Mr. de Villiers made me aware of it as the product of deliberate training which he had revolted against.

"If you find an Afrikaner who is liberal," he once told us, and I took it that he referred to himself, "you must recognise that he gets to that point only after a good deal of heartsearching and repentance, because he's been brought up to dislike and look down on natives. We've been taught that natives aren't like you people here."

I cannot forget the horror with which I understood that in South Africa children were being brought up to despise other children, and even their elders. Until this time I had, I suppose, looked on brutalities as individual aberrations rather than as the rotten fruits of childhood training.

Mr. de Villiers made some impact on us as a person because he opened up a side of South African affairs of which we were largely ignorant. A vigorous apologist for Afrikaners, despite his own revolt against their ethos, he gave us a sense of Afrikaners as victims of their own past. Although the tendency to see oneself perpetually as a victim will lead to the evasion of responsibility and the condoning of evil, I think that much of this man's interpretation of South African history was valid. It did enlarge my understanding of the forces which go to the making of men, and it gave me some insight into the dilemma of whites, particularly Afrikaners, which has possibly served in later years as a real protection against hatred and bitterness.

But Mr. de Villiers has confronted me with a problem to which I find no solution. He is now Secrétary for Bantu Education under the present government. He has aided the work of destroying African education. Can it be that he has repented of repenting?

There are many questions I should like to put to Mr. de Villiers. Above all, I would like to understand what has caused this drastic change in his outlook, his apparent reversion to his childhood. I would like to understand how he reconciles his past with his present. But much has changed since last we met, and now I suppose that we could not meet as men, equals without constraint, to discuss our differences. It is regrettable.

Among visitors to Adams came Dr. Aggrey. I remember his

visit chiefly because of his impressive eloquence and because he gave us a glimpse, rare in those days, of the eminence which black men may achieve. Yet I cannot say even then his advice seemed wise, and certainly I reject it now. "Take what you are given," he urged us, "even if it is only half a loaf. Only when you've used up the entire half-loaf should you ask for more."

I am open to progressive compromise, but I reject Dr. Aggrey's advice to accept anything given. I must be sure it is bread I am offered, and in apartheid I see not bread but a stone.

At least one visit to Adams had a comic sequel. A Congregationalist minister spoke to the students about the British Royal Family—it was the occasion of George V's jubilee. The speaker drew on more patriotism and less knowledge than was desirable, comparing the British Royal Family with the Zulu, greatly to the disparagement of the latter. There was no outward sign that the students had even taken in what was said—not a ripple. Then Edward VIII abdicated. When he abandoned his throne and his people (that is how a Zulu would see it) the students staged a minor demonstration. "Call Mr. Taylor," they clamoured, "to tell us more about the British Royal Family!"

Of my superiors at Adams, two at least made a deep impression on me. Dr. Edgar Brookes took over the Principalship at a time when morale was very low. Starting with this disadvantage, he pulled the place together again in a short time, impressing his efficient personality on every department. He was the first head of Adams who was not a visiting missionary. He was a South African and not a missionary. Yet—this is what made the deepest impact on me—he treated his religion with utter sincerity. It may be that it was from him, together with C. W. Atkins, that I gathered some understanding of lay activity and witness in the Church.

Dr. Brookes was then a member of the Oxford Group. Frequent meetings were held in his house, and at them many themes were discussed in a free and relaxed atmosphere. Among other things, we found ourselves able to consider quite frankly the difficulties brought about by the confluence of races in South Africa. I cannot say we solved our country's problems, but we did exchange ideas with a simplicity and charity which now seemed totally discordant with the present mood.

I do not know whether Dr. Brookes still belongs to the Oxford Group, now known, I believe, as Moral Rearmament (M.R.A.), but he continues to be one of South Africa's greatest champions of public and private sanity and morality.

Early in my career at Adams I came under the influence of C. W. Atkins, head of the Training College and for a time principal of the entire institution. This man typifies for me the side of Adams which I found most valuable and enduring. He placed his emphasis on loving God and on service of the society in which one finds oneself, and he had no hesitation in involving us deeply in the affairs of the African communities which lay within reach of Adams. Possibly this was really the combined achievement of Adams, but Atkins remains in my memory as a symbol of it.

Among my many debts to Adams and its people the greatest was the gift of an ethos gradually absorbed, and profoundly lasting in its effects. It became clear to me that the Christian faith was not a private affair without relevance to society. It was, rather, belief which equipped us in a unique way to meet the challenges of our society. It was a belief which had to be applied to the conditions of our lives; and our many works—they ranged from Sunday School teaching to road-building—became meaningful as the outflow of Christian belief.

Adams taught me what Edendale did not, that I had to *do* something about being a Christian and that this something must identify me with my neighbour, not dissociate me from him. Adams taught me more. It inculcated, by example rather than precept, a specifically Christian mode of going about work in society, and I have had frequent reason to be grateful for this in later life.

4. "No grazing in white pastures"

It was at Adams College that I met my wife.

Nokukhanya Bhengu was the granddaughter of a polygamous Zulu chief, Dhlokolo Bhengu of the Ngcolosi, the husband of many wives. It was customary in those days for a chief to nominate his heir late in life in order to protect him from the possible jealousy of rivals. For this reason my wife's father, although the eldest son of Chief Dhlokolo, was not the old man's heir. Nevertheless, as we Africans look at it, my wife is of royal blood, while I am a commoner, a circumstance which does not seem to have caused either of us any embarrassment.

With my wife's father, Maphitha Bhengu, the heathen line ended and the Christian line began. Maphitha was the husband of one wife, and both of them were probably among the early converts at the American Board Mission Station at Umgeni near Durban. Like me, therefore, my wife had a Congregationalist upbringing, first in schools at Inanda, and later as a teacher in training at Adams.

At one stage we must have been together in school at the Ohlange Institute, but if so we were not aware of it. I first became conscious of the existence of Nokukhanya Bhengu when, having returned to Adams for the second time to take her first grade Teacher's Certificate, she became one of my students in Zulu and School Organisation classes. She later taught at the Adams Practising School and acted also as a member of staff at the Adams Hostel for Girls. She resigned from both these posts at the time of our marriage.

After the usual lengthy negotiations between our two families —in true Zulu style—had culminated in our marriage, my wife settled in Groutville.

Behind our decision to live apart right from the first year of our marriage lay the spectre which haunts all Africans in the Union who dwell in cities—the spectre of impermanence and insecurity. It is more acute now than it was then, for that was in the days before the Urban Areas Act and the Influx Control regulations. But it was present enough, even then. Whatever Adams may have offered us, it could not be a permanent home, and so my wife remained to establish one in Groutville. For all we knew at the time, this separation might have to persist throughout our lives, since we had no idea that my public duty

40

would ever place me in Groutville. As it turned out, we were fortunate. We lived away from each other for only eight years.

To my ageing mother our marriage brought at last relief from toil. It was a great joy to me that I was able to offer haven to one who had laboured long and unremittingly largely for my sake. We welcomed the opportunity to serve her in our home until her death.

Over the inner reality of our marriage and the depth of the attachment between my wife and me, I draw a veil. But I may say here that I count myself fortunate among men to have married so good a wife, and so devout a Christian woman. Her mother died when she was young, her early years were years of struggle, yet out of the struggle have come qualities of character which I have come to value more and more with the years. I have her to thank for maintaining the dignity of our home, a good deal of the time with little help from me. She has created the one place of relative security and privacy which we know.

I think what I value most about Nokukhanya is her integrity, which expresses itself in everything from her steadfast reliance on God, her devotion to me and our family, right down to such things as paying our accounts without delay or immediately acknowledging herself to be in the wrong if she discovers that she has made a faulty appraisal or has misunderstood a situation.

We do not have many of the things of this world. Nokukhanya and I and our family, and on top of this she has found herself married to a man immersed in public affairs and (except when under some ban or other) given to too much travel. Yet, largely because of my wife's openness and honesty, we have found our relationship with each other unthreatened and uncomplicated— and I have never known her to grumble over the things we have to forgo.

She has not once intruded upon me, as she might many times have done, the conflict between family and work. She has not said at any time—not when I entered the political battle nor when I became President-General of the African National Congress, or during the Defiance Campaign, or when I was charged with High Treason—"But what will become of the family and me?" Instead, she has created a home, sometimes my background, occasionally my foreground, which has all through been stable and constant and inwardly secure.

I cannot express how grateful I am, especially as I quite literally neglect my family and feel extremely guilty about it. Ungrudgingly she has taken on, since I entered public life, the whole burden of the home and of working our smallholding.

Her contribution has not stopped short at being purely
41

domestic. At one time she rallied the women of Groutville and led a movement for the establishment of a clinic. The women responded well, even being ready and willing to tax themselves to raise the necessary money. But the whole project disintegrated because of apathy and obstruction in the Native Affairs Department, which had the last word. They are accustomed to tell us that we do nothing to help ourselves—it is one of the themes of *Baasskap*—yet I wonder how much of our recent history is littered by white official frustration of African initiative.

In political affairs my wife is with me, although I have never suggested to her that she should be. It is simply a fortunate coincidence, but to me it makes all the difference. She is not a platform orator, though when she speaks in public she has the gift of talking good sense. Most of the time, however, she cannot be prevailed on to make public addresses. She sticks to the Biblical advice to take the lowest seat; and, besides this, she is a shy person.

In private, I may say, Nokukhanya is less shy. She is more forthright than I am, and speaks her mind without hesitation. I am not by temperament a very aggressive person, and I tend when confronted by (for instance) the ill-behaviour of others, to extenuate for them and look for the explanations of their conduct. My wife, on the other hand, goes straight to the heart of the matter, always gently and always quite firmly.

We were married in 1927. Between 1929 and 1945 Nokukhanya bore me seven children, of whom the first and last two were boys.

We pray very hard about our children, most of all because of the South Africa in which they are growing up. In the days when Professor Matthews and I were young teachers at Adams the world seemed to be opening out for Africans. It seemed mainly a matter of proving our ability and worth as citizens, and that did not seem impossible. We were, of course, aware of the existence of colour prejudice, but we did not dream that it would endure and intensify as it has. There seemed point, in my youth, in striving after the values of the Western world. It seemed to be a striving after wholeness and fulfilment. Since then we have watched the steady degeneration of South African affairs, and we have seen this degeneration quickened in the last ten years.

But our children have been born, with the whole of their generation, into the midst of the triumph of prejudice. Young Africans know from infancy upwards—and the point here is that they know nothing else—that their strivings after civilised values will not, in the present order, ever earn for them recognition as sane and responsible civilised beings.

42

The argument behind the idea[1] that we Africans need a two-thousand-year apprenticeship has occasionally been uttered, though never very coherently. It goes like this: "It has taken us two thousand years to reach our present civilised state. A hundred years ago the natives were barbarians. It will take them two thousand years to catch up with where we are now, and they will not be civilised until then."

It is pure nonsense, of course. The argument does not arise from a survey of history, it arises from the urge to justify a course already chosen. The conclusion ("No rights for two thousand years") is there before the argument begins. An uncritical assumption ("Whites are civilised") is there too. No account is taken of the fact that there have been both bad and exemplary Christians throughout the whole of the two thousand years in question, and that various societies have produced civilised beings for much longer than that. The argument assumes that, whereas white can take up where the last generation left off, Africans cannot encounter and absorb anything in the present—they must go back and take each step of the road from the beginning, as though nothing that has happened during the last two thousand years can affect them. Must we really invent the spinning-wheel before we can wear or make clothes? Must we really invent the internal combustion engine before we can drive cars?

I do not agree that white South Africa, at the end of its theoretical two-thousand-year trek, is displaying at present the high virtues of civilisation, and it is doing a good deal to discredit in African eyes the Christianity which many of its members profess.

But even if we were being Christian and civilised, its values would not have been invented by white men. The Christian faith sprang from Asia Minor, and to this day it speaks with a Semitic voice. Western civilisation is only partly Western. It embraces the contribution of many lands and many races. It is the outcome of interaction, not of apartheid. It is an inheritance, something received to be handed on, not a white preserve. I claim with no hesitation that it belongs to Africa as much as to Europe or America or India. The white man brought it here, originally, but he brought a lot of other things too. I do not suppress one detail of our indebtedness—and I know of no instance in which the indigenous peoples of South Africa failed

---

[1] It is a widely accepted idea. Even so, we are not invited to pin any hopes on A.D. 3960. A Nationalist M.P. announced recently on a public platform that, although we may be "civilised" by then, we shall still not be allowed to vote.

to reach out after a way of life whose value they had the sense to grasp.

Now the cultural gifts formerly offered are being snatched away. Our children are invited to pin their hopes on easier times in two thousand years. That is the extent of the offer. In the meantime, what? In the meantime there is the Bantu Education Act.

Bantu education came into effect in 1954. It is a specialised type of education designed exclusively by Europeans exclusively for Africans. It is not, as were former educational systems in South Africa, designed simply by adults for children. It is not to be judged on the details of its syllabuses, though what I know of these is shoddy enough. It can be understood only in the light of the declared intentions of its begetters, in the context of other legislation enforcing the master-servant relationship, and by its effects.

The effect of entirely discarding children who fail examinations twice is to deny to slow starters all access to literacy—*for life*.

The effect of placing school control in the hands of local elected boards and committees is to invite people who (however excellent in character) have no clear understanding of education or of their function, to interfere with the normal activities of trained teachers. This in turn produces chronic nervousness in the teachers, who are hired and sacked by the local boards—no reason need be given.[2] The principle of School Boards is excellent. In practice, in the present situation, it is harmful—and the African communities involved are never freely represented by them.

The effect of providing one teacher for a minimum of sixty-five children is to reduce efficiency.

The effect, in a fast-developing society with a growing population, of limiting (to £6½ million per year) the Government money contribution to African education *for all time*, is to bleed the poorest section of the community dry, and to insure progressive stunting of African education for lack of funds. The effect of forcing African parents to choose between school feeding and school buildings is to impoverish us further. Under the new system state provision of books has disappeared too and that makes us poorer still, even though the Government now pays the teachers.

The effect of double sessions taught by the same teachers is to overburden them to the point of exhaustion, while the effect of

[2] These committees and boards are ostensibly there to foster African leadership. The Special Branch of the Police scrutinises appointments.

twenty-minute lessons is to waste much of what time there is.[3]

At the teacher-training level, the effect of loading admissions in favour of those taking short courses is to produce comparatively poorly trained teachers—who are paid lower wages. Standards must decline in a cheap-labour system.

The effect of using only the many vernaculars as media of instruction is to cut children off deliberately and violently from access to outside influences and ideas—and the heritage of much of the civilised world.

This, of course, brings us to the heart of the matter. African children have previously had some small access to the commonwealth of learning. They have reached out, many of them, after its riches, and many of our African doctors and lawyers and teachers have proved themselves able to absorb not only learning but Western culture, in less than two thousand years. In South Africa this has set up tensions, and evoked the threat of encroachment upon the white standard of living and all-white rule.

So the door has had to be slammed shut hard in the faces of the younger generation, and a system devised which will recondition us to accept perpetual inferiority and perpetual isolation from Western learning and culture. To isolate us and to convince us of our permanent inferiority—these two motives lie behind much legislation from the Act of Union until now, and the Bantu Education Act is a major means to this end. Whatever may be said in favour of certain altered details of Bantu Education (and I do not deny that here and there is to be found a minor improvement or two), the overall effect of this system is not educational at all, but political. It is a tool in the hands of the white master for the more effective reduction and control of the black servants.

This is not inference. It has been quite badly stated. Dr. Verwoerd made it plain beyond all doubt, when he introduced the legislation, that the new system had been invented because former education had produced "misfits" and "Black Englishmen" who had acquired ideas which did not satisfactorily equip us to be content for ever with a subservient lot. These "misfits" could no longer be allowed to "graze in white pastures".

The *declared* aim of his legislation was to produce Africans who would aspire to nothing in white South Africa higher than

[3] The Government claims that more African children are being educated now. This would have been true without the new system—our numbers are growing. It is also true that more children are being dismissed from attendance, and more are being less efficiently taught for a shorter period of years. The system of Double Sessions of infant classes inflates the enrolment.

45

the "certain forms of labour" which Dr. Verwoerd fixed as the top limit of African aspiration. In order to achieve this end he took over every single African school in the country—even the remaining so-called "private schools" or Church schools may teach nothing but his syllabus in his way, and even the informal tuition by one white person of one black child is illegal. If a white employer teaches her African maidservant's toddler the alphabet, she breaks the law.

Dr. Verwoerd, as is his habit, spoke at great length when he introduced this Bill. When he had finished nobody at all could have been left in doubt that the new education "for Africans only" was intended, from beginning to end, to *create* Africans anew after his own peculiar image of the "real native".

If the outlook for our young people is bitter and empty, they are "native children"—the men who have dreamed up Bantu Education and those who have connived at it feel that it will not injure their children. The laws which govern man's relationship to man in society will prove them disastrously wrong.

Apart from the shock with which we recognised that the Bantu Education Act dealt a crippling blow to African education, the thing which disgusted us most was the Minister's glaring refusal to say one word of thanks to the group responsible for initiating all social services among Africans—the missionaries. It was they who started education, health services, social training institutions, the training of nurses, and who were the first behind training of Africans as doctors. Dr. Verwoerd dealt bitingly and insultingly with them and then, with no word of praise for their long labour, ejected them. They were at liberty to do no more than hire out their school buildings to his Department for his education. Tragically, they did exactly that, except for the Roman Catholics and the Anglican Diocese of Johannesburg.

By itself the Bantu Education Act was felt not to go far enough. It left the universities untouched. It has therefore been recently supplemented by an Act called (with characteristic hypocrisy) the Extension of University Education Act. We are by it denied access to the established universities. In place of this, provision is made for a chosen few of us to proceed to ethnic colleges. Up to the end of his education the African child and youth is to be kept isolated, sealed right off. Not only must an African not meet a European, but Xhosa must not meet Bechuana, nor Zulu meet Swazi.

These new Tribal colleges are set in the culturally stagnant wastes of what are now called "Bantu heartlands" (the reserves). It is as though Cornishmen and Irishmen and Welshmen and Scots were forced by law to go to separate colleges, while only

46

"ethnically pure" Englishmen could go to Oxford or Cambridge. It is as though each of the colleges was remotely set among moors and mountains, and the students in them taught only by staff appointed and dismissed by government authority. Their liberties would be of the dingiest, consisting only of a few censored textbooks. Discipline would be that of the primary school, and cultural contacts with other bodies would be nil.

Again, what I say is not fanciful. It is said by the authorities. As I write the University College of Fort Hare, for long a bright light among us, has been seized, eight members of staff have resigned and seven have been dismissed—not in any case for professional reasons.

Now, Fort Hare is not placed in a "Bantu heartland" (the Nationalist Government did not choose the site). But the new regulations set out to create a vacuum all the same. All students must live in hostels. No student is allowed to have any visitor whatever without the prior consent of the Principal himself. No student is allowed to possess any vehicle without official approval. All women students must be in their hostel by 7 p.m. There is a general curfew at 10 p.m. Students are permitted to make no statements to the Press and are allowed to produce no magazine, pamphlet or news-sheet without official approval. Only Xhosa students need apply for admission. Others go to their "own" colleges elsewhere.

Students must apply yearly for "permission to report for registration". The normal understanding that, unless they are expelled, they will be allowed to finish their courses is removed. And if a student complies with every condition laid down, still the Minister[4] may debar him if he so chooses. No reason need be given.

Again, the aim is beyond doubt. The present Minister of Bantu Education, Mr. Maree, speaking in support of this destructive measure, told his listeners that the aim of the Act was "to produce native leaders who will accept and propagate apartheid".

There it is—the naked intention to indoctrinate, to which all else must be subordinated. That is why some of our most eminent African scholars, Professors Matthews and Nyembezi, and Mr. Selby Ngcobo, resigned. Yet, confronted with all the evidence, many white would-be sympathisers tell us uneasily: "Oh, come along, *surely* it's not as bad as you make out. It can't *all* be negative!"

[4] The Government itself, of course, is the controlling authority. For Africans, University autonomy disappears entirely under this Act.

It is worse than they seem able to imagine. It was some small comfort to us to see the way in which world universities, and South Africa's formerly "open" universities, demonstrated against the Act. But they were too late. This Act's foundations were laid much earlier, when the Act applying to school education was passed. The Nationalists were not deterred. They have already set about the task of breeding up in their "Tribal Colleges" their new kind of blueprint African—as they think.

Take these Acts in the context of all other Apartheid-Baaskap Acts and it is not difficult to see that we are in for brainwashing on the grand scale—or rather, the attempt is going to be made. It will not succeed, this attempt to enslave the minds and spirit of ten million people. But it will wreck African education, such as it was, and I predict that it will be carried over before long into European education. It will have to be. Men so manifestly insecure as South Africa's rulers cannot afford to stop short of absolute power. So they will go on until they drop.

One of the deep-seated intentions of this type of education is to erase all African leadership. I cannot help wondering how the Nationalists would have felt if, after the Boer War, the British had introduced this type of indoctrination for Afrikaners. We hear echoes of how English-speaking South Africans react now that the Nationalists are preparing to take over the education of their children by means of a system called "Christian National Education". But the erasure of African leadership is felt to be a good thing by nearly all whites, who want leaders who will not lead, and that is why they have consented to the emasculation of our education. They are requiring *our* teachers to help enslave the hearts and minds of *our* children.

The ethnic grouping principle in education and throughout other spheres of life is significant. Africans were very painfully beginning to shed themselves of purely tribal allegiances. Even in the most backward areas they are beginning to see themselves as part of a larger African community, and many made the step of expressing allegiance to South Africa as a whole, and to the family of mankind.

But the Nationalists and their fellow-travellers start off with the principle of disunity. Where bonds have formed, they must be broken. The only allegiance they recognise is allegiance to disunity, apartheid. Now not only in education but throughout our lives ethnic grouping must apply. They eagerly impress on us our differences—a Xhosa must not even sleep in a Basuto suburb. The evils of suspicion, hostility and disunity were going. Now a host of evils is cynically and mischievously welcomed back. It suits the white man's book, so he thinks. If their motive were

48

paternal and protective, as they claim it is, would they set brother against brother, as they do?

What an appalling world these men have made for our young ones! In my own family I have been relatively fortunate, for most of my children have been old enough to miss the worst of this, though they do not escape altogether. And our own fortune serves only to make my wife and me more acutely aware of the terrible misfortune of others, of those whose children are younger and must, if the white sickness has its way, be subjected to a life of indoctrination, of tribal pettiness, of subordination—and of very little real education. In former times our children were carefully instructed in the customs and traditions of the tribe. Subsequently they were offered an education on the white pattern which at least attempted to nurture and expand the personalities of real people. Now there is nothing but this cruel deformity.

5. *The call of my village*

My decision to leave Adams College, thereby bringing to an end my teaching career, was preceded by a period of indecision. For various reasons, Groutville's domestic affairs were not going very well and the people desired a change of chief. A body of tribal elders approached me with the request that they be allowed to ask the tribe to consider my replacing the ruling chief. The resident missionary added his voice to theirs. For two years they kept up the pressure, and for two years I answered with excuses.

The truth was that I did not want to become chief. It will be remembered that I had spent some time in my Uncle Martin's household while he was at the head of Groutville affairs. I enjoyed my time there well enough, but I saw nothing in his life to attract me to chieftainship—the very reverse.

For one thing, my comparative youth inhibited me. I did not feel that I had acquired sufficient experience to rule. For another, my own observation had shown me how difficult it is for a chief to make a living. As things go with us, my income as a teacher was relatively high—just sufficient to make it possible for me to support my wife and the family which was beginning to appear (we had three children at this time) a little above the breadline. I knew full well that if I became chief the struggle to subsist would become harder, though not desperate. My wife and I talked the matter over during my holidays in Groutville, and each time we decided that it would be best to go on as we were, in the interests of our children.

Added to this, I was at heart a teacher. I had been attracted to the profession right back in the days when I was so deeply impressed by the integrity and ability of many of my teachers at Edendale and Adams. Since that time the calling had had seventeen years to grow on me. I found fulfilment in teaching, and I cannot say that I had much appetite for the taxing days and the endless stream of petty administrative affairs which beset a chief who does his job properly. Alone, and in company with my wife, I turned the matter over. Each time I reached the same conclusion—I would continue at Adams.

I changed my mind quite suddenly. I think that perhaps all the emphasis which Adams had placed on service to the community bore fruit. I recognised now that the call of my people was insistent, and the reasons I gave for declining the request of the tribal elders seemed to me to be excuses for not going to their aid. I was at Adams when I decided to accept, and I wrote to my wife about this decision. I cannot account for the fact that, quite independently, she too had changed her mind about where our duty lay.

There were four candidates when it came to election. I was elected by democratic voting, the Native Commissioner (who conducted the election) informed the head of his Department, and the Government confirmed my appointment as from the beginning of 1936. I left Adams with reluctance, but there was one compensation besides the belief that I was doing my duty—after eight years of holiday and weekend encounters, I could at last live with my wife and family.

It is not easy to describe briefly the function of a chief, since he has a number of activities which are not normally the combined lot of one person in European affairs. To add to the difficulty, a chief does not stand for the same things in white minds as in African. In African eyes a chief possesses certain authority by virtue of his position, while in European eyes all that he has is conferred on him by beneficient whites—he is a sort of appointed boss-boy.

When I became Chief of the Umvoti Mission Reserve, I at once found myself, among other things, a petty administrator, presiding over the day-to-day affairs of about five thousand people living on about ten thousand acres. I did not relish this part of my work much, but what I did enjoy was court work. Within defined limits a chief acts as a magistrate with jurisdiction in civil affairs. At the pleasure of the Governor-General we may have criminal jurisdiction added to this. In common with other chiefs in the Lower Tugela area I was given criminal jurisdiction. (It was later taken away from all of us and then restored to me alone, I do not know why.)

It was my fortune to be well versed in the fundamentals of what is called Native Law and Custom, so I was able to take up my court work with no great difficulty. But my main pleasure in this activity came from the rewarding attempt to reconcile people who were at variance, and from the debate involved. I love the impact of mind upon mind, and I love thrashing things out in the attempt to get at the truth. The procedures of the court give these things orderliness, and getting at the truth is worthwhile for its own sake. The dying arts of exposition hold great attraction for me.

Tribal courts do not closely follow the pattern with which Europeans are acquainted. Plaintiff and defendant normally represent themselves, and any tribal elder present may question both them and the witnesses. In days before the advent of the white man it was customary for the witness to remain in court throughout the trial, but latterly there is a tendency to take European precautions and exclude the witnesses.

I did not like the practice whereby (in my time) court fees and fines, up to a maximum of five pounds or two head of cattle, went into the pocket of the chief, making him an interested party. The Nationalists have made an improvement here. All tribal moneys go now into the Tribal Treasury.

Besides doing this kind of work, I found myself called upon to be a sort of liaison officer between the Native Commissioner and the tribe, and this brought me a good deal in contact with the Commissioner. On the whole, I got on pretty well with these men. I do not recall quarrelling with one, or being taken to task. Some knew very little about their functions in a Mission Reserve, others knew more. With the former it fell to my lot to brief them tactfully on many occasions. They either learned as they went along, or else they simply delegated a part of their work to me. For instance, the allocation of land is not the duty of a chief on a Mission Reserve; nevertheless, I found myself allocating land in Groutville right up to the end of my tenure.

Since a chief is answerable for the good order of his territory, I had also to be a kind of chief of police—not, I hasten to add, regular South African Police. I was eager to have the regular police in Groutville as little as possible, and for this reason I saw to it that my own men dealt with all minor breaches effectively and promptly. In my early days as chief I set myself to curb the illicit brewing of beer, and especially of the more deadly concoctions—not because I am a reformer in these matters, but because it reduced the pretext for police raids. Eventually I managed to get one of the Native Commissioners to recognise and permit brewing within defined limits, and I myself encouraged the healthy brewing of *utshwala*, corn beer. Illicit brewing, the result of poverty, continued, but it did lessen.

In all my routine work I was assisted by tribal elders. These men were entirely unpaid. They did their work without any compulsion as a public duty, recognising far better than our rulers that privilege—even if it is merely prestige—carries with it obligation. They worked selflessly, without reward of any kind.

At Adams College I had had no particular cause to look far beyond the walls of the institution. I was, of course, aware of the South African scene, but Adams was in some ways a protected world, and the South Africa outside did not reach in in those days. Our awareness was partly theoretical. Moreover, we were busy.

All that came to an end when I became Chief at Groutville. Now I saw, almost as though for the first time, the naked poverty of my people, the daily hurt to human beings. Evidences of an inadequate tribal structure breaking up under the pressures of modern conditions were all around me.

In Groutville, as all over the country, a major part of the problem is land—13 per cent of the land for 70 per cent of the people, and almost always inferior land. The quality of the land at Groutville is comparatively good. But allotments shrink while you watch them, and there is nowhere for the surplus population to go. The average official Groutville allocation is now four or five acres per family. Against this, rural white South Africa owns an average of 375 acres per person.[1] You can see, by looking at these figures, the hollowness of the white argument, both here and in the Federation, that the coming of the whites brought us a material prosperity for which we ought to be grateful.

Groutville has a subsistence economy, based mainly on the culture of sugar-cane, started, it is said, by the Rev. Aldin Grout. Cane has the merit of being a cash crop, and this to some extent lessens the great evils of migrant labour. In a good season an acre will yield thirty tons gross, and this may fetch £60. From this the cost of transport and labour must be deducted at an average of 10s. per ton. An acre may thus earn £45 in a season; so that a five-acre allotment will earn £225. But it must be born in mind that cane is not an annual crop. It takes eighteen months to two years to mature, so that the average annual income of a Groutville farming family may be between £110 and £170. This is up to £150 per year below the breadline, according to the size of the family.

Of course, even on allotments two or three times the size of this we could not lead a materially prosperous existence. The trek to the cities is inevitable if a man wants his children to have meat as well as porridge—and, as for books, they are high up on the list of seldom attainable luxuries. So the family is broken up, and the worker becomes an uneasy dweller in two unrelated worlds.

It is true, of course, that to some extent we farm uneconomically, and I have often wished that we had the aptitude which Indians have for coaxing, almost conjuring, vegetable crops out of every square inch of soil. But I doubt whether our faulty

[1] Per person, rural Africans occupy an average of six acres each throughout the Union.

tillage is fairly compared with that of Europeans. One day during my chieftainship I was given a lift in his car by a neighbouring white farmer.

"You fellows," his conversation began, "you're just playing around with the soil. If we had this land we'd produce far better crops of cane than you do."

"Our handicap," I said, "is that we lack two things which you've got—fertiliser and machines. I think if we had these our crops would be better. They cost money."

"But doesn't the sugar mill down below help you—the one that buys and crushes our cane?"

"No, it doesn't help us at all."

"Oh! Well, then, why don't you ask Dube[2] for money?"

"I wonder," I asked, "if you're aware that Dr. Dube finances his school partly from his own pocket?"

My benefactor looked startled. He also seemed to sober down considerably.

"We," he said eventually, "can get short-term loans from the Land Bank."

"That's the difference. We can't. Your land is their security. Ours isn't."

The Native Affairs Department had a scheme whereby it undertook to supply agricultural officers and African field demonstrators to demonstrate more efficient methods and to produce bumper crops. I set myself when I was chief to co-operate with this scheme. The Government demonstrator decided to persuade Groutville to plant cotton, and I set aside a piece of my own land for him to produce his model crop on.

I ploughed. He planted. My wife tended the crop. The Government demonstrator visited the experiment casually. At the time of reaping he was nowhere to be found. We reaped it in ignorance of the correct methods to employ. He reported the operation to his superiors. That was that. But think of the outcome if I had persuaded some of my people to let their land be fooled around with! And this was a representative experience in my dealings with field demonstrators. I found them slack, unco-operative and indifferent—partly, I think, because they were left largely to their own devices.

I did in fact take the rap from my people over other failures of this scheme. In theory I do not criticise it. In practice it is operated by white authorities who supervise at a distance and

---

[2] Dr. Dube, Principal of the Ohlange Institute, was at this time prominent in the African National Congress. At the same time he edited a Zulu newspaper.

have no knowledge of what goes on in the field. I have no reason to think that it has improved since I was chief. It is not properly supervised or participated in. It is another favour bestowed on natives by well-dressed visitors, and African field demonstrators are identified with the white supervisors rather than with the toiling peasant. It fails, on the whole, and its failure is pointed to by whites as yet another piece of evidence that Africans are unteachable.

But even if this scheme worked to the full, even if every square inch of the land were exploited efficiently, even if we could afford equipment and fertilisers, we still have only a fraction of the land which we need. The miracle of making the "Bantu heartlands" blossom as the rose cannot be performed. The whites find that, to live in their accustomed state, they need 375 acres per person. They allow us six. In Groutville, where the land is above average, we get about this for a family.

The whites can find no answer to this problem of land. They have the land. We are denied it. They cannot make the reserves support the excessive human and animal population, but at the same time, as the recent decision of the United Party shows, Africans cannot even be permitted to buy land, for no white electorate will consent to this except perhaps on so petty a scale that it achieves nothing. It is an impasse. It will have to be solved, even though no white Government dare try to solve it. They dare do no more than tinker with the existing situation and pretend that a little model farming will supply the answer.

Shortly after I became chief I was one of ten Zulu chiefs who were taken on an official conducted tour of the Transkei where experiments in economical farming were being made. There the Government had done something about erosion—but only in places where there were no people. They had in effect created parks. It did not seem like a solution. They were also encouraging experiments in co-operative dairy farming on eight-acre plots under a quit-rent system. The experiment was useful but it did not answer the question: "What happens to eight acres when my children inherit them?"

The benefits of stock limitation were pointed out to us. It is obvious, of course, that any given area can only carry so many head of cattle. White policy all along has been to limit the stock. But they are not likely to persuade us of the desirability of this when we are familiar with the spectacle of white farmers with thousands of head of cattle on spacious ranches.

There is another solution: give us more room.

The tour was pleasant, but it showed us no real way to ease

our lot, and even the African councillors whom we met seemed carefully schooled in what to say.

It fell to me and one colleague to describe this tour on our return for the benefit of a meeting of other chiefs. I remained silent on the subject of stock limitation. To my surprise my colleague praised it. He was set upon as though by a swarm of bees, and only when the subject was shelved could order be restored. Cattle-culling is an unreal solution to the problem in South Africa. The problem is: 13 per cent of the land for 70 per cent of the people. The white version of the problem is: how can we continue to confine them to 13 per cent of the land, as we are determined to do? Cattle-culling is not the result of facing the real problem, it is the outcome of this white determination to make no concession whatever. That is why, in the present South African setting, I reject it.

It is scarcely surprising, if these things are to be borne in mind, that when I became chief I was confronted as never before by the destitution of the housewife, the smashing of families because of economic pressures, and the inability of the old way of life to meet the contemporary onslaught. The destruction of our families is not the least of the crimes which white avarice has perpetrated against us. It continues, it increases, in spite of pleading voices raised against it. The results in promiscuity, neglect and material trouble are read by the whites as just another sign of African incapacity. They ignore our pain.

Before I was a chief I was in a sense a migrant labourer myself; but when I became a villager the plight of my people hit me hard—and Groutville is by no means the poorest of African communities. Others are condemned to land that will support almost nothing, so that a far higher proportion of workers must spend their lives away from home, in cities where African unemployment is rife and increasing. The Government reaction to this problem of growing unemployment is typical: send the unemployed back to the already overcrowded sub-economic reserves, which they left because of poverty. This sort of decision, to transfer the problem of unemployment from city to country, strikes them as a solution—remove the offence from before white eyes, and it ceases to exist.

It may seem odd, in the face of all this, that when, during my chieftainship, a manufacturing company offered to set up a paper factory in Groutville, the village turned down the application. The idea was put before me by the Native Commissioner, who did not indicate his Department's attitude one way or the other. I submitted it to a tribal gathering—in practice all male adults. (I took the quite revolutionary step of admitting women to these tribal councils. Although the change was accepted by the people without a murmur, ingrained custom tended to keep the women on the outskirts of discussion. But they did come, and though they hung back they did seriously follow proceedings.)

The people turned down the application by a very large majority. In he first place, Groutville had no surplus land for a factory. In the second place, the reserve remained oui escape from city life with (among poorly paid Africans) its demoralising effects, and the people had no wish that Groutville should be transformed into a factoiy compound. I think, too, that the people recognised with a sound instinct that the motive of the company was to exploit a cheap labour market rather than to enrich Groutville. Such schemes do not, in fact, bring in their wake any appreciable improvement in the African lot. I agreed, therefore, with the decision of my people, perhaps because I am of a conservative cast of mind. I was interested to observe that the Native Affairs Department appeared to approve of our rejection of this scheme.

We were to arrive at another tribal decision which went against Government policy in urban areas. They were then, as now, encouraging the establishment of beer halls by whites in these areas, partly perhaps to counteract the harmful effects of illicit concoctions, and partly to raise money for theii schemes which the white parliament and municipalities are reluctant to vote. The Groutville missionary of the time drew my attention to the attempt being made in the neighbouring township of Stanger to open a beer hall. Emphasising the fact that I was acting in a personal capacity, I drew up and submitted a memorandum opposing this. Stanger's application was turned down, but the matter did not end there. One or two local whites remarked to me sourly: "Stanger isn't Groutville." I did not think that the disappointment which they showed had anything to do with the frustrating of a charitable impulse.

In the course of time Stanger renewed its application. The Native Commissioner called me and said that my personal expression of views was not enough to justify continued opposition to this application. The Department wanted the views of the whole Groutville community. I did not know what the outcome would be. But when the tribe met it opposed the intention of Stanger as strongly as I, albeit for reasons not identical with mine. I recall clearly what one man said, and he summed up the general opinion: "I shall be tempted to waste my money in Stanger, and rob my children of money from which they would benefit. My wife can make beer here."

Although Stanger eventually got Government permission to

establish a beer hall, the town did not, after all, carry out its original intention. This is not a matter for regret. There have been no disturbances similar to those which have occurred throughout Natal recently over this very issue. The beer hall has become for us—and especially for the women—a symbol of legal robbery by whites. This is not a new thing, but as the scale and intensity and range of beer hall disturbances latterly (most notably at Cato Manor) show, it has assumed greater proportions than before.

The point is simple. Africans are denied all licit access to alcohol, except in municipal halls. The municipalities use beer halls to raise money in order to meet the cost of public services among Africans—whites will not make their money available for this. The beer halls are therefore profit-making enterprises, and the result is that they produce beer at a cost far beyond the cost of home production. The women know that they can make beer more cheaply at home, they know that when their menfolk drink regularly at beer halls their families are further impoverished, and they know that beer hall profits are spent on achieving the white man's notion of what is "good for natives". Since this is done at the cost of putting their families even further below the bread line, it is not acceptable.

I do not call in doubt the desirability of public services, such as clinics. But can the existence of such things be justified if they can only exist on impoverishing the poor, and thus reducing the general health of the population they serve? It is obviously a vicious circle. The more clinics we are forced to afford, the less can we afford to feed our children, and the more do they suffer from malnutrition. And of course entire beer hall profits are not spent on clinics. They are spent on whatever seems good to the white man for us.

The most shocking feature highlighted by the beer hall issue is this: why are the social services not there anyway? This is said to be a civilised country, and its Government tells us that it is civilised. Yet the social services which are there for the richer section of the community are not there for the poor, except at the cost of the poor being made poorer—though it must be added that this does not apply to the white poor. There are not many of them, but the social services are there for them as for their richer fellows.

One of the results of the beer hall system is, as may be expected, illicit brewing, not only of beer but of more potent concoctions. This in turn brings police raids at all hours, followed by fines or imprisonment, and it provides a lucrative sideline for some whites who buy liquor and resell it at high prices to Africans. Is it really inexplicable that our women boycott beer stalls, are antagonistic towards municipal Native Affairs Departments, and have sometimes done damage to municipal buildings (including clinics) put there "for their benefit"? We do not want a few services, ostensibly provided by beneficient whites—at our cost. We want a share in South Africa, nothing less.

Many whites, some missionaries among them, are very stern on the subject of illicit brewing. Up to a point I agree with them about the abstract moral principles. I am an abstainer myself, but I must be realistic and meet the problem in a practical way. I am aware of the evils of "home brewing", particularly of those deadly concoctions which seriously undermine African health. But the illicit sale of concoctions is often the only way which African women have of feeding their children.

There is not enough food on our side of the fence—one African child in three dies from malnutrition in its first year. But across the fence there is enough and to spare.

Nevertheless, there is one ray of light in this squalid picture. This is the effort of various voluntary white groups, and some churches, to provide Africans with such social amenities as they are able to finance and run. But these absolve neither the Government nor the urban authorities from responsibility. And the Nationalist Governments have made our plight worse: not only are their grants to municipalities for such purposes niggardly, but they have greatly reduced grants to indigent, disabled and aged Africans.

What a mockery to call this state Christian!

6. *Peasants and townsmen*

I had not been Chief of the Umvoti Mission Reserve for long before it was quite clear to me that, if I was going to go beyond merely ruling Groutville's five thousand people efficiently, my service to the community would be related to their difficulties as peasant sugar farmers. There were real difficulties.

The sugar farmer depends on the miller as much as the miller depends on the farmer. In the early days a mill to process our cane had been jointly established by Africans and the Natal Colonial Administration. When, for lack of money, this joint venture collapsed, the people, led by a certain Makhabeni Dhlamini, tried to keep it running on their own. But there was too little capital, Dhlamini and others had to sell their lands to pay the mill's debts, and the project failed. The period which followed was very difficult for Groutville. The people had to take their crop to a distant mill, and the costs of transport reduced profits considerably. Later, during my student years, two more companies successively tried to operate the mill. Both failed, and after each attempt came a period of low profits for Groutville. A third company, still operating today, succeeded better.

The harvesting and transport of the cane crop, both costly affairs, are beyond the resources of small farmers with little ready cash. Until 1936, when the Sugar Act limiting production came into force, most mills advanced money to African growers to pay for these operations. But for some reason some mills, including the one which served us, withdrew this assistance, and a new hardship was added to disabilities already existing. Knowing that we would not be paid for our crop until two months after delivery, we had none the less to meet the cost of teams of harvesters and heavy transport. We were thus often in a position where we could not afford labourers to reap.

It was just at the time when I assumed office that the Government of the day introduced legislation to keep the price of sugar from falling by limiting production. To this end a quota system was applied on an individual basis. The quotas allotted to us were meagre. Cane stood and rotted on the lands. Yet at the same time since quotas were given to individuals, we could not use up the quotas of any farmers who had gone to the cities and were not producing.

Obviously, we needed to organise. I was helped greatly in this by some elders and by the return to Groutville of Ackroyd Mvuyana, a student of Fort Hare. I called a meeting at which we decided to revive the moribund Groutville Cane Growers' Association which we now established on a formal basis. I became Chairman of this, and Mvuyana was elected Secretary. We discussed our difficulties and made representations, both to the millers and to the Central Board which the Government had set up to administer its legislation. Although we were not met quite halfway, it was well worth the effort.

We approached our millers and eventually, after four years of struggle, they restored the concession of advancing money to cover our production costs. They now help us liberally, deducting the money advanced for final payment. But we have not yet been able to persuade them to help us with our planting—an operation much easier for whites who have access to the money market, to which Africans are *by law* denied access.

Our representations to the South African Sugar Association[1] bore fruit also. An amendment was made to the Sugar Act to allow African growers delivering cane to each mill to have a "globular" (comprehensive) quota amounting to the sum of individual quotas. This meant that where for one reason or another individual farmers did not produce, others were able to make up the shortfall and get their cane on the market, instead of watching it rot in the fields.

It was quite clear that if we had not organised ourselves and revived the Growers' Association, our lot would have continued to deteriorate. The blame for this would have rested squarely on the Native Affairs Department, which is supposed to represent us when legislation affecting us is introduced. In this instance they had done nothing.

The fact that our organisation and the representations which we had made had produced limited results, made me acutely aware of the plight of other districts where nothing whatever had been done. Everywhere white planters and millers had their associations. Clearly we needed ours, even more perhaps than they did. We needed to take advantage of what the law did allow us. With a view to organising ourselves on the European pattern, I got in touch with African leaders and farmers in other places.

The response was not universal. But we were able to found the Natal and Zululand Bantu Cane Growers' Association. For the first time we were able to make united representations to those who controlled our interests. I became Chairman of this body

[1] These were indirect since no non-whites were represented on it. Our approach lay through a non-European Advisory Board.

which included on its Executive such men as the Rev. A. Zulu (now assistant bishop in troubled Pondoland) and Ackroyd Mvuyana.

I do not claim that my attempt to organise my people was entirely successful. Those who saw the value of such organisation banded together and produced some results. But not all did see the point, so that we were met too often with incomprehension, apathy, or suspicion. It was my first, but certainly not my last, experience of the difficulty of getting African people to act in unison. The whites know this weakness and they exploit it to the full. At the same time, however, the increase in oppression in recent years has had the happy effect of driving us closer together, though our troubles are not over. Africans in South Africa are by no means a united people.

Nevertheless, we did get as far as having a representative in the Government machinery for administering sugar production, processing and marketing. True to South African tradition, we were not represented on the South African Sugar Association, but when an advisory board was created, one Indian and one African were allowed to serve on it. I was the African and I continued to serve until I was banned in 1953.

My attempts to organise African sugar producers did not always meet with white approval. The Native Affairs Department later became patchily co-operative, and so did other authorities connected with the sugar industry. My activities in this regard took me through the whole of the sugar belt, and I found millers generally willing to co-operate. But some of them encouraged African growers, by one means and another, to look upon our Association as an interference, and to look on local white millers for paternal protection.

During one such visit to Zululand I chanced to meet the white Agricultural officer of the area in the home of an African farmer of some distinction. We were entertained to an excellent lunch there. I noticed that the Agricultural officer seemed a little bewildered, but I could not tell why until (at a moment when our host was absent) he leaned across and whispered to me:

"By the way, who cooked this food?"

"The lady of the house," I replied.

"The lady of the house? But . . ." He nipped off the rest of the sentence. It was my turn to be taken aback by his puzzled surprise. Here was an agricultural officer, a servant of the Native Affairs Department, who knew nothing about African food—yet African food was his job. Still, he seemed to show no actual resentment at eating the food, and that in our company.

At Stanger one day I had an interview with a senior man of

the Native Affairs Department from Pietermaritzburg. At some length I told him of our difficulties. Not long after this there was a change in the approach of the Department. Formerly they had instructed their officers not to concern themselves particularly with people who produced commercial crops. Now Native Commissioners and their staffs in our part of the world were told to give all assistance to African cane farmers. It was another result of having organised ourselves.

My own Native Commissioner helped me with these activities, and the administration of Groutville did not suffer from them. The same was true of other Native Commissioners, save one.

My Native Commissioner sent a letter to this colleague saying that I would be visiting his district. There was no reply, and my Native Commissioner advised me to approach in person. I did this on arrival. When I presented myself, I was asked my business.

"I'd like to meet your people in this area to discuss the problems of sugar farmers," I said.

"Why?"

"It's a matter of common interest and concern to us to ex-change views about our difficulties, and the ways there may be of solving them."

"Well, I don't think I'll allow this," said the Commissioner. "You'll give these people wrong ideas, you'll spoil them. Any-way, *I'm* trying to organise them."

"If you're trying to organise them, sir, let us profit from your good ideas. Let them be discussed."

"No, no," the Commissioner objected. "That's not the way to go about it. They'll get spoilt. But why do you try to insist on this meeting idea?"

"It helps us to speak with one well-considered voice."

"Out of the many voices, the Native Affairs Department will choose the voice it judges best," he retorted.

"Sir, occasionally we'd like the majority voice to be heard."

"Why don't you trust the Department, Luthuli?"

"You word it loosely, sir. But in this particular matter, as far as sugar is concerned, I don't trust the Department because when this legislation was before parliament you did nothing at all to protect our interests. Nothing. You're only becoming aware of them now because we are making you aware."

The Commissioner continued, almost as though talking to himself: "You mistrust us. Generally these days when natives come to court they get themselves lawyers. Don't they trust magistrates or Native Commissioners any more?"

"Sir, we learned that from you. We see the virtue of having specially trained men. I suppose Europeans rely on the integrity

of magistrates and judges, but they still get themselves lawyers."
I led the talk by a roundabout route back to the subject under
discussion. "I came to ask your permission to hold and address a
meeting."

"No, I don't grant it." His voice was final.

"I see, sir, that you're adamant. Let us part in peace."

Some time later, when I was seeing the Chief Native Commissioner about a different matter, he surprised me by asking,
"Do you remember that place where you were not allowed to
hold a meeting?"

"I do, sir."

"Well, make your application again. I think this time there'll
be no difficulty."

I applied and permission was granted. I held the meeting. It
was not very rewarding. Africans there proved generally apathetic
and unco-operative.

I continued organising African sugar producers until about
1949. Then I had other things to do, and anyway, by that time
either it was apparent that no headway would be made in certain
areas, or local associations were standing on their own feet and
could be left largely to themselves. I look back with nostalgia
on this type of work. Political activity has cut me off from it all.

Another effort of organisation in which I was involved during
these years did not directly concern Groutville at all. It concerned the Umlazi Mission Reserve, an Anglican station on the
pattern of Groutville, a few miles south of Durban. Umlazi has
come into the news again lately, since it is intended to make it the
dumping ground of many people being moved from Cato Manor
after the disturbances of 1959 and 1960.

At this time—the early forties—the crisis at Umlazi was of a
different nature. The Anglican Church had already been guilty
of a piece of unwisdom in that it had sold a part of the mission
glebe to a private European company, and another part to the
Durban City Corporation, thus making the further allocation of
that land to Africans an impossibility. The extent of the available
land was reduced to 8000 acres.

Now, in order to ease its own problems, the Durban Corporation was casting acquisitive eyes on Umlazi. Its claim was that
it did not have enough land in the Durban area to accommodate
its African workers. Its intention was to turn the mission, a
farming area, into a location. Its method was to petition the
Government to cause Umlazi to become part of the land administered by the Durban Corporation.

To meet this crisis—a very real one for the Umlazi people,
who would cease to be farmers and become out-of-work denizens

of a sub-economic housing estate—I was able, again helped by Fr. Zulu and others, to revive another moribund association, the Mission Reserve Association. Inevitably, I suppose, I became its chairman.

Originally, this body had been formed to protect the rights and serve the common interests of Mission Reserves. (These Reserves are, I think, peculiar to Natal, having been officially recognised in the days when there was a Colonial Administration.) At its inception the Mission Reserve Association was concerned with freehold rights for Africans. We had long entertained the hope that Africans would in due course be able to acquire land as individuals rather than communally, and we had long been moving away from communal ownership.

Right at the beginning of its history, then, the Mission Reserve Association was concerned to voice the clamour of an advancing people for the right to own land.

We now set ourselves to organise the people of Umlazi. There was no difficulty. They were entirely opposed to the schemes of the Durban Corporation, and we had only to direct their objections to where they would be heard. Suggestions in the Press that the Government were inclining towards the Durban Corporation view made it a matter of urgency, and we made immediate representations to the Government through the Native Affairs Department. As a result of this a conference of Africans was called in Durban by the Minister for Native Affairs, who attended it in person but did not preside over it. Umlazi and the Mission Reserve Association sent delegates, and the Durban Corporation sent observers.

It was not difficult to see that the Department sympathised with Durban. But we were united in opposition, and we were able to point to vacant lands, within the municipal area, which would have met Durban's needs quite as well. In the end the Department suggested a compromise whereby 1000 acres would, while remaining trust land, come under a housing scheme, while 7000 acres would be unaffected. We thought it wise (for fear of losing the entire 8000 acres to the all-white Durban Corporation) to accept this tentatively, provided the land were administered by the people and the Native Affairs Department—not by the Durban Corporation. Not knowing what the people of Umlazi would say, we took our opinion to them. The compromise was agreed to, but by a negligible majority. The general feeling, with which I entirely agreed, was, "this is *our* land."

In the course of time (things went slowly in those days) the Government set up a committee to handle the details. Seven bodies were represented: the Government, Durban, the Housing

Board, Commerce, Industry, Umlazi, and the Mission Reserve Association. The Rev. (now Bishop) Alphæus Zulu, the Anglican priest at Umlazi, represented Umlazi, and I represented the Mission Reserve Association. We were in a minority, usually a dissident one.

We discovered, among other things, that what was called freehold (to describe the rights of the occupants of the projected housing scheme) was not in truth freehold at all. It was not more than a retractable acknowledgment of occupation. On paper, "business sites"[2] were sketched in. Here Father Zulu and I were interested to notice the reaction of commerce and industry. In theory the new estate was represented as an independent township, with its own shopping centres. In practice, while talking of a "freehold township" the whites were thinking exclusively in terms of the usual "location", dependent on Durban, and a source of income to Durban traders.

Father Zulu and I drew attention to the lack of provision for development within the township, particularly stressing lack of industrial facilities. A Durban industrialist opposed us hotly.

"We," he declared (meaning, of course, "we white industrialists"), "cannot afford to have native industries established next door to Durban. If we permit this we'll find ourselves having to compete with a Japan!"

There was consternation. He had, of course, voiced the view of both white Durban and the Government, as was shown by the fact that no concessions were made; but he had been embarrassingly outspoken (for those days) in mixed company. The chairman rapidly came to the rescue, assuring us all that existing industrial laws were sufficient to prevent a "Japan". He instructed the planners to earmark a few sites for individual shops, leaving the question of industrial sites for later decision—by which time, as we pointed out, the land would be otherwise employed. I recall this nowadays, when the Government talks glibly of "developing the Bantu heartlands".

I must stress here that this committee did not try to browbeat or hustle us. Here and there, there were even signs of the beginnings of healthy co-operation, and in some details Father Zulu and I were able to curb possible evils or to achieve amelioration. We were not satisfied with all the committee's decisions, but at least we were there and could affect them on occasion.

The Government then in power, the United Party as it then.

---

[2] These were to be communal bazaars with restricted accommodation for stall holders. There was no provision for a single shop, retail or wholesale. Nor was there a single site set aside for industrial purposes.

was,[3] was willing at times to give half an ear to the African voice. Consultation did take place, though its results were not always what we desired.

At all events, nothing ever came of the scheme. Matters dragged on slowly until 1948. Then the Nationalists came to power, and the whole project was shelved. To us it seemed a pity. The Umlazi housing scheme, for all its defects, might well have proved a compromise between town and country, a place where some of our people might have been able to learn the disciplines of city life gradually, avoiding the disorientation which sudden change often brings. The scheme might also have relieved pressure on Cato Manor.

There is now fresh talk of a housing estate at Umlazi. The Durban Corporation is putting heads together, this time with the Nationalist Government. Whether what is now intended in any way resembles the former plan, I do not know. But one thing I do know—this time we shall not be consulted.

Not all my activities outside Groutville were as strenuous as organising cane farmers and the people of Umlazi. One of my privileges and duties was to attend gatherings at Nongoma in the heart of Zululand, where the Paramount Chief (at this time a regent) had his home. The relation of Zulu chiefs to the Paramount is a matter of sentiment rather than of law. He has no legal authority over lesser chiefs or over their people, but the authority which he exerts by virtue of his place in the hearts of Zulus is great.

Our loyalty is real and a force to be reckoned with. It is true, I believe, that tribal organisation is outmoded, and that the traditional rule by chiefs retards my people—a fact of which the Nationalists are not slow to take advantage. The wiser and more courageous of the chiefs recognise this, and refuse either to obstruct the political leaders of the people or to become Government catspaws—but it is becoming progressively harder for them to stand aside or to rule in the traditional way, because of the pressures which the Nationalist Government brings to bear on them. Chiefs find themselves caught between the interests of their people and the commands of the Government, and the weaker ones go down. Nevertheless, loyalty to the institution of the chieftainship persists. It would take a few years more of Nationalist rule to undermine it far enough to bring it tumbling down. Meanwhile many Africans are caught in a real dilemma—

[3] Not as it now is. In its desperate bid to outbid the Nationalists, the United Party has estranged some of its own members and forfeited whatever claims to integrity it may once have had.

our impulse is to be loyal to our chiefs, but we know full well that the Nationalists are turning more and more of them into their puppets.

I find the dilemma in myself. Respect for the Paramount is in my bones. It exists within me alongside the recognition that the present Paramount's actions and attitudes endanger much that I hold dear. I know that his position is acutely awkward. Yet lesser chiefs have stood out against the destructive intentions of white nationalists, while our Paramount Chief, and those of other tribes, seemed to fall in lamely with the manœuvres of the Government. It creates a conflict in us, a conflict which will not end in our meekly kowtowing to our pro-Government chiefs as the whites want us to do.

But my earlier official visits to the then Royal capital were made in a different atmosphere, when there was still a regent ruling, and before the white authorities had begun to tamper so mischievously with the chieftainship. Although Groutville lies well to the south of Zululand, we have a metaphorical saying: "Our doors face in the direction of Zululand!"

Accordingly, my visits to the capital fitted happily with my desires. They were an education too. I was introduced to customs of which I had not formerly been fully aware, and the formality and ceremonious etiquette of the Royal capital seemed to fill a vacant place in my make-up.

It usually irritates white men, of course. I remember paying two visits to the regent in the company of European companions, one of them an eminent senator. The leisurely compliance with court formality and the accustomed delay between our arrival and our being granted an interview made them seethe with impatience, whereas I revelled in it. I suppose it is in my blood. I do not think I am a "Black Englishman".

It will be readily seen that if gatherings of chiefs and tribal elders at Nongoma had been conducted in the European style, there would have been acute problems of accommodation and catering. We met these readily in our traditional way. The problem of accommodation was simply solved: we bivouacked in the open, like Shaka's army on the march. As for catering, the Paramount supplied us with the necessary number of oxen (some provided by his tribesmen), and his visitors slaughtered, cooked and ate them.

Most impressive on these occasions was the simplicity and ease with which urbanised and educated Africans mingled with their rural opposite numbers. The fusion was unconscious and complete. I can remember to this day observing the naturalness and humility with which such men as Dr. Dube took their allotted place in proceedings, dined squatting on their haunches, and slept in the open. Despite petty bickering, it is refreshing to look back to these gatherings, symbolising our basic oneness. They make utter nonsense of the white cry: "Education cuts the natives off from their own people."

One such meeting of chiefs was a direct outcome of the war in Europe, and its object was to organise recruiting for the army. The Minister for Native Affairs attended in person. The regent Mshiyeni, was presented with a horse and an ancient gun (said to have a historical value). There was a parade of sorts, and Zulu volunteers fired a few probably decrepit cannons. I was not deeply impressed, and maybe I was not alone in this. Moreover, the spectacle of Zulu soldiers handling guns was a piece of calculated deceit. In the army their function was to peel potatoes, dig trenches and, at best, to drive trucks.

In South Africa, as distinct from the Protectorates, Africans were unenthusiastic about the war. It did not have the attraction of the First World War. We had answered the call of the whites then and thereafter our position had steadily deteriorated. The disaster in which a large number of Africans were drowned, when the troopship *Mendi* went down, was speedily forgotten by South African whites, who tend to take our loyalty for granted.

At all events, the question of Hitler and what he stood for was hardly raised among the majority of Africans. To us the war seemed a call to rally to the defence of General Smuts, his oppressive white South Africa, and British imperialism from which we had suffered much, and we had reason to expect that after the war we would once again be ignored. Moreover, from our angle of vision, the practice of White Supremacy seems all too closely related to Hitler's assertions about the master race. It is not surprising that in South Africa we hung back: the issue seemed to be the local master race versus the foreign one. So the response was poor, even though the Government manufactured weird military titles for our Paramount and his chief minister.

I enjoyed these visits and conferences thoroughly, taking delight in the orderliness and dignity of my people. In spite of my youth I soon found myself on the inner councils of the regent. But perhaps the greatest value on these occasions was the opportunity which they provided for us to meet and exchange views, to confer with one another outside the times of formal conference, and to have our ideas informed and modified by the minds of other men. The quiet world of Adams gave way to a larger and more significant world.

7. *Two journeys abroad*

During these years of my chieftainship my contact with white people was less than it had been at Adams College. I found no way of reaching the whites of the Stanger area who seemed to me very conservative, very English-South African.

One effort was made, by a few Indians and myself, to form an inter-racial group. One or two white churchmen lamely attended and two priests—a Roman Catholic and an Anglican—gave the attempt real support for a time. But it was never well supported and fizzled out when I was first banned. Apartheid is really very thoroughly accepted by white South Africans, and very often their timid gestures across the colour-bar can be halted by one crack of the Government (or public opinion) whip.

I made a few contacts with white groups outside my own area, particularly in Durban. I was a member of the Durban Joint Council of Europeans and Africans, and of the Institute of Race Relations. The first has contributed little to the struggle. Indeed, as one of my friends remarked with some truth, these Joint Councils probably did us a disservice in that they did not go to the heart of South Africa's troubles. Yet at the same time, because they had a preponderantly white membership, they tended to curb or misdirect African initiative.

The Institute of Race Relations is highly valuable because of the research which it does, and the bridges which it has thrown across the colour-line. But I imagine that it does not profoundly affect public opinion. White South Africa is well insulated against the statistics of African poverty.

I had occasion to address other white groups by invitation—the Durban Workers' Association, Durban Rotary, and the Y.M.C.A. At one Y.M.C.A. meeting there were speakers of different races, an African, an Indian, an Afrikaner, and an Englishman. We speakers were introduced to one another. The Afrikaner reluctantly and furtively shook hands with the Indian. Very markedly he altogether avoided my hand. It did not surprise me; but I regretted it nevertheless, and it presented a difficult personal challenge.

My main interest of this kind lay in the Natal Missionary Conference, which was affiliated with the Christian Council of South Africa. The Christian Council was an inter-racial body on which I served as a Natal delegate, and then as an executive member. (I had to abandon membership of the executive when my first ban was served to me, since I could no longer attend meetings.) In the Christian Council I was first able to meet men like the Rev. Arthur Blaxall and Ds. du Toit. While membership of this body did not affect my life in any extreme way, I was very happy to enjoy the fellowship of other members, some of whom were genuinely eager to smash the scandal of a colour-bar within Christendom, and most of whom were eager to be friends with fellow-Christians of any race, and to learn the African view of South African difficulties.

But the Christian Council was not immune to the South African virus, and as a result of differences over the colour issue the Dutch Reformed Churches withdrew from it. Most of us felt this to be a sad pity. I think, too, that it was one of many signs of Afrikaner isolationism and of a tendency, fatal to rational Christianity, to assert and impose and withdraw, instead of staying in on the discussion. Ideas and faiths need cross-pollination. This act did the Christian Council no good. It was not until the Anglican Archbishop Derbyshire became chairman that the body began to recover.

Before the Dutch Reformed Churches departed for the wilderness, my membership in the Christian Council bestowed on me my first journey beyond the Union's borders.[1] In 1938 I was one of several delegates (four of us Africans) to the International Missionary Conference in Madras, the main purpose of which was to discuss the place of the indigenous church in missionary endeavour.

The leader of our delegation was a Dutch Reformed Minister. Even when South Africa had been left lying far behind in the wake of our ship, white South African attitudes clung to him. We, for some reason, were travelling second class, while the Europeans travelled first. On the first Sunday out the delegation leader sought us out to say, "Well, gentlemen, the white passengers might object if you were to come to the first class to worship there. Would you make your own arrangements here?"

We accepted this. It was nothing new. It scarcely aroused comment until other white delegates came to inquire about our absence. We told them the reason and they were taken aback. On the following Sunday we were invited across to the first-class lounge for multi-racial worship. The boat did not sink.

I remember this same man saying to us during the voyage,

---

[1] I hope that the two trips abroad dealt with in this chapter may not be my last.

"Personally I have no colour-bar. I'm quite ready to associate freely with Christians of different race. But in South Africa, having regard to the situation there, I would not invite any of you to my house if the neighbours objected."

A sad comment, I thought, on the battle between Christian principle and what the neighbours think. But there has been a sequel, one which raises my spirits and which is, perhaps, peculiarly Christian. After years of silence (following the Dutch Reformed breakaway) this minister and his wife have sought us out and kept regularly in touch with us by visits and correspondence. I still hope to return his visits if a time comes when I am free to move about again. In this case, the neighbours have not won.

The Conference itself was a great privilege, bringing as it did contact with Christian leaders from all over the world, some of them giants. I think that what made the deepest impression on me was not the high level of debate (it was high), but the thrill of seeing world-wide Christianity in miniature. For the first time I *saw* the result of the command: "Go ye into all the world and preach the Gospel." What had hitherto been vague became precise. Added to this was my delight in a sense of the vigour of Christianity. It was alive and active, grappling with its problems and facing its challenges. We do not see much of that in South Africa.

I was sad about South Africa. When I learned (for the first time) that there are African Anglican Bishops in West Africa, I thought it an adverse comment on South Africa, where so far there are none after this long time. Why? Has the Church been unable to train Africans, or has it tried only half-heartedly? Or has the rigour of the West African climate made Europeans feel more temporary there, readier to hand over and go?

In India we found evidences all round us of aggressive Christianity. There were schools and colleges everywhere, and the Church had found it possible to produce mature indigenous Christian leadership. Perhaps the challenge of highly developed Eastern religion spurred Christians on to great efforts. In South Africa the Church has tended to accommodate itself to the general secular pattern of the country, it has been content to supply a modicum of elementary education, and generally it has waited for its African converts to push it from behind, to alarm it into belated action.

The spectacle in India of the Church seriously tackling poverty (how desperate a poverty!), the Church undertaking agricultural projects, the Church organising home industries and social services, all this made me aware of our sluggish pace in South

Africa. I came home an incisive critic of South African Christianity. I still am one. It does not diminish my loyalty.

The hospitality of India and Ceylon, and the munificence of the Christian community were overwhelming. In Ceylon I was for ten days the guest of a devout Anglican widow, the owner of an extensive estate and a large mansion. To her great regret her only son was a Communist. I remember how she said to me, "Chief, I have gone beyond grief now about my son. He's a good boy. He could have misused our wealth, but he works, he cares for the servants in ways which put me to shame as a Christian. I had hoped he would be an Anglican priest. But he's a good son."

The poverty of India appalled me. It was so much worse than what I know in South Africa. Beggars followed us for miles, people slept huddled in the streets, the country dwellings were often crude huts. But if I felt helpless in the face of such destitution, Indians were trying to combat it. In one suburb of lovely houses we learned that the teachers there had formed a building society and provided housing. The Society of the Servants of India was busy, too, using voluntary self-taxation to relieve the poor. The imagination and spirit of these efforts impressed us deeply.

One cloud hung over the Conference—the cloud of war. Tension was evident in a reserve between Chinese and Japanese delegations. Even so, the very fact that they were able to meet as brothers in such a situation bore vivid testimony to the potency of Christianity.

I came back from India with wider sympathies and wider horizons.

Ten years later I enjoyed a second reprieve from the tense complexity of my homeland. As on the occasion of my first visit beyond the confines of South Africa, the invitation arose out of my church activities. This time, however, in 1948, I was invited to go to the United States to undertake a lecture tour about Christian missions, under the joint ægis of the American Board and of the North American Missionary Conference.

The opportunity delighted me. With it came my first experience of air travel. My wife accompanied me to Johannesburg where I was to board the plane which left at midnight. I remember my departure vividly. Because it was dark I could not even catch a last glimpse of her. As the plane took off I felt an acute pang of loneliness and isolation, a voyager going into the void.

My arrival at New York made it speedily evident that my knowledge of geography had deserted me while I packed. I packed in winter. I arrived in blazing, humid summer—equipped to meet it with a winter wardrobe!

73

I was soon immersed in the first part of my programme, which took me to a number of summer camps, mainly for young people. I was most impressed by the way in which the churches in the States were meeting the challenge of young people; not only by providing for their needs, but by deploying them wisely in the active work of the church. This accent on youth was new to me, and it seemed both worthwhile and successful. For a couple of months I was fully occupied in visiting these camps and talking to young people. As a member of the staff of each camp, I found myself counselling groups of young white boys—another new experience. At one camp my group (boys and girls this time) stole the show on Talent Night. We put the emphasis on Africa and ended by singing *Nkosi Sikelel' i-Afrika*.[2]

Everywhere I went the interest shown in Africa was immense. I was able, I think, to satisfy curiosity about South Africa, but the questions which were asked about the rest of the continent made me much aware of my ignorance in those days about Africa as a whole, and of the extent to which white South Africa sealed us all off from the rest of Africa.

After this I became for a while the property of the North American Missionary Conference. According to its itinerary, groups of speakers toured numbers of large American cities and I found myself called on to address huge gatherings in such places as Boston, Chicago, Minneapolis and Washington, D.C. I was taxed more than the other members of my group, but when sheer fatigue drove me to the point of rebellion, I was told, "Blame that on the people's eagerness to learn about Africa."

It may be that the presidential election going on at the time stimulated American interest in Africa. One of its themes was the development of under-developed countries. I hoped then, as I do now, that the U.S.A. was concerned with the uplift of people and not with the dragooning of Africans into the Western camp for reasons of international politics; nor solely with the exploitation of material resources. I said this repeatedly to Americans with whom I discussed the matter.

I think it is still pertinent. We are subjected to intensive wooing by both East and West. But what we want now is to be ourselves, to retain our personality, and to let our soul, long buffeted by the old scramble for Africa, grow free. African leaders must be wary of the material enticement of her people. We do not live by

[2] This means "God Save Africa". The hymn is a sort of unofficial National Anthem of black South Africa and the theme song of the African National Congress.

bread alone, however alluring the sight of bread may be to the hungry.

While we were in Washington the Australian Embassy held a reception for us, and there I met the Secretary of the South African Legation. It was strange to be accosted in Zulu so far from home, and perhaps stranger to be treated as I would not be at home—certainly not nowadays—by a Government official. At his invitation I visited the South African Legation twice, where I was quite normally treated. I remember this conversation:

"How are you getting on in the U.S.A., Chief?"

"Well," I replied, "that's not for me to say. It's really for the people I've spoken to to judge. I find it hard to divorce church affairs from politics. The Americans ask questions, you know, and I reply honestly to the best of my knowledge. I cannot answer as though the church lived in a political void."

"On the whole, Chief," was the reply, "you're doing very well."

I wondered how they knew.

Although it was not a part of my programme, I asked to visit the south, where I was entertained at three colleges. I had little opportunity to meet ordinary country people, but during visits to country areas I was able to form some idea of the conditions under which American negroes live. I was interested to notice that in certain places farmers were not only taught how to farm but were given state financial aid, regardless of their colour— and that in the Deep South. I was interested, too, to encounter the sort of institution which would have been dear to the heart of Dr. Loram. The emphasis was all on the manual crafts. I have no scorn for these, but they do not seem to me to justify university degrees.

I think, however, that I spent more time in answering questions than in having my own curiosity satisfied. My negro friends were very eager to hear about South Africa, and their readiness to help resolved itself many times into the question, "Can we come over there to assist you?"

"It would be heartening if you could," I used to reply, "but for one thing the South African Government wouldn't let you— certainly not with that motive. For another, you'd find your- selves, and those from other countries, foreigners in the continent of your origin. But we're glad of your interest in any case, and to the extent that you fight segregation here, you help indirectly. The more democratic America becomes, the better for those whom she influences. We need the interest of your churchmen too. There's a tendency for your white missionaries among us to drift away—they sometimes get identified with the whites."

I did not meet the issue of colour at all in the north. Naturally, I lived for the most part in the home of Christian people where one would not expect to meet it. But even in hotels and shops, people were people. In a mild way I was conscious of a colour-bar in the south.

In Atlanta I asked if, by way of relaxation, I might go with my hostess to a cinema.

"Chief Luthuli," she said, "you've asked a difficult thing of me. You see, our cinemas are segregated, and the shows are poor in negro cinemas. But the main thing is this: I have vowed never to spend a cent of my money upholding segregation. I will not buy segregation. I'd love to take you. I hope you understand why I can't."

"Lady," I replied, "I understand you only too well."

In one institution an exaggerated sense of race—or rather, of nationality—displayed itself oddly. Here I preached a sermon one Sunday morning and on the following day made a tour of the classrooms. As I came to the end of my tour, the teacher who was with me said hesitantly, "One student here has refused to attend your lecture to this class; I'm reluctant to tell you why."

I pressed her for the reason, and she replied, "Yesterday in your sermon you said, 'I'm glad to be amongst my people.' This child has taken exception to that. She says *she's* not of Africa."

"It's good that she feels she belongs here," I said, "but I blame you for not teaching her all the facts about herself."

It was in Washington itself that the full and utter absurdity of the colour-bar really manifested itself. Train travel to the south (and back) was segregated. This meant that negro Americans were separated from white Americans by curtains. They travelled in the same compartment, but curtains hung between them. Then in Washington the curtains were removed. The same passengers journeyed onwards in the same compartments, still breathing the same air, but now they could see as well as hear each other.

During my stay I was able to address a number of groups of Americans not connected with the churches; and then, reluctantly, I had to take my leave—reluctantly because of the many friends I had made, and because it was refreshing to enjoy normal relations with white people and to notice that no heavens fell. I had already extended my time in the States by three months. Even so, I still had to refuse invitations to speak as far afield as Canada and the Pacific Coast.

I came back via Lisbon. Both ways, to my great regret, I failed to set foot on English soil, but on my return I did spend a day in Lisbon. "A lovely, lovely city," I said to myself, "—and no wonder. Its loveliness is partly fashioned out of the toil of Africa. Africans who do not know much loveliness have helped to make it look like this."

This was my last visit to the outside world, at least for the time being. This visit was undertaken when the Nationalist Government of Dr. Malan had come to power. Formerly whites had discouraged travel abroad by Africans. Now it is made excessively difficult, with only rare exceptions. The argument is, of course, that "natives who travel get spoilt." We are said to become misfits. Contact with whites in America or Europe is supposed to go to our heads.

My journeys to India and America did not, as such things are believed to do, fill me with a new discontent, or any half-desire to escape. I was asked often enough whether I would not like to stay in the U.S.A. I had only one reply: "No. The very challenge makes me say I have work to do at home. I like to travel. But South Africa is my home, and I hanker after nobody else's."

It may be that travelling had made me see South African issues more sharply and in a different and larger perspective. Even so, I have not been seized by the urge to shake my people's oppressors and bang their heads until they recognise that people are people. I would like the recognition to come to them naturally and peacefully.

But perhaps the desire in any African for normal human relations—not group relations—is itself proof that he is "spoilt". If that is so, I can only reply that I was not spoilt abroad. I was spoilt by being made in the image of God.

8. *Whose is South Africa?*

For the moment I shall leave my own story there, in 1948. When I remind my reader that in 1948 the first Nationalist Government assumed power under Dr. Malan, and when I recall that it was while I was still in America that news of the appalling Durban Riots reached me, it will be clear that during these main years of my chieftainship events in South Africa were not standing still.

If I have created the impression that I stood somehow aloof from political developments, I must correct that impression at once. It is true that while at Adams I was primarily a teacher of teachers, and that life at Adams went on outside the main arena. But even while I was chief-elect of Groutville I found myself precipitated into public life, and from that time onwards my own affairs steadily converged with those of the growing resistance movement. It could hardly have been otherwise.

But to make clear the nature and the purpose of a resistance which was there long before my story began, I must go back. Otherwise it may not be obvious what I was drawn into, and why.

I do not find myself among those people who tend to reduce all human affairs to questions of economics and economic pressures. None the less, the basic point at issue in South Africa is the question of ownership. Because the races inhabiting the country disagree fundamentally on the answer to this question, the whole controversy is hopelessly tangled with racial factors, and on both sides these racial distinctions have become an unavoidable part of the struggle. One cannot separate the issue of race from the argument about ownership at present, because one race insists on exclusive ownership.

Who owns South Africa?

With the exception of a small group of black nationalists who have learned their politics from Dr. Verwoerd's and General Smuts's parties, *the great majority of Africans* reply that the country now[1] belongs to fourteen million people of different races —it is jointly owned by all its inhabitants, quite regardless of their colour. This view, which I adhere to without qualification,

---

[1] For us questions of who came first to which part of South Africa are irrelevant. The vital issue is not a quibble over the past, but salvation in the present.

demands that people be regarded primarily as people. As far as culture and habits of life are concerned, they may differ as radically as they wish. But when it comes to participation in ownership and government, race must be made wholly irrelevant.

With the exception of a small number of voices crying in the wilderness, the overwhelming majority of whites reply that South Africa is exclusively owned by three million whites. On this point General Smuts and his successors, and Dr. Malan and his successors, are in whole-hearted agreement. It does not stop, either, with ownership of land and wealth, and participation in government. In this view the whites, because they *are* "whites", extend their possession to ownership of the remaining eleven million people, who are expected to regard themselves as fortunate to be allowed to live and breathe—and work—in a "white man's country".

The whites who hold this view energetically repudiate the accusation that those who do not belong to the "master race" are owned as though they were slaves. It is, of course, true that we are not bound in quite the same shackles as in the days of conventional slavery. But the idiom of slavery changes with the times. Nowadays, state ownership has replaced individual ownership to some extent. The slave system has been nationalised. We are told where we may work, where we may not, where we may live and where we may not; freehold rights are altogether taken from us and we are forbidden by law to strike or to protest against the edicts of an all-white parliament or against exploitation.

We have no safeguards whatever. There is nothing which our white owners cannot do to us simply by agreeing with each other to do it. And in law after law since the Act of Union in 1910, you will find this conception—whites own Africans, Indians, coloured people—expressing itself. In election after election you will see the "native question" ("What shall we do with our movable property which our political opponents have not yet thought up?") used as a major successful means to sway an all-white electorate. We stand by and watch ourselves being used as the white man's football. This or that white group scores the points and wins the election, over what should be done with "the natives". Our lot is to feel the impact of the boot.

In South Africa as it was before the Act of Union. the question of ownership was still partly undecided. In the two Boer Republics Africans had no rights, and could look forward to having none. In the "English" colony of Natal, which included Zululand, there was a complicated and unsatisfactory system whereby a few Africans might qualify for the franchise. In the Cape certain rights had been extended to Africans, and an appreciable (though by no means decisive) number were voters. Even in the Cape Province, however, the familiar opposition gathered momentum.

The Act of Union virtually handed the whole of South Africa over to a minority of whites, lock, stock and barrel. English Natal sided on this issue quite happily with the Boer Republics. Only in the Cape was there a little ineffective opposition, and this was lost in the compromises which had to be effected in order to achieve union. As far as the whites were concerned the matter was settled: they became the exclusive owners of the new state. The members of other races who found themselves handed over officially, entirely without their consent, were the livestock which went with the estate, objects rather than subjects.

I do not think that the African opposition to this situation brought about by the Act of Union is surprising, and I do not think that it has so far been extreme. We regard it as an act of piracy, in which the lives and strength of ten million Africans are part of the loot.

Since Union, Government after Government has set itself to consolidate the white position, painlessly to itself, and always at the expense of what are quite frankly described as "subject races". Law after law has had this intention. When the legislators have been dealing with industry, land, marriage, freedom of movement, the siting of homes, education, commerce, passports, parliamentary representation, wages, strikes, church services, prostitutes, transport—almost everything—there has been in the forefront of their minds the will to affirm and extend white ownership.

I do not here intend to survey this ruthless process law by law. The curious will find that a study of the South African Hansard and Statute Book more than supports my contentions. As early as 1913 the Natives Land Act confined us to hopelessly over-crowded Reserves and virtually deprived us of rights to purchase land. As recently as 1960 the Extension of University Education Act removed us from universities. From 1910 to now, the whites have carried out systematic and relentless mopping-up operations. Today their ownership is as complete as it ever will be.

Opposition to white ambitions began, of course, well before Union. But it was the perpetration of the Act of Union itself which hardened African opposition and brought organised resistance into being. By ganging up together, Boer and Briton had achieved their coup. It took us very little time to recognise that only by working for our own unity could we hope to withstand the effects, upon us and within us, of being treated like cattle, or to bring the white man to his senses.

Our reply—a very mild one indeed, to begin with—was the formation of the African National Congress.[2]

This body came into existence as the direct outcome of our exclusion from our own country, and of the white entente to ensure this exclusion. The man who most clearly saw the need for African unity, and for a body which expressed this unity and gave voice to a people rendered inarticulate by the Act of Union, was a brilliant young advocate lately returned from Oxford and the Middle Temple, Dr. Seme. He was able to convince other leading Africans of this need, and the outcome of his activities was a gathering of African leaders in Bloemfontein at the beginning of 1912.

Under the presidency of Dr. John Langibalele Dube, Congress was originally fashioned along the lines of the British Parliament. It was divided—an attempt to meet the complexity of emergent African society—into a House of Chiefs and a House of Commoners. The difficulty, however, was that so many petty chiefs had been created by the whites that it was almost impossible to know who qualified to sit in the House of Chiefs. Further, since the whites looked on Congress with little favour, they exerted pressure on many chiefs to dissociate themselves from the new body, and some chiefs succumbed.

The whites did not, however, succeed in creating a rift between chiefs and people. No gulf appeared. Chiefs had no difficulty in recognising the elected leaders, and elected leaders had no temptation to trespass on the preserves of chiefs.

I would go so far as to say that, in spite of the intensive activity of the Nationalist Governments to estrange chiefs from political leaders, this is still true. For the most part, with exceptions here and there, chiefs do not become as jealous of political leaders as the white supremacists would desire. Even "pro-Government" chiefs are in sympathy with the Resistance movement as often as not, and both the chiefs and their subjects recognise that chiefs, because of their legal relation to the Government, are in no position to lead a movement of liberation.

The House of Chiefs has long since been discarded. It may have been in conformity with the idea of a sort of African shadow Parliament, but that idea was not appropriate.

The business of Congress is not deliberation and legislation. Its business is to right the total exclusion of the African from

[2] It was originally called the South African Native National Congress. I shall refer to it here throughout as "Congress" or as the A.N.C.

the management of South Africa, to give direction to the forces of liberation, to harness peacefully the growing resistance to continued oppression and, by various non-violent means, to demand the redress of injustice. Congress is therefore now more fittingly organised as one body, rather like a political party fighting an election. (But, even now, the A.N.C. is not a true political party. It is very much more all-embracing than any political party would be. Its goal is not that Congress shall rule South Africa, but that all Africans shall fully participate in ownership and government. The time for political parties among us is not yet.)

One of the major purposes of Congress, right at the beginning, was to overcome the divisions and disunities between tribes, and, since we did not then hope to *create* national unity against the will of the whites who held all the power, at least to *develop* African unity. Right from its inception the A.N.C. realised the importance of awakening the African people and uniting them in a common loyalty which would cut across all lesser loyalties. Our oppressors have done all in their power to retain and emphasise minor allegiances. In spite of this, although we have not won the battle for unity, we have gained much ground, and increasing oppression of all Africans by white supremacists is one of our strongest allies in this battle.

In its early days Congress gave voice to the many day-to-day grievances of the people. It appealed (fruitlessly) to the whites, it made representations, and it busied itself with the spadework of creating unity. It did not at that time attack the fundamental issue—participation in ownership and government. Realistically —for it was dealing with people who were still politically unawakened—it addressed itself to such sources of hardship as the 1913 Land Act and the Pass System. In these early stages it was asking for alleviation rather than demanding votes.

Little headway was made. Neither then nor now were the white rulers in any mood to listen. Congress put more faith in the reasonableness of its claims than the white man's amenableness to reason has justified. But at least Congress was there, and at least it attempted, year after year, to bring the whites round by argument and persuasion.

In the course of Congress history, no civilised method of attempting to get recognition and redress has been neglected. But perhaps reason, argument, and the appeal of humane values and democratic principles are things which most white South Africans cannot understand. They have turned a deaf ear.

To begin with only the ear was appealed to, until we discovered that it was deaf. In the early years Congress was not organised to appeal with more forceful arguments. It was little more than a yearly gathering of leaders who, having formulated grievances, having decided whom to appeal to, and having made their representations, then went home until the following year. Individual members did a certain amount of freelance educating of the people between times, but there were as yet no local branches and no sustained pressure. Still hoping in the Crown, misunderstanding the Statute of Westminster, deputations went to England. There they were politely treated, and then they returned, hopeful or depressed.

After the First World War one such deputation met General Hertzog at Versailles. The General was looking for a republic. The Africans were looking for access to their homeland.

Even so, things were beginning to move. In the Free State in 1913 there were widespread anti-pass demonstrations and numerous arrests. In 1919 Congress organised an anti-pass campaign—in Johannesburg alone there were 700 arrests. In Capetown 400 dockers staged a strike. In 1920, 40,000 African miners came out on strike on the Reef, and in Port Elizabeth twenty-one people were killed by the police. In the following year 163 people were wantonly massacred by the police at Bulhoek, and in 1924 a hundred Hottentots were butchered for refusing to pay an incomprehensible tax on dogs. South Africa was beginning to reap the rewards of the Act of Union which launched us along the way of strife. From these years until today, tension and pressure have done nothing but mount.

I am far from claiming that Congress was responsible for the growing resistance. At first it was no more than a part of it, and possibly a conservative part at that. Other organisations and interests were in the field, among them industrial workers' organisations and the Communist Party. Throughout the country as a whole, resistance was unco-ordinated and haphazard. But it was there, and it arose out of the whites' refusal to share the country with us, or to permit us to walk free in our own land.

The whites claimed the land and the people and set out to consolidate their position. Africans opposed themselves to this claim. From this head-on clash began to come an unending series of laws aimed not only at white consolidation, but at crushing African objection, paralysing African action, demolishing remaining privileges, stifling the African voice, and punishing the African resister.[3]

In 1924 or 1925, the Smuts régime ("it has been our ideal to

---

[3] In white parlance, all people who do not wholeheartedly accept indefinite white supremacy are "agitators".

make South Africa a white man's country") was ousted by a coalition between Hertzog and "Labour"—white labour. In 1929 Hertzog found himself able to do without Labour, but by 1933 he was in trouble with his own extremists, led by Dutch Reformed minister D. F. Malan. He extricated himself from this by a merger with Smuts, which sent Malan into the wilderness for the next fifteen years.

Laws aimed at crippling Africans politically do not begin with the advent of Hertzog. Nevertheless, from the middle twenties onwards, they grow in range and frequency. It is worthy to note that many of the brutal laws used by the Malan-Strijdom-Verwoerd Nationalists against African resistance were already on the Statute Book in 1948 when these men came to power. They were put there by the successive Governments of Botha-Smuts, Hertzog-Labour Party, Hertzog-Smuts, Smuts.

During the years of Hertzog rule, South Africa continued along its logical path, resistance and oppression both intensifying. In 1928-29 Natal burst into fits of unrest and violence over certain brewing restrictions, and there was trouble in Durban over taxation. In 1930 there was an outburst in Worcester, and an anti-pass demonstration in Durban. The cost of white supremacy—paid almost entirely in black corpses—rose steadily.

The stock reaction of the white parliament was to give its Governments harsher powers. If the wounded man groans, shoot him again.

The unholy alliance between Hertzog and Smuts gave Hertzog an opportunity for which he had been hankering from the time he came to power. In order to execute his purpose, which was an assault on the so-called "entrenched clauses" of the Act of Union, Hertzog needed a two-thirds majority in parliament. Until this time he had been unable to command it. Now Smuts gave it to him. Between them they set out to tidy up and make much more severe the already drastic effects of the 1913 Land Act, and to remove the last lingering vestiges of political opportunity for Africans.

The product of the mutual scheme of Smuts and Hertzog emerged finally in two Acts of Parliament, still known, for some reason, as the Hertzog Bills. The Natives Representation Act made it impossible for any African to qualify as a voter. Before this there had existed the possibility of the franchise being extended—there were a few thousand Africans on the roll in the Cape. Now the franchise was entirely removed as far as we were concerned.

The generals threw us what they perhaps thought of as a sop. By a complicated system of electoral colleges, we were to be allowed to elect four senators and three members of the House of Assembly. Our candidates would, of course, have to come from the ranks of white South Africa.

They also set up an institution called the Natives' Representative Council (N.R.C.), whose members were the Secretary for Native Affairs, the four Chief Native Commissioners and elected and appointed Africans, and whose functions were advisory. They felt, apparently, that if we could be induced to talk enough to no purpose, our political hopes and economic troubles would fall away.

The Natives Land and Trust Act did not substantially alter the land position. It merely consolidated the practices which had existed from 1913 onwards in one piece of legislation, confining us more effectively to our 13 per cent of South Africa's land surface. The "Trust" part of the Act gave the impression that the Government was intending to buy us more land to add to our crowded and agriculturally unsatisfactory "reserves". That was its declared purpose. Some land had been bought. It had taken successive Governments twenty-five years to acquire 70 per cent of the extra land then promised. Thus we still live on less than 13 per cent of South Africa's land; and the present Government is finding it acutely difficult to persuade white farmers to part with any more. If we had ever approved of the restrictions on our buying of land, or if we had ever placed reliance in white promises, we should by now, after twenty-five years, be sadly disillusioned. Fortunately not many of us had any illusions.

The proposal to bring in these Acts of the Generals served, as it chanced, to introduce me into public life in South Africa.

9. *The Hertzog Bills*

While I was still at Adams College, and chief-elect of Groutville, I was invited by the Native Affairs Department of the day to attend a conference of chiefs and leaders to discuss the provisions of the Hertzog Bills. At this stage they were still in draft form, and a show was being made of consulting the people whom they affected. The conference to which I was invited applied only to Natal, but similar local conferences were held in the other provinces.

It was an odd affair. The acting-Paramount of the Zulus was chairman, though in practice Dr. Dube, who at this time headed the A.N.C. in Natal, acted for him. After discussion a committee was appointed to report on the findings of the conference. The Rev. A. Mtimkulu presided over this committee, though as it turned out he was absent from some of the sessions. I acted for him.

We worked hard and drew up a report, detailed in its criticism of the proposed legislation. When the report was completed we gave it to the Rev. Mtimkulu, expecting that he, as chairman of the committee, would present it. He glanced casually through its pages and said, "No, I don't think I'll accept this."

In our accustomed Zulu way we contained our surprise and tried to discover how he could reject the findings of his own committee. His answer was to produce a report of his own.

"This report," he informed us, "is in conformity with the line of the Government. We can't afford to run too far counter to the Government mind." We learned that the report had been inspired unofficially by a clerk in the Native Affairs Department. With the deference due to his age we tried to press our point.

"No, no," he replied, "you're just *young* men."

In the event he substituted his own report and the committee's findings were discarded. The upshot was that Natal Africans appeared completely indifferent to the fate of their disenfranchised brothers in the Cape, and the conference appeared to accept without criticism the proposals relating to land. The white newspapers gladly reported the Zulu people as being solidly in agreement with the generals. We younger men were shocked and taken aback, but we did not see how to make an issue of it with a politically entrenched older man.

There was, however, a sequel. Somehow, I suppose, news of

what had happened reached the ears of white authorities, and a second conference was summoned. Here the Native Affairs Department clerk was pointedly absent. This conference, while condemning the deprivation of the right of Cape Africans, was not critical of the system of being represented in parliament by whites—at that time the franchise had never been a live issue in Natal. Our emphasis was on the restriction of land, but we did say that, in so far as it was the declared intention of the Government to increase the size of the reserves, we would welcome this.

As far as the Native Representative Council was concerned, Natal expressed no strong views for or against. The fact that the Paramount was to be a member of it probably inclined Zulus to see it favourably rather than otherwise.

Of course, this second conference was intended only to keep us quiet. Mtimkulu's "report" might as well have remained the final word. The generals proceeded to do exactly as they had all along intended. Africans were disenfranchised, land rights were further restricted, and the Native Representation Council was created.

The proposed legislation had a further effect. A move was set afoot by Professor Jabavu (son of the old Cape leader) to hold a conference of all African organisations, and the result was a body called the All African Convention. The Convention met in Bloemfontein in the last month of 1935. There were 400 delegates —even African sporting organisations were represented. I did not attend.

The Convention condemned the two Bills. But there was nevertheless a sharp cleavage in its ranks. Broadly speaking, the younger delegates wished to reject the legislation outright, while older men, more moderate in their outlook, preferred to tinker with the details and suggest modifications here and there without commenting on the basic principles involved. Hertzog summoned some of the older leaders, who came away from their interview with him appeased and mollified—by what, I do not know. The Bills became Acts all the same.

Once this had happened, once the Bills had become law, the conflict between old and young in the Convention showed itself more sharply. Younger men wished to boycott the Native Representation Council entirely, and they wished also to refuse to elect white Senators and M.P.s to represent us in parliament. The older view was, "Let us try to milk this almost dry cow. Let us once more put to the test the white man's declared good faith."

The older men prevailed. Younger opinion tended thereafter

to find its outlet in Congress, to which it brought a new and invigorating militancy.

The All African Convention had one unfortunate result in African political life. There was a desire on the part of the officials of this body to keep it in existence, although at its inception it was intended only to voice African views on the Hertzog Bills. The A.N.C. refused to be a party to this, although some of its more venerable members were in favour. The Congress argument was that it wished to remain a political body and not to be submerged in mere deliberation. There was a youthful urge in Congress to organise itself for action, which would be hampered by its being included in a formless *ad hoc* organisation including representatives of completely non-political bodies—ministers' fraternals and soccer clubs for instance. The feeling was growing apace that there was work to be done. The days of fruitless talking were sliding into the past.

Congress, therefore, went its own way. The Convention remained in existence, giving birth to the Non-European Unity Movement. It is doubtful whether South Africa has so far produced a body more torn by friction and disharmony than the Unity movement. Except in a small corner of the Cape it has made no political impact.

It is not quite accurate to say that Congress went its own way. A few Congress members hived off to stay with the Convention. Among these was the then President of the A.N.C., the Rev. Z. Mahabane. But under the new leadership of Dr. Xuma, who was then in sympathy with the views of the younger men, the great majority of the A.N.C. took a somewhat altered direction. The Hertzog Bills had been a crisis. It was obvious now that the clear statement of African opinion went unheeded, and it was also obvious that we had too long allowed ourselves to be bought off by bland words and an occasional pat on the back.

Under Dr. Xuma's leadership, Congress at last got down to the task of equipping itself for the fray, and of facing up to the realities of the South African situation. Men with a desire to air grievances gave way to men with a purpose. In the Xuma era (1940-49), Congress gradually began to take on a new character. It began to formulate its aims and policy far more clearly than hitherto. Inspired by the Atlantic Charter, and by a war for human freedom, it drew up a precise document called "Africa Claims". Young men began to come into their own, and the Congress Youth League injected new determination and vitality into the organisation. A new constitution was devised, one far more appropriate to the efficient working of a liberatory organisation. The machinery was overhauled and altered in ways which turned a rather vague and shapeless body into something whose workings its members could grasp, and a drive was launched to establish branches throughout the country.

I do not pretend, however, that Congress suddenly became a streamlined organisation. It is far from being that even yet, and this is one of our major difficulties, especially since every impediment which the Nationalists have been able to devise has been brought into play. But it did improve, vastly, and it must be said that Dr. Xuma had much to do with this improvement. We began to know what we were after, and we began to evolve methods for pursuing it.

When I say "we", I must add that I was not at this time, the early and middle forties, a member of Congress. I was still emerging from the Adams chrysalis, I was occupied in administering Groutville, I was giving some time to the needs of cane growers, and I spent some of this period on my visit to India. But I was watching these developments in the African political world with close attention and interest, and I felt myself to be a part of the events which were unfolding.

I was precipitated into Congress casually, almost by accident. I will not pretend that I had any reluctance about this. I had for a very long time admired the stand made by the A.N.C., particularly against the 1913 and 1936 Land Acts, and against passes. It appeared as an organisation struggling for the uplift of the people, and the removal of heavy shackles. (In those days our present desire for full participation in the running of the country was hardly evident.) I was then, as many people are now, a part of Congress in all but the technical sense. To me, as much as to its enrolled members, the A.N.C. was "the watchdog of the African people".

My formal inclusion in the ranks of Congress came about like this. The leader in Natal was Dr. Dube, who had formerly been the first National President of the organisation. A man of great breadth and intelligence, Dr. Dube was the Elder Statesman of African politics. In 1945 he had a stroke, and the reins of Congress were taken over by his deputy, the same Rev. Mtimkulu who had ten years earlier substituted his own "findings" on the Hertzog Bills for those of the appointed committee.

For some time before Dr. Dube's stroke, which was followed a little later by his death, the A.N.C. in Natal had been making rather heavy weather. Now it seemed to many of us younger men that what he had stood for was in danger of disintegrating entirely. Our reaction was to rally to Congress in an attempt to preserve the work of Dr. Dube and to try to get down to building on his foundations. To some degree this was for us a matter of a largely personal allegiance to Dube.

Dr. Dube had for a long time been heavily opposed in Natal by the African trade unionist A. W. G. Champion. At the annual meeting now in the offing, both Champion and Mtimkulu were candidates for the provincial presidency of Congress, and each was strongly backed by his own followers.

These annual meetings, I should explain, were very general affairs—in order to go in and talk one had to do no more than pay one's subscription at the door. In those days the A.N.C. in Natal was still very much an *ad hoc* organisation which somehow persisted from year to year. There was certainly work crying out to be done. The annual meetings could be chaotic and rough too —more than one delegate on occasion left by the windows in earlier days.

The meeting which took place after the indisposition of Dr. Dube was presided over by Mtimkulu. He neglected to have the credentials of the delegates examined in the morning. In the afternoon, when non-delegates had already participated in formal discussion and voting, he tried to do this—but now Champion rightly objected. Confusion reigned. This was not decreased when Mtimkulu suddenly left the chair. On the spur of the moment, when the meeting was about to erupt, I leapt on to the platform and called for silence. To my surprise, I got it. I suggested that we should not allow ourselves to wreck the meeting. We did not even know why Mtimkulu had left, so there was no point in quarrelling over it. I urged the delegates to appoint an acting chairman of the meeting, and carry on. That is what was done, and I found myself in the chair.

We separated the sheep from the goats—quite a number of goats had found their way in—and held a conventional election. Champion became Natal President, and I found myself serving on his executive. It was a day of surprises.

To accept this position seemed to me the natural outcome of an attitude which I had imbibed at Adams: it was another way of trying to serve people. To serve under Champion, now that Dube was gone, did no violence to my admiration for Dube. Both in different ways were after serving their people too.

With Xuma as National President, and with Champion leading us in Natal, things were auspicious in many ways for Congress. In Natal a long-standing breach between Congress and a union of industrial and commercial workers was healed, and Dr. Dube's policy of running his own Congress in the province was scrapped. We became fully integrated with the National organisation. On the administrative side, attention was paid to establishing branches and running them properly. The membership began to grow. And at last we began to turn away from thinking in terms of an amelioration here and a concession there, and to get down to fundamentals. We began, in other words, to demand our rightful place in the South African sun, where before we had been petitioning to be treated a little less harshly in the place assigned to us by whites.

To Xuma, on the African side, must go the credit for beginning to co-operate with other liberatory organisations. Some of the credit, however, must go to General Smuts, for it was one of his more iniquitous Acts which made us and the Indians of Natal realise that we have a good deal in common. In 1946 General Smuts—a world statesman beyond the Union's borders, a subtle and relentless white supremacist at home—reacted to the fears of Natal whites and introduced the notorious "Ghetto Act"—the Asiatic Land Tenure Act. Like the Natives Land Acts (1913 and 1936) this was a precursor of the Nationalist Group Areas Act, in that it confined rightless South Africans to areas not of their choice.

Both Dr. Xuma and Dr. Dadoo (head of the Indian Congress) were big enough men to surmount the barriers of race, and the outcome was what has come to be known as the Dadoo-Xuma Agreement. Co-operation between the two Congresses drew steadily from that time onwards.

(I might put in here that this co-operation was criticised by a minority within the A.N.C., who wanted Africans to "go it alone". Recently these men broke away from the A.N.C. to form the Pan-African Congress.)

A further sign of the awakening of these years was the founding of the Congress Youth League. Until Dr. Xuma's time older men did not encourage younger men to join Congress, let alone participate in leading it. The organisation therefore stood in dire need of the ideas and energies of young men. Xuma brought the young men in, and the impact which the vigorous Youth League made on Congress as a whole was considerable and beneficial.

Certainly in these years, roughly between the late thirties and the middle forties, an awakening was taking place. At home in South Africa, the constant and unremitting curtailment of our liberties was beginning to evoke, on a new scale, our refusal to sit by and watch our claim to humanity being whittled down until there was almost nothing left. The patient beast of burden can be goaded and overloaded for only so long—especially if he is not in reality a beast of burden but a human being.

Away from home, the world was torn by a war fought in the

interests of human freedom. We could not but be aware of the contradiction between Smuts's behaviour on the world stage and his behaviour at home. On the world stage he was vocal about freedom, human liberty, and Western values. At home he denied us these things, even though our help in South Africa's war effort was diligently sought. Nevertheless, we were made aware by the war of forces stirring in the world at large and on our own continent. A great number of Africans realised, perhaps with some surprise, that South Africa was not the world and that there are alternatives to white South Africa's ingrained ways of governing.

For the moment I leave the Congress story there, at the years immediately following World War II. As Smuts was beginning to falter in white South African affairs, and as the strength of the Malan party was mounting to bring about his downfall, Africans were slowly but unmistakably waking up.

While all this was going on, and while I was serving on Champion's Congress executive in Natal, I was at one stage briefly occupied with something else.

It will be recalled that one of the Hertzog Bills of 1936 created a Native Representative Council. It will be remembered too that when this proposal was considered by the All African Convention there was a division of opinion. The younger men wanted to boycott the body entirely, whereas the older men, seeing that it was in any case inevitable, wanted to make it work in the hope of gathering a crumb or two. The view of the elders prevailed. There was this to be said for their attitude: at least the new body was elective, in a cumbersome way, and at least it was intended to represent *all* Africans. It was, perhaps, worth trying. At all events, here again was the appearance of an opportunity to make our voices heard. It can never be alleged that we turned aside from what means were open to us.

Apart from my place in the deliberations about who Natal's first representatives in the Native Representative Council were to be, I had no connection with this Council in its early years, save in my capacity as chief. However, when the death of Dr. Dube brought about a by-election, I was voted into his place. I was interested, though not at all surprised, as I went about among the people before the election, to notice how deeply disillusioned they were by this time with the Council.

"What is the use," they asked me, "of your going to the N.R.C. in Pretoria? They do nothing but talk. Where has this Council got us?"

It was only too true. For years now they had talked. Nobody listened. I was disillusioned myself and could only reply, "There are people beyond South Africa who sometimes hear what we say. All we can do is try to shout to the world. All I can do is to help us shout louder."

It was hardly surprising that the Native Representation Council was no more than a hollow show. White South Africa was impenetrably dead, and their newspapers did nothing to educate them.

Some field officers of the Native Affairs Department persistently set out to undermine the Council. As usual, it was the old divide-and-rule principle, this time taking the form of the too-familiar argument, addressed primarily to simpler people: "Don't you trust us Native Commissioners? Do you really think the N.R.C. is a better mouthpiece of the natives than we are?" This went together with subtle undermining of the prestige of the African members of the Council, and a demonstration of their ineffectualness.[1]

My "shouting to the world" was confined to one speech. I doubt if it travelled farther than the room in which it was made.

When I travelled up to Pretoria in 1946 to take my place on the Council, South Africa was in the midst of a minor crisis. 70,000 miners were out on strike. Five men had been killed and several hundred injured. The situation in the country was having its effect in the Native Representative Council.

I arrived about an hour before the session was due to begin. Members were discussing the strike crisis and a motion to adjourn until—how familiar is this theme!—the Government removed all discriminatory laws. I made little or no contribution to this discussion, having barely arrived.

When the Council sat, Dr. Moroka, after the usual formalities, moved its indefinite adjournment. He expressed the Council's sympathy for the miners, and the legitimacy of their demands, and called for a public inquiry. He stressed that one reason for the motion was the fact that the Government paid no heed to the Council's recommendations. Moroka was brilliantly seconded and after this I put in my new oar. I remember the tenor of my speech quite well.

I remember saying that, unfortunate though it was that I arrived to find the house on fire, I would do nothing to extinguish it—if anything, I would add fuel to the fire. Being newly come

---

[1] Just before this, the Council's moderate proposals for certain reforms had been rejected by the Government. The Commissioners had no difficulty in underlining how ineffectual it was. But they did not advertise the fact that it was intended to be ineffectual by those who designed it. Again, white obstruction leads to African failure, and the blame is borne on black shoulders.

from an election, I was in a good position to assess the disillusioned mood of the people—disillusioned because the Council was not heeded, disillusioned because its function seemed irrelevant to the rulers, disillusioned because, in ten years, nothing had been done to redeem the promises made by the Hertzog Government. The purchase of land to add to the Reserves had been entirely stopped, ostensibly because of the war. But since the war the Smuts Government, in order to make provision for returned white soldiers, had been settling whites on Crown Land—and turning Africans off some of this land in order to do it. On the one hand, purchase of land urgently needed for Africans was suspended. On the other, we were dispossessed of what we already had. The Council had approached the Government with resolution after resolution, only to be rebuffed or ignored. So I was entirely at one with the motion of adjournment.

When I sat down it was evident that the N.A.D. official in the chair was much upset by what I had said, and not able to disguise it. Perhaps he had expected something milder from a chief, and a newly elected one at that. He put one question to me: "Where were you born?" To this day I do not know what prompted the question, or whether the man who put it knows why he asked it. Perhaps his motive (since the answer was, "In Rhodesia") was to show me up as a "foreign native".

The motion to adjourn was carried unanimously, even the Government-appointed chiefs voting for it. We were called back, however, to hear the Government's reply to our demands. At this time Smuts was away and it fell to the Acting Prime Minister, J. H. Hofmeyr, to answer us. Courageously, he replied in person; but it must have been a distasteful task for him to have to argue in line with Smuts's policy. In short, the Government could accede to none of our requests, and the laws which we regarded as discriminatory were really in the best interests of "the native".

We retired, considered, and found that we were still of one mind about standing adjourned.

When Smuts came back he drafted a few proposals purporting to give a little more life to the Council, and one or two administrative functions. He called six members to confer with him at the Cape, among whom was Professor Matthews. These men pointed out that they could not express the mind of the Council. But they criticised the proposals and indicated that they would probably not find easy acceptance.

Then, in the General Election of 1948, Smuts went. The Council was convened not long after, and the new secretary for Native Affairs, Dr. Eiselen, soon set a new tone. He told us that the

Nationalist Government could not, of course, meet any of our requests and that in any case they should never have been made, since the Council had no right to discuss matters of a political nature.

A little later, Dr. Verwoerd took over the Portfolio of Native Affairs. He made a lengthy speech when opening a session of the Native Representation Council. We were not allowed to discuss this speech, and when told that we might, however, confer singly with the Minister in private, we refused. We had had enough of divide-and-rule, and our stand was that we would meet Dr. Verwoerd only in public since his speech had been a public one. We again adjourned indefinitely.

Shortly after this, Dr. Verwoerd formulated and steered through parliament his Bantu Authorities Act, whereby the pointless, wasteful and futile Council was abolished. Worse, much worse, was to come.

10. *The programme of action*

When the whites of South Africa went to the polls in 1948, I doubt whether anybody realised how significant the election was to be. General Smuts's United Party, feeling that it had done well by white ex-servicemen, appeared confident of victory. Malan's "purified" Nationalists hoped for gains.

As usual, but this time even more extremely than before, the election campaigns were fought over the Africans. The United Party feebly tried to introduce bread-and-butter issues, but these gained them very little support. The 1948 General Election was the apartheid election. Malan's claim to have an answer to South Africa's race difficulties, the fear of the Black Peril which his party had instilled into the white electorate, and the obvious bankruptcy of the party in power in all directions, influenced the outcome of the voting far more than anybody had predicted. It was the end of Smuts. When the votes were counted, not only were the Nationalists in power, but Smuts had been defeated in his own constituency by a little-known opponent.

It was not the end of an era. There is a tendency nowadays to look back to the Smuts régime as a day of restraint and just government. In point of fact, however, the General did not once exert his undoubted influence to extend a helping hand on the masses who groaned under their disabilities, and it was he who gave Hertzog the power to disenfranchise the few African voters.

What he failed to do as a politician was to recognise that white South Africa was ready to go further than he along the road to discrimination which he himself trod. In 1946, when he introduced the Asiatic Land Tenure Act,[1] he was still sensitive to his electorate and quick to carry out their cruel bidding. By 1948 he had been left behind, while white South Africa had entered its next logical phase. The white voter was more eager than he was aware to continue the dismemberment of justice and morality displayed so boldly in the Hertzog-Smuts Bills. And, with the usual handful of exceptions, even those who were not eager were either quite ready to connive or to remain colourlessly neutral. It has always seemed to me a pity that a man as gifted as Smuts should have gone into eclipse, not because of adherence to any principle, but because of political obtuseness. Yet, since he did

[1] The "Ghetto Act".

not at home ever stand on principle, perhaps that was just.

For most of us Africans, bandied about on the field while the game was in progress and then kicked to one side when the game was won, the election seemed largely irrelevant. We had endured Botha, Hertzog and Smuts. It did not seem of much importance whether the whites gave us more Smuts or switched to Malan. Our lot had grown steadily harder, and no election seemed likely to alter the direction in which we were being forced.

Fundamentally, of course, we were right. The Nationalist win did not either surprise or extremely interest us, though we did realise that there would probably be an intensification of the hardships and indignities which had always come our way. Nevertheless, I think it is true that very few (if any) of us understood how swift the deterioration was destined to be. I doubt, too, whether many of us realised at the time that the very intensity of Nationalist oppression would do what we had so far failed to achieve—awake the mass of Africans to political awareness, goad us finally out of resigned endurance and so advance the day of our liberation.

It seems hard to recognise at the moment that the Nationalists more than anybody have given force and insistence to African demands. Now we are caught in the agony and struggle which must precede freedom in a country such as South Africa. But for the Nationalist victory in 1948 we might have had to wait and organise for years to produce widespread refusal to accept the white yoke.

Malan, Strijdom and Verwoerd have done an important part of our work for us. They have demonstrated unambiguously to the African people what it is that the Congress movement is pledged to resist. And at last the African people have responded unambiguously. No longer do a few Congress voices oppose each new measure. Now the voice of the African people says, "We do not consent."

The Nationalist régime must take at least some credit for this. A good measure of the work of Congress has simply consisted of co-ordinating, and giving direction and non-violent expression to the anger and repudiation which they have aroused. By intensifying our experience of serfdom, they have given us a deeper thirst for freedom. It was coming anyway, but Nationalist rule has appreciably shortened the day of white tyranny.

Although members of Congress did not foresee the speed with which the Nationalists would set about depriving us of the few shreds of humanity and opportunity which remained, yet we were not this time caught on the wrong foot. We had already seen the writing on the wall, in the Hertzog Bills and in the Smuts about-face, once our men were no longer required as drivers and potato-peelers in his army. The founding of the Congress Youth League had met a longstanding need, giving to young men a sphere of action, and assurance that the days of polite, unheeded complaint were over. We were already girding ourselves against the Smuts régime when Malan took his place.

Some index of the earnestness of the younger element, and of the rapid change which they worked on Congress thought, is given by the eclipse of Dr. Xuma. When Xuma took over the national leadership, he was at the spearhead, and the contribution which he made to the organisation of the movement should not be forgotten. But by the time Malan came to power, Congress rank and file in general, and the Youth League in particular, were in advance of him.

Congress was more than fortunate in the quality of the men who were the moving spirits in the Youth League. At their head was a forceful and gifted Roman Catholic, Anton Lembede, and with him was a group of men such as Mandela, the younger Matthews, Walter Sisulu, Mda, Yengwa, Dr. Conco, and Oliver Tambo.

It was not long before they found that, while all were agreed about the work of organising the movement, Dr. Xuma hung back over the question of what to do with the organisation once it was there. Congress was urgent, Xuma cautious. The younger members looked around for an alternative leader, and found one in Dr. James Moroka.

In 1949, under Moroka, newly elected President-General of Congress, the movement met and evolved its Programme of Action. This Programme of Action is a milestone in Congress history. It represents a fundamental change of policy and method. Underlying it was the refusal to be content for ever with leavings from white South Africa's table—stated uncompromisingly and finally.

The challenge was to be on fundamentals, we were no longer interested in ameliorations and petty adjustments. There was no longer any doubt in our mind that without the vote we are helpless. Without the vote there is no way for us to realise ourselves in our own land, or even to be heard. Without the vote our future would be that decreed by a minority of whites, as our past has been. The whites always insist that they know what is best for us, and that this is what we *really* want—only we are too foolish and backward to know it. The whites are an interested party in this controversy: they invariably hand out what is best for them—passes, crippling industrial laws, African poverty,

98

but never land and never the smallest measure of self-determination. Never human dignity, never opportunity.

The Programme of Action adopted in 1949 stressed new methods. Representations were done with. Demonstrations on a countrywide scale, strike action, and civil disobedience were to replace words. Influenced by the combined action of the Indian community after the passing of the Ghetto Act, we agreed to concentrate mainly on non-violent disobedience. This disobedience was not directed against law. It was directed against all those particular discriminatory laws, from the Act of Union onwards, which were not informed by morality.

Once Congress as a whole had thrashed out our new approach, the matter was placed in the hands of the National Executive. They were to apply the general principles to specific occasions, to work out the details, and to issue the calls for action to the provinces, who would then relay them to local branches.

During 1950 there was a major demonstration on 26th June. Its immediate purpose was to protest against the Group Areas Bill and the Suppression of Communism Bill. It took the form of a one-day stay-at-home and was most successful in Johannesburg and Port Elizabeth, and in Durban. In the minds of the organisers (Africans, Indians and Coloureds participated) one purpose was that those who stayed at home should fittingly mourn the many people—many Africans—who had up to that time lost their lives in the struggle for liberation. There has for many years been a steady loss of life of demonstrators at the hands of the police. It is seldom sensational enough to attract attention—it is simply a feature of South African life. It was high time we mourned our dead—they number thousands.

In May 1951 there was an effective protest strike of Coloured people, supported by Africans and Indians, in Port Elizabeth and the South Western Cape. This was directed against the Nationalist intention to remove Coloureds from the Common Electoral Roll.

These were first steps, the early outcome of the Programme of Action.

In July 1951 the National Executives of the Congresses met together. A Joint Planning Council was appointed to organise co-operation between the different non-white groups—this, indeed, was a major step forward.

The significance of the Joint Planning Council should not be missed. The very fact that it was able to be formed and to function was a sign that all but the white races in South Africa were beginning to think and act across barriers of race. The desire to shed apartheid could now at last be translated into outward expression. The joint organisation of the Defiance Campaign took us one step nearer to a South Africa where race will be of incidental importance.

In Natal we were placed at a disadvantage. We were, on the whole, very much in line with the Programme of Action. But by this time Champion was beginning to have his doubts. He did not voice them, he did not openly oppose the new policy. He simply held his peace, when he returned from meetings of the National Executive, over what had passed there. The result was that we inevitably fell behind, knowing little of what was being discussed and planned in the rest of the country.

At this time, because Champion insisted upon reverting to the practice (which had prevailed in earlier Congress days) of appointing his own Executive, I declined to serve under him—his action seemed retrograde, undemocratic, and it was unconstitutional. I remained on friendly terms with him. My status was that of an ordinary Congress member, and in view of the personal clashes which now began to appear within the Executive, this did not distress me.

The Press brought the clash into the open, and the conflict between the Natal leaders came to a head at the Annual General Meeting of 1951. The meeting was held in Pietermaritzburg, but it adjourned to Durban for the election of office-bearers. It turned out to be a "packed" meeting, but Champion overrode the objections of those of us who objected to the unconstitutional presence of non-members. Rather than break up the meeting, we submitted.

Just before the resumption of Durban—the only outstanding business was the annual election—I had been approached by a group of Youth League men who asked me to stand for the Natal Presidency. Knowing that Msimanga, the excellent Congress secretary in Natal, had been approached, I refused. But the younger men were insistent. "If we are to save Natal for Congress," they declared, "there must be a change in the leadership."

In the end, I agreed, but on one condition. I wished to remain quite clear of squabbles for position and of the personal conflicts within the movement. I told the younger men that my name could go forward only if Msimanga agree to this. So we talked it over with him, and his view was that his name should be withdrawn and that I should stand against Champion.

When nominations were called for only Champion's name and mine went forward. The irregularly constituted meeting recorded its votes, and by a vast majority I was elected to replace Champion at the head of Congress affairs in Natal. Since I had no intention of appointing my Executive, we proceeded to elect other office-bearers.

But we were in a quandary. We knew full well that the meeting was unconstitutional. At the same time we knew that if we did not function, the A.N.C. would disintegrate in Natal. For the moment we felt that we had to act as a sort of caretaker Executive, so that the work of Congress might not lapse.

At the earliest possible opportunity we convened a special general meeting, where we explained our odd position to the delegates. The meeting decided that, rather than spend time on a fresh election, it would simply ratify what had been done at the unconstitutional meeting.

At the end of the year (1951) a National Conference of A.N.C. was held in Bloemfontein. Shortly before I was due to depart, the Natal headquarters were sent material relating to this conference. To my astonishment, this included suggestions and resolutions about a campaign of civil defiance. The National Executive and other provinces had been considering this for some time—but here was Natal's first hint of it!

It was already too late to summon my Executive. Our only opportunity for discussion was in the car on the way to Bloemfontein. We decided that we would agree in principle to the Defiance Campaign, but that we would have to plead, because the matter had not so much as been raised in Natal, for postponement of the proposed date (6th April, 1952). We could not commit Natal to something so momentous while it was still in ignorance of the whole issue. Nor could we get Natal ready in time.

At Bloemfontein the President-General, Dr. Moroka, asked me to take the chair for the conference. I left it only when the time came for me to present Natal's views on the proposed campaign of civil disobedience.

This was no easy matter—my audience was unsympathetic. I well remember the interjection of one woman delegate when I tried to argue for a later date:

"Coward! Coward!" she shouted at me.

"It is better for me to express my cowardice here," I retorted, "than that I should keep silent and then go away and play the coward outside."

The truth was, however, that the other provinces were geared to launch the campaign in the second quarter of 1952. The only concession made to Natal was that it was agreed that if we were not ready in time, we should come in as soon as we were ready, and later in the same year.

Outside the conference hall, however, some members from other provinces did confide in me that they were fearful that the campaign might suffer from preparation that was too hurried. This contradiction expresses a real dilemma. We have continually needed to act and act urgently. At the same time, ill-prepared action can be worse than none. The Congress movement cannot rely on occasional spontaneous demonstrations—too often these, coming at a time when patience has snapped for the moment, develop into violence. The people need to be briefed with clarity and care, and they must be given the opportunity to signify their willingness and readiness to participate.

Had Congress ever been an organisation which placed reliance on bloodshed and violence, things would have been simpler. What we have aimed to do in South Africa is to bring the white man to his senses, not slaughter him. Our desire has been that he should co-operate with us, and we with him.

At first we argued for a change of heart which would permit this. Then, with the Programme of Action and the years that have followed, we have tried to demonstrate the realities in a less academic way; we have tried to show what the realities are in the hope that the whites could see the imperative need to conform to them. A few have seen this need—some Congress Democrats, Liberals, maybe some Progressives. A few have known of it all along and have acted on their knowledge. But the vast majority, like Pharaoh, have hardened their hearts.

It has naturally crossed our minds to wonder whether anything but indiscriminate bloodshed and violence will make any impression, so impervious do they seem. It will do neither them nor us any good, and if they get it, it will not be from Congress. It will be simply the result of unendurable provocation, of trading for too long on a patience which has its limits. If the whites continue as at present, nobody will give the signal for mass violence. Nobody will need to.

The Natal delegation returned from Bloemfontein to face an attack upon our proposed action in the Press, both white and white-owned "African". But at the general meeting which we immediately called, we found no disaffection in our own ranks.

The meeting, publicised by adverse Press comment, was well attended. The main points at issue were the question of co-operation with other organisations and the Defiance Campaign. At Bloemfontein we had endorsed the earlier decision to undertake the Defiance Campaign in conjunction with the Indian Congress movement, and with any others who cared to join in. But among Natal Africans there was a degree of anti-Indian feeling, and it was not difficult for those who opposed the

Campaign for other reasons to exploit this form of racialism. Malcontents represented the policy of co-operation as the invention of the new leaders in Natal.

But it was not difficult to reply to this, since the "new policy" of Congress co-operation had in fact been firmly established before Moroka took over the National leadership from Zuma, and before I had replaced Champion in Natal. The meeting endorsed the Defiance Campaign and stated Natal's desire to be included in it. The details and the date of Natal's entry were left to the executive, working in conjunction with the other congresses.

It is perhaps worth underlining here one of the great strengths of the African National Congress. It has displayed the power to adapt itself. Who would have predicted, at the time of the Durban riots of 1949, when Africans and Indians were involved in terrible mutual hostility, that within three years Africans and Indians in Durban itself would be acting together to demonstrate their repudiation of injustice, cruelty and tyranny?

Step by step along our difficult road, Congress has adapted itself to the real needs of the situation. This has not always been easy, but it has happened. And with each adaptation we have brought ourselves and our country nearer to the vision of a homeland where men may eventually live at peace with neighbours of all races—because they really are neighbours, not white masters and other-race servants.

11. *Defiance and deposition*

Preparations for the Defiance Campaign went forward. 26th June was chosen for the launching of open disobedience, but the earlier date, 6th April, did not go unused. It turned into a warm-up for the Campaign proper. Large meetings were held in the main centres at the same time as the whites were, in their way, observing the three-hundredth anniversary of the landing of Jan van Riebeck at the Cape.

To put it simply, while they celebrated three hundred years of white domination, we looked back over three hundred years of black subjection. While the whites were jubilant over what they said God had given them, we contemplated what they had taken from us, and the land which they refuse to share with us though they cannot work it without us.

Speaking to a crowd of over five thousand people of all races in Freedom Square, Sophiatown, Dr. Moroka said: "In Cape-town today the van Riebeck celebrations have reached an unprecedented climax. . . . The white man's cup of joy is overflowing. The Europeans have every reason to display their joy on this colossal scale. . . . Taken man for man, the Europeans of this land are some of the richest people in the world. . . . But we Africans also look back over that period of three hundred years. We see a record of sadness. . . . I wish to remind the Europeans of this country that in taking stock of the past three hundred years they cannot escape the fact that whatever page they turn in the history of South Africa they find it red with the blood of the fallen, they find ill-will and insecurity written plainly across the pages. I appeal to them to weigh and consider. . . ."

In Capetown, Port Elizabeth, East London, Pretoria and Durban, crowds of up to ten thousand attended mass meetings and demonstrated their support of the coming Defiance Campaign. These were the main centres, but satisfactory preparation was going ahead in smaller places too. Such meetings were not confined to 6th April—during the first half of 1952 there were gatherings at different times throughout the country.

At this time there was a fruitless interchange of letters between the Congresses and the authorities. I say "interchange". It was not exactly that. Our letters were sometimes completely ignored, though there was an answer or two from "the office of the Prime Minister".

But the white rulers, at least, were left in doubt no about what we intended or why we intended it. When they did reply, it was to scold us for sending our letters to the wrong person, to assure us that we have "no inherent rights" and will not get any, and to threaten us with "full use of the machinery at its (the Government's) disposal to quell any disturbances, and thereafter deal adequately with those responsible for initiating subversive activities of any nature whatsoever".

One thing which this correspondence did underline was that there is not really even a common language in which to discuss our agonising problems. The Nationalist rulers cannot speak to Africans except in the restricted vocabulary of white *Baasskap*. They cannot discuss. They know, and they then proceed to arrange and give orders.

For our part, we cannot employ the phrases of supplication and subservience, we cannot take up the unreal posture of "good native boys" towards good, all-knowing and all-beneficient white rulers. Our whole protest and resistance is based on our claim to human dignity. With those who recognise it we are at one. We cannot discard it in our dealings with those who deny it.

We made it abundantly clear long before the Campaign was launched that it was a system, not a race, which we were opposing: "The struggle which the national organisations of the non-European people are conducting is not directed against any race or national group, but against the unjust laws which keep in perpetual subjection and misery vast sections of the population."

The target of the Campaign was unjust, oppressive laws. The intention was to disobey these laws, suffering arrest, assault, and penalty if need be, without violence. The method was to send in groups of carefully trained "volunteers" to disobey publicly.

The fact that the African and Indian Congresses were participating jointly, and that we were joined by some coloured organisations—the coloured people had no national organisation—limited the scope of what we could jointly defy. Different laws oppress different non-white groups. What we all had in common, however, was the humiliation of discrimination in public places. For this reason the main force of the Defiance Campaign was directed against the national motto of white South Africa, EUROPEANS ONLY, which is found over the length and breadth of the country.[1] Railway stations, waiting-rooms, post offices, public seats, train accommodation, all bear this legend. The volunteers were to abandon the "separate but unequal" facilities set aside

[1] The unheeded official motto is: "Unity is strength."

for us and to make challenging use of the alternative white facilities. In addition to this, the flouting of curfew and pass regulations was determined upon.

With Natal and Capetown postponing defiance until they were ready, the rest of the country went into action on 26th June as planned. Whenever possible, the authorities were forewarned of the detailed intentions of each batch of volunteers—in some cases full lists of the names of the volunteers involved were politely handed in. In July the two Natal Congresses joined in. During the following three months the Defiance Campaign gathered momentum. October, with 2354 resisters, was the peak month of this part of the Campaign. There is no doubt at all that a profoundly successful movement was under way, and was accumulating support as it went along. The Defiance Campaign will go down as the first major breach in the defences of White Supremacy.

Even the white Press took note, reporting almost daily on the progress of the Campaign. Before the late forties the whites were hardly aware (except at election time) of the nine or ten million Africans who surround them and carry them on their backs. Now they were forced at least to register our presence. A number of them even began to consider seriously the implication of our existence, and a few have been thinking ever since.

But it cannot be said that the Press was helpful. They provided pictures and stated the number of arrests. The Afrikaans Press was, as might be expected, nearly hysterical. The English Press signally failed to acquaint its readers with our side of the case, repeatedly put to the courts which tried the volunteers.

Throughout, the discipline of the volunteers was excellent. I will not say that they were ever subdued—the new militancy was clearly discernible. But they were restrained and well behaved, and no detachment of volunteers ever got out of hand. At no time was there even the suggestion of violence or disorder. The Eastern Cape (Port Elizabeth and East London) organised brilliantly well, and the Reef kept up its pressure. Natal fell behind in execution. The mass meetings were successful enough, but the enlistment of volunteers was not as high as the enthusiasm of the meetings led us to expect. It was a salutary lesson.

In Durban it became our practice to send groups of volunteers, Indians and Africans, only after giving them some instruction on what to do and how to behave. We invariably informed the police in advance, before a batch was sent out. The local traffic police were certainly taxed to the limit—indeed, they came to rely on our help. On one occasion they were caught unawares and we had to see to traffic control ourselves. Yet not once was the public discipline less than impressive. Our greatest problem was not the volunteers but the crowds of bystanders.

The Durban Corporation quickly introduced and passed a by-law giving themselves additional powers to control meetings and processions. As soon as we heard of it, we challenged it. We wrote to the municipality and announced our next meeting in "Red Square". The Special Branch duly arrested Dr. Naicker and me and others—but their difficulty was to get the vast crowd to disperse. From under arrest we did the job for them, and then went along to the central charge office where, to our surprise, we found the place thick with heavily armed police. (We were charged. We appeared. The case was adjourned. As far as I know, it still is.)

We had some trouble with the police, not of the usual kind. They were obviously reluctant to arrest us. My Natal Chairman, Dr. Wilson Conco, had to spend three nights leading his group in law-breaking before the police would arrest them, and other groups suffered a similar fate. The police tended to keep watch out of the corner of the eye.

On the whole, as South African police go, the Durban and Natal men were not over-aggressive. There was, however, one foolish incident. A crowd of spectators left the magistrate's court together. That they were together was an accident—they had all left the court at the same time. An over eager white constable rushed up and put everybody in sight under arrest for "forming a procession". The crowd accepted the situation and followed along. A senior man rushed up and ordered the crowd to disperse. It began to do this, but not in time to avoid a baton charge. A woman dressed as a diviner was arrested—she refused to part with her equipment. A male bystander was arrested for saying, "Why are you manhandling that woman?" Both were later discharged.

But these, I emphasise, were not yet the days when South Africa bristled from end to end with heavily armed police and troops.

As far as the Defiance Campaign was concerned, I was a Staff Officer. I did not let myself defy any law. My job was to remain in the background, to keep up the pressure, and to organise. In the next phase[2] it was intended that I should tour Natal in order to involve more people, especially rural people. I did, in fact,

---

[2] The Defiance Campaign was planned in three stages: carefully prepared defiance in the cities by small groups; the extension of the Campaign to the country; and finally countrywide mass action, including industrial action.

towards the end of the year begin on this. But the second phase of the Defiance Campaign had to be abandoned, for reasons which will appear later.

I was having to be very lively in these days, trying to supervise activity in different centres and at the same time continuing with the administration of Groutville. I kept well within the regulations which governed chiefs, but trouble was close at hand.

Shortly after my return from a briefing tour in northern Natal I received a letter from the Lower Tugela Native Commissioner— the man who supervised me. He enclosed a little document which had been sent to him from the office of the Chief Native Commissioner. Some white fellow, a farmer, I suppose, had reported that I was encouraging people to oppose Government schemes. I was asked to say whether or not this was true. I replied that notwithstanding inaccuracies in the report, the African National Congress, which I led in Natal, was engaging on a campaign involving the defiance of certain laws and regulations, including those relating to the culling of cattle.

About three weeks later my Native Commissioner asked me to call on him. He told me that I was being summoned to Pretoria and that I would have to leave almost at once. We did not discuss the reason for this summons, but the Assistant Magistrate who prepared my papers for the journey said that he thought it was in connection with my political activities. I had little doubt. When I left the train—I did not try to travel in the white section—I noticed the Chief Native Commissioner for Natal on the platform. I exchanged a word or two with him and his manner seemed apologetic.

At N.A.D. headquarters, when I presented myself, I was ushered into the presence of the Secretary for Native Affairs, Dr. W. W. M. Eiselen, who was flanked by the Deputy Secretary and by the Natal Chief Native Commissioner.

"We have called you here," began Dr. Eiselen, "to discuss your Congress activities. I want you to realise at once that so far as the Native Affairs Department is concerned we have no complaints—you've worked efficiently and conscientiously and have seen to the welfare of your community. We have noted this and appreciated it. We look on you as one of our best chiefs.

"Now, before we come to the subject of your own participation in the A.N.C., we'd like to ask you some general questions. To begin with, why does the A.N.C. oppose Government schemes for land rehabilitation? It seems to us that any educated person should appreciate schemes to restore the land and prevent erosion."

"I shall speak for myself," I replied, "not for the A.N.C. Nobody, in a normal context, would oppose the prevention of erosion. Nobody. If I had a farm of my own, I would keep no more stock than the farm could carry. You realise of course, all the same, that preventing erosion, by cattle-culling, strikes at the only wealth—cattle—which rural people believe in. In theory, however, the principle of limiting the livestock to what the land can carry is sound. But in practice here is the factor which you ignore; the overcrowding of African areas by man and beast is the direct result of the 1913 and 1936 Land Acts—it is imposed on us. Your solution is to take our cattle away today because you took our land yesterday. We are not prepared to co-operate with you in applying this sort of remedy. If you remove the root cause of the trouble—the Land Acts—our co-operation in saving the land would be immediate. As it is, your solution is just another expression of the oppressive and restrictive legislation under which we suffer."

The Deputy Secretary put his question: "Why do you oppose Influx Control?"

"As you operate this system, it goes right against the usual understandings in Trade Union circles. Workers must be free to seek out the best market and sell their toil there. We do not accept a system in which huge, half-starved labour reserves are dammed up in order to keep the price of labour down."

"But," said the Deputy Secretary, "we're doing this to protect the urban natives." He went on, to my utter amazement, to harp on the evils of migrant labour—evils which the very system under discussion causes. Only labourers are allowed to join the influx, while the rest of the family is left behind. The family is effectively crippled. For a while I was speechless with amazement.

"You know, sir," I chipped in eventually, "we don't like migrant labour either. We didn't invent it. I approve of having the workers near their work and earning a living wage, I approve of the establishment of townships—provided the families can live with the breadwinners, and provided rural people can have the chance to acquire land and make a decent livelihood. But to go back: I have never heard that one urban African has opposed the influx of rural people to the cities. This is the first intimation. If my people have no complaint, why legislate as though they had?"

Dr. Eiselen apparently thought it was time to get down to business.

"You are a chief," he said, "yet you ask people to break the laws of the land. You are an officer whose work is to keep law and order, yet you encourage people to defy the law. What do you say about that?"

I remember that I paused to arrange my thoughts. "I do admit without hesitation, sir, that I'm engaged in furthering the policy of the A.N.C. The course we have chosen is the only way open to us of showing our opposition to laws which have no moral basis. I have not asked people to become criminals or to act in a criminal way. Our motive is political. This is the only way we have of highlighting our plight and our refusal to consent to being governed by criminal laws. Our hope is that white people will look into our grievances, take us seriously, realise that we are serious about this. The Defiance Campaign is a *political* demonstration against discriminatory laws."

"No!" said the Secretary. "You are asking people to break the law. You are asking people to break the law!"

"No, sir," I replied, "not to break the law. To signify in this way our rejection of a particular kind of law."

"And how do you reconcile the encouragement you give to people to break the law," somebody asked, either the Secretary or the Deputy, "with your duties as a chief?"

"As far as that is concerned, I have never experienced any conflict. My policy has been to keep my commitments distinct. I have never discussed Congress matters in tribal councils—in fact, I have excluded such discussion when others have begun it. But my duties as a chief do not conflict in me with Congress activity. Congress has not yet been declared subversive."

"We have not called you here," said Dr. Eiselen, "to talk you out of belonging to the A.N.C., but because you are asking people to break the law of the land. You can't be a Jekyll and Hyde."

I thought this remark revealing. It seems to imply that chiefs, who are indeed concerned with maintaining and dispensing law, must have split personalities before they can possibly object to the immoral laws, whose main purpose is to uphold white supremacy, a repugnant creed. In point of fact, I was in Congress not in spite of being a chief but partly, anyway, *because* of the things to which chieftainship had opened my eyes.

Dr. Eiselen drew the interview to its close: "I must make it clear to you that this Department cannot have you acting this way. Go away now and think it over, and let us have your reply in a week."

"I think that a matter of this kind needs a little time," I said. "There is the possibility of my ceasing to be a chief. It is a matter which needs talking over with the tribe."

"With the tribe?" said Dr. Eiselen. "Must you?"

"Well, sir, I ought to discuss it with my headmen at least."

110

"Sir, isn't a week rather short?" asked the Natal Chief Native Commissioner.

"I leave that with you," said Dr. Eiselen.

The interview ended there. I had already made up my mind about what course to follow, but I said nothing of that for the moment. I was, however, distressed at the suggestion that I should act without consulting my people, possibly relinquishing office unknown to them. It might be the way of the Native Affairs Department, but it is not the way of the Zulus and nor is it mine.

I felt inhibited, all the same, by Dr. Eiselen's "Must you?" and for that reason I did not convene a tribal gathering. Seeing nothing further to add to what I had said in Pretoria, I refrained from writing to Dr. Eiselen. I still saw no conflict between the Defiance Campaign and my place as chief, but that is perhaps because I failed to see my position in Groutville as a favour bestowed by the Native Affairs Department. I discussed the situation with my church ministers and awaited developments.

After a couple of weeks a letter came requiring my reply to the question posed in Pretoria. I replied neutrally, stating that I had no intention of resigning either from A.N.C. leadership nor from the chieftainship, since the two did not contradict one another. At this stage I forewarned my headmen of what was about to happen.

In due course the Native Commissioner asked me to call on him. "Pretoria says that from now you cease to be chief of the Umvoti Mission Reserve."

I had a chat with the Assistant Native Commissioner. "I'm sorry," he said, "that it's had to turn out like this. I've often thought of speaking to you about it, but somehow I haven't got round to it. But please do this one thing—tell us whom you suggest to take over in the meantime."

"Well, that's normally the office of the chief headman."

I was asked to have a meeting convened, but to remain silent about my disposition. I did these things. At the meeting the Native Commissioner told the people of Groutville what had happened. The reaction of the people surprised me, and it certainly startled the Native Commissioner. They refused to nominate a successor. "We still want to know from you and your Department," they told the Commissioner, "why you have reversed our choice and overridden us. As for nominating, we shall do no such thing, not now. In any case, whom could we nominate? The next man we choose will be A.N.C. and then he will suffer the same fate."

For two or three months the whole question was left open.

In the meantime the usual resignation set in. It was clear, I suppose, that the white will would have its way, and behind the scenes canvassing for the vacant chieftainship began. It was a matter of regret to me that Groutville did not persist in the stand which it had originally taken. I would not for a moment have said that the village should be without a chief, but I think that they bowed to the deposition too lamely, a tacit acknowledgment that might is right. There was a suggestion in the Press that Groutville might lead a joint Mission Reserve protest under the deposition, but the opportunity was not taken.

That was the end of my career with the Native Affairs Department. Since that time I have held as aloof as possible from tribal affairs.

The author in the uniform adopted by the African National Congress

A moment of relaxation during the Treason Trials in 1957

s President of the African National Congress, the author publicly burnt
is pass in Pretoria on March 26th, 1960, and invited all Africans to do
the same

Africans walking into Johannesburg during the bus boycott in 1957

The author relaxes with his books

12. *When the chain breaks*

I was back in the hurly-burly of the Defiance Campaign in time for the end, which came from a totally unexpected source. It was becoming obvious to the Government that the Defiance Campaign was more than a passing incident. In October, after having been running for four months, it was still gathering force. Congress paid-up membership had soared from seven thousand to a hundred thousand. The example set by the first batches of volunteers was being followed all over the country, spreading even to some of the smaller towns. Country people were interested but we were unable to extend our organisation to reach them. The discipline of the volunteers did not waver.

Then, with no warning, rioting broke out. Late in October the first riot occurred at New Brighton, Port Elizabeth. In the course of arresting two alleged thieves, a white constable started shooting. He fired twenty-one shots and then withdrew. Reinforcements of police returned to the scene of the attempted arrest to find a crowd of a couple of thousand people[1] doing damage to the railway station. There ensued a running skirmish accompanied by great damage to property. Seven Africans and four Europeans (no policemen) were killed.

Early in November three Africans were killed in a Johannesburg disturbance over increased rents. The police took cover and simply fired blindly into a labour hostel.

Almost simultaneously two further riots took place. Thirteen Africans lost their lives in a Kimberley beer hall disturbance, and at least a dozen died in the East London riot which followed police baton charging and shooting.

We watched these developments with horror. This sense of horror is not lessened by our understanding of how these outbursts of violence may have come about. The policies pursued by the whites make this sort of thing inevitable.

Every so often the yoke becomes unendurable, something explodes, and for a while blind resentment takes control. The conditions which lead to these tragedies are carefully kept in

---

[1] The police figure was between 2000 and 3000. I do not know what training policemen have in estimating the size of a crowd in the open. The temptation, not always successfully withstood, is to exaggerate on occasions like this.

existence by the majority of white South Africans. They react with horror at the outcome of their lust for white domination. So do we. But they will do nothing to remove the root cause.

But that is by no means the whole story as a rule. It certainly was not in Port Elizabeth, East London and Kimberley. Many whites, having persuaded themselves against the evidence that they share South Africa with a barbaric and hostile black horde, cannot leave us alone, they feel they must goad and prod us. It is as though they are perversely most afraid of us when we are friendly and disciplined and patient. The large, amiable dog in the yard is on a chain. You have been told that he is a snarling, dangerous cur. His amiability must therefore be a deception. You keep out of reach and jab repeatedly at him to rouse him to anger. If you succeed, that proves he is a wild and savage creature. Now and then you do succeed—the best-tempered animal gets sick of ill-willed pestering. Sometimes you do enrage him. Sometimes the chain made for him snaps. Then there is a riot.

Whites see only the riot. Their reaction?—Make a stronger chain.

The white police constitute the section of the white community which has the most intimate and regular meeting with Africans. On some occasions—and I have never been slow to applaud these —they behave with restraint. But generally speaking it is they who do the continuous work of prodding at the African giant, and some of them enter very deeply into the spirit of this danger-ous game. They must assert and parade themselves, demanding this, ordering that, and hurling abuse. Behind it they are, of course, afraid. They rely on the chain.

What follows when the chain breaks is not riot and the restoration of order. It is riot and counter-riot. That was certainly true of the series which broke out in 1952, particularly in the Eastern Cape. It has been true more recently than that. In Zeerust and Sekhukhuniland, for instance. As counter-rioters the the police are more disciplined and more effectively armed than rioters, and what they do is done behind the guise of restoring law and order.

There are occasions when the counter-riot takes place before the "riot".[2] That seems to have been so in East London when police charged into a prayer meeting, charged again, and then began shooting. They continued to shoot from their vehicles as they drove about the location in large numbers.

[2] Since I wrote this, Sharpeville has provided macabre illustration of its truth.

Yet another kind of provocation featured in the 1952 riots. The Defiance Campaign was far too orderly and successful for the Government's liking, and it was growing. The prospect before the white supremacists, if they were going to react to our challenge in a civilised way, was that arrests would continue indefinitely. Behind the thousands already arrested there were more, many more. The challenge of non-violence was more than they could meet. It robbed them of the initiative. On the other hand, violence by Africans would restore this initiative to them—they would then be able to bring out the guns and other techniques of intimidation and present themselves as restorers of order.

It cannot be denied that this is exactly what happened, and at the moment most convenient for the Government. The infiltration of *agents provocateurs* in both Port Elizabeth and Kimberley is well attested. They kept well clear of the volunteers and the Congress. They did their work among irresponsible youngsters—more than half of the people subsequently charged in Port Elizabeth were juveniles.

It was all the Government needed. The riots and the Defiance Campaign were immediately identified with each other in the white South African imagination. The initiative was with the Government.

We called for an inquiry. But an impartial commission looking into these disturbances was not at all what the Government wanted. For one thing, the identification (so useful to them) of the Defiance Campaign with the riots would have been shown to be false. For another, the true immediate causes of the riots, and the character and backing of those who instigated them, might have leaked out. This, too, would have hampered the Government's making use of their ill-gotten initiative.

In reply to the demand for a Judicial Inquiry, the Minister of Justice, Mr. C. R. Swart, said that there was only one thing which the "law-breakers" understood and that was for the police to hit hard. If he could not suppress violence with violence, he continued, he would not want to be Minister of Justice.[3] A Judicial Commission would achieve nothing except to provide a platform for agitators. This last observation now accompanies all refusals to make facts public.

It is well known that the Government used its recovered initiative harshly and to the full. First by means of proclamations and then, as soon as Parliament had reassembled, by means of the Criminal Law Amendment Act and the Public Safety Act,

[3] He is now the S.A. Republic's first President.

115

they imposed bitter penalties on any people taking part in any defiance or passive resistance. The activities of rioters provided the pretext for crushing non-violent demonstrators. It became illegal to defy any law by way of protest.

The Campaign went on for a while. The organisation behind it did not break down. In Port Elizabeth on 10th November a one-day stay-at-home in protest against a newly imposed curfew was unusually successful—96 per cent of the people observed it.

Nevertheless, the end was in sight. The harshness of Government action frightened some people off. More important, our people were well aware that the whites were trying to blame the Campaign for the riots. Just how disposed to violence we Africans are was shown by the fact that rather than be identified, even falsely, with the disturbances, large numbers abandoned non-violent defiance.

While the Defiance Campaign was entering its last weeks, the African National Congress was confronted with an internal crisis. The President-General, Dr. Moroka, and nineteen other Defiance Campaign leaders from Johannesburg were arrested and brought to trial (Regina vs. Walter Sisulu and Nineteen Others). Moroka elected to be defended apart from the others by his own lawyer. This in itself cost him much prestige.

But the real damage was done when at the end of his trial his lawyer entered a separate plea of mitigation. Whose idea this was I cannot say. But the lawyer argued that Dr. Moroka enjoyed good relations with neighbouring white farmers and that he had helped financially with the education of white boys. These things may have been true and laudable, but in Congress eyes the moment for drawing attention to them was ill-chosen. The leader of the Congress dissociated himself from his fellow-accused, he appeared unready to go the whole way in defiance, and he asked whites to shield him from the consequence of white laws and from the consequence of his own stand.

December was the month of the National Conference of the A.N.C., and 1952 was a presidential election year. As usual in any election, there was some activity behind the scenes. The Natal delegates who travelled up with me told me that they intended to nominate me to stand against Dr. Moroka. I agreed without much excitement, making one stipulation: "I do not intend to become involved in fights over position."

"You just leave it to us," they replied.

I did leave it to them. In Johannesburg my impression was that the Transvaal leadership, having just suffered the Moroka let-down, was unenthusiastic and cautious. I was relatively new in the movement, compared with many who had borne the heat

116

and burden of the day. It would not surprise me to learn that they regarded me as an unknown quantity, and possibly a risky proposition.

When it came to nomination, only Dr. Moroka's name and mine were put up. The Natal delegates had nothing to do, to their surprise—it was the Transvaal rank and file who proposed my name.

In the voting, Dr. Moroka had some support from Free State delegates, but the upshot was that I now found myself at the head of the resistance movement, President-General of the A.N.C. I suppose that the deposition which Doctors Eiselen and Verwoerd conferred on me had something to do with the matter. If the people wanted me there, I was there. But I was grateful that I did not have behind me any struggle for power, nor any contention with other resisters.

Shortly after the National Conference of the A.N.C. I was asked by the Youth League to address a meeting at Alexandra Township, just outside Johannesburg. It was intended that this meeting would precede the sending of batches of volunteers into defiance. After I had spoken, somebody on the platform began a long and rambling speech calling for volunteers, but by this time those who had offered themselves seemed to have melted away. The response this time was one old man, and he was tipsy.

Meantime I had done a little weighing up. In affairs of this kind one has to know when to begin. I think that with the Defiance Campaign we chose the right moment. But one has also to know when to end. The anticlimax of the Alexandra meeting certainly suggested to me that we had overlooked the importance of this.

Shortly afterwards we brought the Campaign to an official end, rather belatedly. Its back had been broken well before this, by the skill with which the riots were handled and used by the authorities.

So ended a year which changed the political complexion of South Africa. The whites took several more strides towards authoritarianism. Among Africans and Indians, and to a smaller extent among coloureds, the spirit of active opposition came alive, consent to continue being governed exclusively by the whites and for the whites was withdrawn, goals became clear. I do not think the outside world saw the full significance of what had happened—it took the Treason Trial to arouse their interest. But, when the history of these troubled years comes to be written, I think it will be seen that, on both sides, 1952 was a turning-point in the struggle.

I tend today, perhaps, to overstress the fact that our struggle is a struggle and not a game—we cannot allow ourselves to be daunted by a harshness which will grow before it subsides. We shall not win our freedom except at the cost of great suffering, and we must be prepared to accept it. Much African blood has already been spilt, and assuredly more will be. As I have said, we do not desire to shed the blood of the white man; but we should have no illusion about the price which he will exact in African blood before we are admitted to citizenship of our own land.

One feature of the riots—not only those of 1952—requires comment. In East London a nun, whose service was devoted to the African people, was wantonly killed. There, and in other places, churches have been burned down.

It is possible to see a significance in the burning of churches which is not really there. When a crowd riots, it seeks some symbol upon which to vent its anger. Obviously, in locations, there are not many such symbols. Destructiveness will not turn against destroyers—the rioters are not going to damage their property. What remains? Only buildings put there by Europeans—beer halls, schools, churches, administrative blocks, clinics, and perhaps cinemas. So these are the buildings attacked.

The fact that some of them serve the community is incidental. It must be remembered too that some such buildings *appear* to serve the community, while in fact they do not. I have already shown that this is true of beer halls. Schools come into the same category, not because they are schools, but because they are Dr. Verwoerd's Bantu Education schools, not loved but bitterly resented.

I cannot rid my mind of the fear that something similar may apply to the destruction of churches. When a church is burnt down, some whites say, "But a *church*—I simply cannot understand it." Others say, "There, you see! They even burn down churches, because they are barbarians!" But how far is it not tragically true that these churches have become distorted symbols? How far do they stand for an ethic which the whites have brought, preached, and refused to practice? "You close your eyes obediently to pray," goes the saying, "and when you open them the whites have taken your land and interfered with your women."

How far do these churches represent something alien from the spirit of Christ, a sort of patronising social service? Do not many Christian ministers talk down to us instead of coming down (if that is the direction) among us, as Christ did and does?

African people bear these things long and patiently, but we are aware of them.

White paternalist Christianity—as though the whites have invented the Christian faith—estranges my people from Christ. Hypocrisy, double standards, and the identification of white skins with Christianity, do the same. For myself, for very many of us, nothing short of apostasy would budge us. We know Christianity for what it is, we know it is not a white preserve, we know that many whites—and Africans for that matter—are inferior exponents of what they profess. The faith of Christ persists in spite of them. But how many weak and experimental black Christians are made to stumble by the white example? How vulnerable we Christians are!

The burning of churches I condemn and deplore. I deplore it utterly. Reluctantly, I must confess that I partly understand it. The churches above all were to have brought us not apartheid but fellowship one with another. Have they? Some measure of human failure is inevitable. Even so, have not many of the churches simply submitted to a secular state which opposes expressions of fellowship and our membership one of another? Have not some even gone so far as to *support* the outlook of the secular state?

It is not too late for white Christians to look at the Gospels and re-define their allegiance. But, if I may presume to do so, I warn those who care for Christianity, who care to "go into *all* the world and preach the Gospel". In South Africa the opportunity is three hundred years old. It will not last for ever. The time is running out.

13. *After defiance*

It may be true that the Malan Government acted more swiftly
and harshly than we had foreseen—but then we had reckoned
without the riots. On the other hand, however, we had not
doubted that sooner or later the authorities would act against
any real and effective opposition to their continued domination.
We had never deceived ourselves into believing that the Suppression of Communism Act was aimed at communists or communism; and the Riotous Assemblies Act was designed to
frustrate organised resistance. When, early in 1953, the Criminal
Law Amendment Act and the Public Safety Act were added to
these, and all were reinforced by various proclamations, we knew
what to expect. The Government reacted to the Defiance Campaign with bannings and banishments, and by using the courts in
an effort to crush us.

But this after-effect of the Defiance Campaign was by no
means the only one, nor the most important.

Among other things, the Defiance Campaign revealed to us
some of the weaknesses of the resistance movement. There was
in existence a body calling itself the Bantu National Congress,
led by one S. S. Bhengu. This body allied itself enthusiastically
with the Government. Mr. Bhengu declared that "the Bantu
must be guided by the Europeans" because "God has said . . .
that an uneducated people must be guided by wiser counsellors."
The Nationalist South African Bureau of Racial Affairs
(S.A.B.R.A.) donated fifty pounds to his funds, and the white
Press gave prominence to his utterances. I do not know how many
followers he had, this African champion of apartheid. He made
no dent in the resistance, but he helped to lend colour to the
distorted picture of the situation being served up to white readers
by their Press. The Press made less of Bhengu's conviction,
which soon followed, for theft and forgery.

More important, though in the long run not much more
effective, was the running attack on the Defiance Campaign
carried on by the Non-European Unity Movement. They did
not appear to be inspired by the Government. I think their line
of attack was all their own, and it is certainly true that they
attacked the Government as vocally as they attacked us. Their
talk is really fierce, and they attack on all sides. So far they have

contributed nothing to "Non-European Unity", and their bite has not matched their bark.

They barked at us right through the Campaign—they presented it to their restricted public as the joint effort of "African Quislings" and Indian merchants activated by self-interest, they wrote of our leadership seeking "freedom from responsibility in gaol", and they derided the methods of the Campaign without suggesting any alternative. Both the N.U.E.M. and Mr. S. S. Bhengu held the Congresses responsible for the riots.

A good proportion of the membership of the N.U.E.M. is "Coloured"—that is, of mixed race. From other people and organisations the Defiance Campaign had a measure of support, and parts of their leadership deserve high credit. The co-operation which took place between coloured organisations and the Congresses showed that the area of common ground had grown. It is true, however, that the coloured people as a whole are divided among themselves and divided in their attitude to white supremacy. Some of them reject it because it is an immoral creed, but many of them resent it because they are not included in it. They seek identification with the whites, and find only rejection. At the same time they avoid identification with Africans.

Their dilemma is pitiable, they cannot make up their minds which world to live in. They find themselves debarred from living as whites. They refuse to make common cause with Africans, and this refusal comes from adherence to the same race hierarchy which causes the whites to reject them. Their confusion isolates them unhappily. In other words, they have become the victims of the very attitude which the Congresses will not accept—the belief that South Africa contains several worlds which may be graded as superior and inferior. Our struggle is to build one South Africa embodying all simply as fellow-citizens.

I do not want what I say to be interpreted as stricture on the Coloured community. I am very much aware of their difficulties, and in any case, what I have said does not apply to all. But it would be welcome to the resistance if more coloured people were to accept the ideal of a raceless South Africa.

We learned too, in the course of the Defiance Campaign, that the acclamation of resistance at mass meetings did not necessarily lead to resistance in practice. It is easier to raise one's voice in company with five thousand others than to court imprisonment with twenty others. Because the movement to defy was well supported and successful, the faint-hearted did not impede it. It was as well, however, not to overlook faintness of heart, to recognise that some of our people can be scared off by harshness and intimidation. One effect of my own deposition was that it frightened a good number of chiefs out of expressing support and sympathy.

In this connection there was a curious incident involving the Zulu Paramount. Efforts were made to get him to condemn the Defiance Campaign. Eventually a statement attributed to his uncle, formerly the Regent, appeared in the Press, condemning the Campaign in mild terms. In the normal course of events the Zulu people would take such a statement as expressing the mind of the Paramount. But on this occasion the Paramount dissociated himself at once, saying that only he could express his mind. It was the proper line for one who, but for the conquest, would be the Zulu King to take. He stood apart, and refused to be manœuvred into denouncing civil disobedience.

He has, alas, not consistently maintained this impartial stand. The pressure which the Government has brought to bear on him has been excessive, and latterly he has become, in his actions and utterances, a supporter of apartheid even when this has not been incumbent on him. He has had our sympathy throughout. His position is unenviable. But we regret this. The institution of chieftainship will die out in the course of time, but it will be a pity if its end is in ignominy. What I have said of the Zulu Paramount Chief goes for most, if not all, our Paramount or Principal Chiefs.

There were weak links in our chain, the Defiance Campaign showed that. But there is no doubt that the strength which it revealed was far more important. In itself it was the largest protest up till then, and it had not only kept moving but it had gathered weight as it went.

But that was not all. It had succeeded in *creating* among a very large number of Africans the spirit of militant defiance. The Campaign itself came to an untimely end, but it left a new climate, and it embraced people far beyond our range of vision. Since then there have been a number of unexpected demonstrations, especially among women. In Zeerust, Natal, Sekhukhuniland, on the Reef, in the Free State, and elsewhere, there have been upsurges of passive resistance, and the refusal to comply. To our surprise, many of these resisters called themselves "Congress" or "A.N.C." They were not on our books, their actions often took us by surprise, but they had caught the Defiance Campaign mood and sometimes its technique.

It was not only Africans previously politically inactive who sat up and took notice. At long last there were clear signs that the churches were becoming involved in the South African struggle *as churches*. Here and there individuals have acted and spoken out all along. Now African Christians, involved in making moral decisions about passive resistance, wanted the guidance of their churches speaking officially with voices not African or European but Christian.

The churches did not speak with one voice, but as far as I know only the Dutch Reformed Church went so far as to condemn the Defiance Campaign outright, and to equate obedience to the State with obedience to God. Perhaps closest to them was the General Assembly of the Presbyterian Church which, while it expressed sympathy and condemned the laws which we opposed, deeply regretted the Defiance Campaign.

Other churches, including the Roman Catholics, condemned the laws and refrained from regretting the Campaign. The Methodists condemned the laws and violent opposition to them, leaving its followers free to choose non-violent opposition. The Anglican Archbishop, presumably speaking for his church, declared: "It has been the traditional teaching of the Christian Church that there is no obligation on a man as a Christian to obey unjust laws." The Bishop of Johannesburg, while he warned of the possible dangers of the Campaign, saw in it a moral judgment upon the type of legislation being opposed, and upon the whites who had passed such laws.

I cannot speak authoritatively of all that the churches did and said at this time. The point is that whatever their reaction they were participating, instead of taking the stand, "Politics is not our business." Even though some statements were so indecisive and evasive that they aroused general disappointment, they were a beginning.

I can, however, disclose what passed at the meeting of the Executive Committee of the Christian Council in January 1953, since I was there. We met under the chairmanship of the Archbishop of Capetown, and the Defiance Campaign came before us because the Presbyterians had sent in a letter seeking advice about it.

The first reaction of the Christian Council was that, since it is a body which does no more than seek to co-operate, a statement would be out of place. The suggestion was that the matter should be referred back to member churches.

With others, I took a strong contrary view. The issue was real and present. By the time there was an answer from member churches, the whole thing might be out of date. I believed it to be the duty of the Council, because it was the duty of the Church as a whole, to give moral guidance at once while the issue was alive and while some Christians were in real confusion about the principles involved.

123

The Christian Council thought again, and we appointed a sub-committee to draft a statement. The sense of the final statement was that individual Christians had to bring their consciences to bear on the situation; it was not, however, un-Christian to participate provided that resistance activity did not violate the individual conscience; and that only obedience to a higher Law than man's justifies disobedience to man's laws. It was a sound and useful statement, and it did save the Christian Council from the charge of evasion.

The charge of evasion, where it is made against the churches, is not unfounded. If the Christian concern is with people and not disembodied principles, its concern must be with the conditions under which its people live. Christianity must be concerned with what is going on inside people *here and now*. If it is indifferent to these things, it is indifferent to people. It is utterly idle for Christians to criticise Communism and Islam from a deep armchair, when Communists and Moslems are concerning themselves with those involved in the conflict.

Obviously, we do not expect to see the Church organising political movements. But it must be *with* people, *in* their lives. I have no admiration for the political predikant. But I know something of the thirst of my people for spiritual guidance in the situation which confronts us now and will continue to be our lot for some time yet. The Church must be in among us all. If it stands on the outskirts, we cannot expect our religion to survive and be respected—we are untrue to our mission and that is suicide. Too often the flock has been left to its own devices in pressing matters of the moment.

It meant much to me that the churches did react to the Defiance Campaign, because Christianity is confronted with challenge and crisis in South Africa. Dr. Verwoerd, while Minister of Native Affairs, virtually withdrew *all* support for Christianity from African schooling. Whites need church schools and they have them. But Dr. Verwoerd secularised *all* African education and turned the emphasis on our heathen past. For decades African people have looked to Christian congregations and mission-taught people to lead the way.

What did the churches do about this? Except for the lone stand made by Bishop Reeves, who refused to hire church buildings out for the Verwoerd secular education for serfdom, almost nothing.

Church sites in African areas are now held on yearly lease at the pleasure of the Minister. The threat is that, if a sermon or a congregation or a bishop displeases the Department, the site will cease to be available. Parsons must not talk politics—yet much orthodox Christian teaching can be called "politics", especially in South Africa, and how is it possible to apply Christian principles to the lives we lead without talking "politics"?

This threat has many Christian ministers and organisations virtually cowering, as of course the Government intends. What is becoming of our Christian witness? I am extreme on this point. Let us lose Church sites and keep Christian integrity. I disagree with those who want to "save something from the wreck" because what I see happening is the wreck of Christian witness, and what I fear is a slow drift into a Nationalist state religion. I do not know how whites react to this prospect, but it does not attract African Christians.

It is my hope that what began, in the way of Christian involvement and thinking out, at the time of the Defiance Campaign, will not simply drain away, leaving Christians in despondency and impotence, adapting themselves fearfully to each new outrage, threat and assault upon the people in our case. There is a witness to be borne, and God will not fail those who bear it fearlessly.

Among Europeans, the Defiance Campaign had some happy political effects. The Liberal Party is very much the child of these times. Towards the end of the Campaign one group defied the law requiring permits for entry into locations. This batch was led by Patrick Duncan, and Africans, Indians and whites, after following him in, were duly arrested. This was virtually the Liberal Party's entry into South African public affairs, and the fact that the Party could be formed was a sign that some Europeans were beginning to recognise our plight as something real.

The Liberals have not acquired a large following, but perhaps that was scarcely to be expected. In any case, their effectiveness is not to be measured in votes, but in the appraisal they have forced on whites. The Liberal Party has been able to speak with a far greater moral authority than other parties with white members because of the quality of the people at its head—such as Alan Paton, Senator Rubin, Margaret Ballinger, Peter Brown, Patrick Duncan, and others. Moreover, it has tried to make its stand on principles and not on expediency—a new thing indeed in white South African politics. It remains to be seen whether the new Progressive Party[1] will follow its example. It is to be hoped so, because the Progressives have profited from the climate of opinion produced by the Liberals far more perhaps than they realise.

[1] A breakaway from Smuts's United Party.

125

The Liberal Party took the unprecedented step of throwing its membership open to all races, and in the South African setting that was an act of courage. So far the support it has won from Africans is limited. The disability from which a multi-racial party in South Africa suffers is that although within the party there is no discrimination, only the white members are voters in the country's elections. A slight unreality is introduced. I do not find it surprising that Africans in the resistance seek identification with other voteless Africans rather than with voting Europeans. It will be otherwise when we have reached our ideal (and the Liberal Party's) of a universal franchise. For the present, while most of us warmly welcome co-operation with Europeans, a resistance organisation such as the A.N.C. serves the needs of the moment more fully than a political party can. Meantime, I am glad the Liberals are there. I foresee the day when truly non-racial parties will function in South Africa, and when the existing resistance movement will change its composition. The needs of the moment do not permit that yet.

Earlier the Defiance Campaign had given birth to another group, with which the A.N.C. has co-operated closely. During the Campaign there was some co-operation with Europeans, and the desirability of continuing this was widely felt. Except for a dissident, conservative minority, the A.N.C. was ready to take a further step along our road towards a broader South Africanism. The Congress which had conducted the Campaign invited sympathising whites to form on their side of the fence a group with which we could co-operate in future. The result was the formation of the Congress of Democrats.[2]

At the start they rallied well, but as time went on there were defections. It appears that some members feared the presence of ex-Communists in the organisation. I do know that it is not the Communist Party in another guise. Some of its leaders—maybe many—have no Communist leanings or past affiliations, and of the "ex-Communists" in C.O.D. a number had left the party long before the Nationalists came to power. There may be an authentic orthodox Communist here and there in C.O.D., but I have reason to believe that on the whole it is an organisation of people who would be known in the British Isles as left wingers, more or less extreme.

[2] Known as C.O.D., this organisation is now a member of the Congress Alliance, which consists, together with it, of the A.N.C., the South African Indian Congress, the South African Coloured People's Organisation, and The Congress of Trade Unions. C.O.D. shares far more fully the political outlook of A.N.C. than do the newly formed Progressives or the Liberal Party.

Because it identified itself with us in the struggle for human liberties, the C.O.D. was destined to play some part in the years after Defiance. A number of its members appeared, with Africans, Indians and Coloureds, on charges of High Treason.

14. *Bans*

My visit in January 1953 to the Cape to attend the Executive
of the Christian Council gave me my first opportunity to visit
Congress branches outside Natal. Before this, except for occa-
sional journeys to conferences and meetings of the National
Executive, my experience of Congress was largely confined to
Natal. Now at last I had the opportunity, in my capacity as
President-General, to widen my knowledge of the movement and
meet the rank and file on whom it depends.

I began in Capetown. While I was there the Acting Cape
President, Dr. Njongwe (Professor Matthews was overseas),
invited me to alter my plans and return to Natal via Port
Elizabeth. I gladly agreed to this, though it was not possible for
Njongwe to accompany me in public places because he was
already under one of Mr. Swart's bans.

Port Elizabeth was an experience. Of all centres, it had shown
up best in the Defiance Campaign, and to this day the Congress
branch there is a model of sound organisation and an illustration
of the way in which, in spite of obstruction, it is possible for the
urban African to unite with his rural brother in the cause of
liberation. At a huge meeting which I addressed in Port Elizabeth
it was made clear to me that the spirit of resistance had by no
means abated. The provoking of the riots had, if anything,
wedded the Congress more firmly to passive resistance.

I was home briefly, and then, in response to an invitation from
the leaders there, away on a quick tour of the Free State. Then,
as now, the A.N.C. was not very strong in this province. The
aim of my tour, suggested by my working committee, was to keep
the Defiance Campaign spirit alive and to extend it where
possible. I used the opportunity to acquaint myself with my
new relationship to the people, and I spent some time looking
into the records and the efficiency of local branches.

In Bloemfontein I was visited by the Special Branch, or
Security Police. They told me that it was a "courtesy call". We
made polite conversation. I suppose they were committing to
memory the shape of my head. At Ficksburg, a Free State dorp
on the border of Basutoland, they were still in attendance.

Here I learned the hard way about the regulation requiring
us to have permits for a stay longer than seventy-two hours in
any one place. At the time, such had been my previous immunity,

I did not even know of the existence of this regulation. It was time I did.

The Bethlehem (O.F.S.) Congress branch sent word to ask me to delay my coming to them for one day, so I proposed to spend the extra day in Ficksburg. Almost to the minute of the expiry of my seventy-two hours, a policeman called to say that the Location Superintendent wanted to see me. I was taken to him riding pillion behind the policeman. I could not fail to see the undisguised anxiety on the faces of the residents as they saw me riding past.

At the Location Office I was steered into the presence of the superintendent.

Policeman: "Is this the man you want?"

Superintendent: "Yes. That's him. Have you got permission to be in this location?"

Self: "Permission? I don't know. I'm a guest of the local Congress branch. They made all the arrangements."

Superintendent: "What! Aren't you aware of the regulations? You can't be here over seventy-two hours."

Policeman (in a discouraging voice): "Well, man, what now? Are you charging him or not?"

Superintendent: "Yes!"

Policeman: "Are you *really* going to *charge* him?"

Superintendent (nettled): "Yes, of course I am, I'm charging him."

The policeman went off to the telephone. When he came back he said to the superintendent, "Well, if you're actually going to charge him, I suppose we'd better take him to the Charge Office."

At the Charge Office I stood around for an hour while the police and the superintendent conferred in the near distance. In the end they seemed to reach some agreement, and an officer came over to me.

"Tell me," he asked, "what were your plans?"

"I intend to spend an extra day here to suit our branch in Bethlehem. I was leaving tomorrow," I replied.

"Can you leave today?"

"If necessary."

"The superintendent is charging you. You can't go back into the location. Which would you prefer, to wait for your case to come up, or to pay an Admission of Guilt?"

"I prefer not to wait around. It would interfere with my programme," I said.

"Admission of guilt, five pounds," he replied.

The next contentious issue was my baggage. I said to the superintendent, "I want to go back to get my things."

"You're not going back into my location," he said.

"Well, how do I collect my baggage?"

"Somebody can get them for you."

"Who can?" I asked.

"Man," interrupted a police officer testily, speaking to the superintendent, "you've got to let him go back just to get his things."

They fell to sorting it out among themselves. In the end I was allowed back until midnight.

My stay at Bethlehem was quiet and uneventful. A large crowd assembled at the railway station to see me off, but the train was delayed and they had to leave. When the coast was quite clear an African policeman approached and began a conversation. He told me of his Congress sympathies. "Look, my son," his mother had said to him, "you're in the police force, and the police have got a proper job to do which any good man understands. But you know what it is here—a lot of bad behaviour, doing the job the wrong way, doing the wrong job sometimes. Don't you ever forget that its *your* welfare Congress is working for. Do your job properly, but don't forget and behave badly."

We chatted on for a while. I am not among those who rail against the police, but the lot of the African policeman is becoming harder every day. On the one side are his white superiors who ask him not merely to be a policeman but to be a pro-Nationalist defender of white domination—what a role for an African! On the other side are his own people—people like his mother, to whom the police are, more and more, part of the machinery of oppression. His sympathies are with his people, his white superiors often goad him against them. He wants to do a worthwhile job properly, but he is used to bolster up all-white rule. His lot is unenviable—indeed, it is becoming tragic.

There are white policemen too who, left to themselves, would do a necessary job well. It is true that in recent years there has been an influx of rabid youths into the force, as the Nationalists have looked forward to the day of police-state government. It is regrettably true that these youths, and some of their elders, have used their position in order to further the aims of harsh oppression. Not impartial law, but white supremacy, *Baasskap*, is their business. They tend to render the good policeman powerless. Yet there are still good policemen.

As the train pulled out of Bethlehem station, I caught sight of my new friend. He was standing behind a pillar. He looked to the right and then to the left, and then raised his hand in the Congress salute.

A short while later, towards the middle of the year, my first ban was served on me in terms of the Riotous Assemblies Act and the Criminal Law Amendment Act. In comparison with my later bans it was a mild affair. I was debarred from entry into all the larger centres of the Union, but I was not confined to a single area. I could still visit smaller places, which meant that although I could not continue my efforts to get to know Congress rank and file, I could arrange to meet my Executive in convenient places. I was not allowed to attend public gatherings anywhere.

This last provision at once raised the question of attendance at public worship. My church took up the matter with the Department of Justice and told me that while they did not *think* that the police would interfere with my religious activities, I should apply for permission to be present at public worship.

I have not done this during any ban. I have attended Communion services, since they are private in the sense of being restricted to communicants. I do not wish to attend public services without police permission, since this seems to be playing heroics and to place me at the uncertain mercy of the police. I do not ever intend to ask permission to worship God with my fellow-Christians—I do not concede that any man has the right either to grant or to withhold this "privilege".

Throughout the country various kinds of ban were served on many Congress leaders. It should have crippled us, but it did not. Whether the leaders were banned or not, the Defiance Campaign had given notice that the African people mean business. They rallied to the movement, and confidence in it grew. It has continued to be a source of encouragement to me that Congress strength and support have grown steadily in spite of the disability of the frequent banning of leaders. It is, in fact, the people as a whole who mean business, and they cannot all be banned. It would shorten our agonies if the whites realised this and came to terms with it. As it is, the Government takes refuge in a fantasy: only African "agitators" really oppose them. Ninety-nine per cent of the "law-abiding natives" are said to be contentedly and wholeheartedly behind them. It is, of course, nonsense, as anybody without blinkers can see.

In my banned state I settled into the routine work of running Congress, giving my main attention to matters of organisation. The Executive came to meet with me more frequently than was usually possible.

One of the great difficulties of running a resistance movement is money. What there is goes on literature and secretarial works largely. If some is left over, it is used to pay travelling expenses. In practice, however, there is seldom any left-over—we yearly

131

write off debts owing to Executive members for transport, which means in effect that they pay their own fares more often than not. The position of President-General is honorary, like other Executive posts. Part of the white propaganda among Africans against the A.N.C. is that we sponge on the people. I invite the meanest paid white government servant to try living on a "Congress income".

It was in 1954 that Congress tackled the outrage of Bantu Education. It was Dr. Verwoerd's intention to make the change-over to his secularised system at the end of the first quarter of 1954. We recognised fully—and the event has not proved us wrong—that the end of true education for all Africans was in sight, at least for the time being.

The problem was what to do about it. The Act eliminated all alternatives, and in any case, alternatives are financially far beyond the African people. Protest of some kind was more than desirable. Verbal protest has no effect whatever. The choice before us came to something like this: either no protest, or a temporary boycott, or a permanent end to sending our children to school at all.

I could not address the National Conference (in Durban) which considered this. But some of the delegates came to see me in Stanger and we held a sort of "private conference", in addition to which I sent a message to the people assembled in Durban. I advised that some action be taken, its type to be determined by the people's readiness.

The resolution of the Conference was that there should be a permanent and total boycott of all education so long as we are confined to Dr. Verwoerd's Bantu Education schools. The hazards of such a decision are obvious. The choice before parents is an almost impossible one—they do not want Bantu Education and they do not want their children on the streets. They have to choose between two evils, and no rule of thumb indicates which is the greater. The chances of universal agreement are small, not because of hesitation about whether Bantu Education is evil, but because, as Archbishop Clayton of Capetown told his Synod, "a rotten education" may be "better than none".

Other centres were chafing to be given the go-ahead to boycott, and in Port Elizabeth and on the Reef plans were well advanced. A special conference was summoned in Port Elizabeth. As it turned out, some places were fully prepared and others utterly unprepared for boycott. That was our dilemma. Congress leadership could not afford to go more slowly than the general members, yet if it decreed boycott, many areas would be unready. After much discussion the Port Elizabeth meeting decided that particular areas could, if they so wished, apply the boycott provided they had Executive permission. So from the start the boycott of Bantu Education was doomed to be partial. Yet we could not simply sit by and listen to some Cabinet Minister[1] telling us that since no protest had been made, the whites could be assured that we are delighted with Bantu Education.

It might have been better to wait and organise. But in point of fact the people, especially in urban areas, were so furious at all that the Verwoerd system of education stands for that they were in no mood to stand by and watch it come down on us. The decisions in various centres to boycott, and the final decision to boycott in particular areas, may be criticised as unrealistic because unlikely to succeed. Yet these decisions reflected the mood of the people, and that mood had to find some expression.

On the whole, although there have been examples of boycott and reprisal—very savage reprisal—we African parents have had to submit unhappily to this violation. Our children are dying of mental and spiritual starvation. Understandably, the attempt by good teachers to frustrate the National intentions cannot meet with full success. The evil of Bantu Education cannot be adequately described.

At the end of 1953 something which was destined to have far-reaching results began in a quiet undertone. Our Annual Conference was held in December in Queenstown. The advantage of this venue was that it was not out of bounds to banned leaders, myself among them. I could not attend the public gatherings. None the less, it might be said that I attended the Conference without actually breaking the letter of the law. (By this time, of course, the Security Police were in almost constant attendance.) I had taken a somewhat devious route to Queenstown, carefully skirting the "danger zones".

Here for the first time in public session the idea of an assembly of the people was mooted. This idea had come from Professor Matthews, who had just recently returned from a trip to the United States. In part his suggestion came from the need to keep our people on the move. The Defiance Campaign was receding into the background, the leaders were banned in various ways, and it was high time to canalise the restiveness of our people.

But the main intention of Professor Matthews's idea was to convene a gathering of *all* who are opposed to white domination,

[1] The Separate Universities Act, which came later, was actually justified to Parliament, not on the grounds that Africans had been consulted and had approved, but on the grounds that there had been no Congress demonstrations against it. The overwhelming majority of M.P.s on both sides of the House swallow this sort of thing whole.

133

to make a public declaration, together with our allies of other races and organisations, of our refusal to bow to the white yoke. The strength of the South African liberation movement does not lie in its ability to organise, which is sometimes poor. It lies in the fact that there are a couple of million white supremacists who have ranged against them ten or twelve million people of all races, whites included, many of whom have already got beyond the bounds of colour, and all of whom reject apartheid and *Baasskap*—by whatever names they are called.

Besides this, there was in our minds appreciation of the need to think creatively about the New South Africa. We are, after all, not mainly devoted to battling *against* something, though that is imposed on us at present. We are inspired by the ideal of working *for* something. If we are against passes, it is because we are for human dignity and freedom of movement. If we are against Bantu Education it is because we are for education. When you are constantly impeded in the effort to work towards a worthy goal, there is the danger of becoming preoccupied with the impediments. It was felt to be high time to counteract this by defining the goal rather more clearly.

At this Conference, the suggestion was no more than discussed and filed for future decision. But the seed had been sown.

Meantime, as an ominous background to our daily lives, the Nationalist Government, usually with the support of most of the opposition, were settling down to give our people more and more to battle against. As I have said, the Criminal Law Amendment Act was passed (without a division) early in 1953, and this was followed by the Public Safety Act (nine against). The whites then fought another election, returning Malan with an enlarged majority of seats. It did not surprise us to see the United Party lose further ground. By this time its policy was no more than a tepid version of the Nationalist Party's, and the electorate naturally preferred bald statement to enfeebled imitation.

The new Parliament settled in to circumscribe us further. The Native Labour (Settlement of Disputes) Act make strikes illegal, and excluded "natives" from any share in the workings of an economy which our labour upholds. The Separate Amenities Act arranged that we should be treated as lepers in public places. The Suppression of Communism Amendment Act gave Mr. Swart additional power over the resistance—sinister power, in that he was now able to by-pass the courts in dealing with "agitators". The South-West Africa Administration Act threw the African people of that vast territory into Dr. Verwoerd's gigantic empire, whether they wished it or not. The Industrial Conciliation Act—introduced, so the Minister said, in the cause of "racial survival"

—placed the settlement of all industrial disputes in the hands of the Government. The situation now is that Africans, because of this Act taken together with the Apprenticeship Act, are altogether excluded from skilled labour in industry; while Indians and Coloureds, now mainly through the Job Reservation Acts, can have the door slammed in their face any day of the week. The inability of South African whites to compete with us in the open market does not intensify our submission to the much-vaunted doctrines of white supremacy.

The energetic Dr. Verwoerd kept his end up well. His Natives (Urban Areas) Consolidation Act cleared the way for him to push "redundant natives" out of the cities and redirect them to white farms or commit them to overcrowded reserves. His Resettlement Act gave him power to seize the freehold rights of Urban Africans in Johannesburg, to move them where he wished, and to resettle them as tenants. This last Act alone affected the lives of about 130,000 Africans. It was represented as an effort of slum clearance. The main obnoxious "slum condition" was the possession by some Africans of freehold. Those who escape the consequences of the Group Areas Act fall victim to this one, and vice versa.

A catalogue of the South African Parliament's Acts of oppression makes dreary and exhausting reading. There seems to be no end to them, there are so many that the mind loses count of their number and grasp of their effects. But with each one, people are further injured and degraded.

In the winter of 1954, when the new battery of ruthless laws was freshly in place on the Statute Book, my ban expired. It was not immediately reimposed. I suppose I was being given a chance to go straight.

I immediately misbehaved. I went to Uitenhage, near Port Elizabeth, where I addressed the Cape Provincial Annual Conference. On my return I was invited to open the Conference of the Natal Indian Congress in Durban. This invitation was a further sign of the growing co-operation between people of different race. It was no longer an ideal, it was a practical reality —not universal, but very real, and spreading to embrace more and more people.

For years after the Act of Union, the resistance such as it was was a purely African affair.[2] Those who put the fact of resistance down to the work of "liberalists" who have introduced foreign ideas should bear this in mind. Latterly its character has changed,

[2] The demonstrations organised by Ghandi against purely Indian disabilities must qualify this statement.

until I doubt whether there is a race group in South Africa not represented in the resistance. While the old-style parties cling to their theories about the superiority and purity of their minorities, the resistance movement is forging the New South Africa.

I had been about to visit Johannesburg when the ban was placed on me. Now that it was lifted, I at once prepared to keep this engagement, even though it was a year behind schedule. I boarded a plane in Durban and stepped off in Johannesburg straight into the arms of the Special Branch. Mr. Oliver Tambo, now Secretary-General of Congress, joined me but was ordered to step aside. I was surrounded and taken downstairs to a room in the buildings of the air terminal.

"Do you understand English?" demanded a member of the Special Branch.

"Well," I replied, "perhaps just a little bit."

Two documents were presented. One debarred me from attending public gatherings. The second confined me to the Stanger magisterial area in the Lower Tugela District for two years. My second dose of punishment had not been long in coming.

An officer in possession of a few words of Xhosa, which when properly spoken does have some affinity with Zulu, apparently felt that I was taking things too blankly. Fearing that I had not grasped what had happened to me, he endeavoured to explain the contents of the documents in Xhosa. He ended very emphatically: "You understand, you can't go from here and address any meeting. You understand?"

"Yes," I said, "I think I understand."

The documents allowed me a margin of seven days before I had to be back in Groutville. I emerged from the buildings and broke the latest news to my colleagues.

15. *The Freedom Charter*

The meeting in Freedom Square, Sophiatown, which I was unable to attend, was the climax of a great deal of preparation and organisation. It would have been my first mass meeting in Johannesburg after election as President-General of Congress. The meeting went ahead, but all the people could do to acknowledge my existence was to process in thousands past the gate of the house where I was staying. In an informal way, standing by the gate, I returned their greeting. There was no doubt that their spirit was high—the Youth League had to be restrained from carrying me bodily to Freedom Square.

In a house near the square where I went just to get a breath of the meeting, I was beset by news reporters. My people were uneasy about this—the presence of numbers might be held to constitute a gathering—so I had no opportunity to reply to the question of a rather haughty American reporter, "How is it that you, alleged to be a Christian, can co-operate with Communists?"

Disregarding the tone of this question, it is one which requires a reply. I do not know whether there were any or many Communists at Freedom Square that day, but I shall assume that there were a few. In any case, the issue has been raised by people so diverse as Robert Sobukwe of the Pan-Africanists, and Patrick Duncan of the Liberals.

Let me make it clear at once that I do not feel in the least defensive or apologetic about the position as it actually is—it is often misrepresented. For myself I am not a Communist. Communism seems to me to be a mixture of a false theory of society linked on to a false "religion". In religion I am a Christian, and the gods of state worship (as in Russia and to some extent in white South Africa) and man-worship (as in pre-war Germany, and to some extent perhaps unconsciously in white South Africa[1]) are not my gods. In politics I tend towards the outlook of British Labour, with some important modifications.

---

[1] In a funeral oration after the death of Prime Minister J. G. Strijdom, a Dutch Reformed Church *dominee* chose his text from the beginning of St. John's Gospel: "There was a man sent from God whose name was John . . ." To me this is repugnant.

There are Communists in the South African resistance, and I co-operate with them. The Congress stand is this: our primary concern is liberation, and we are not going to be side-tracked by ideological clashes and witch hunts. Nobody in Congress may use the organisation to further any aims but those of Congress. When I co-operate with Communists in Congress affairs I am not co-operating with Communism. We leave our differing political theories to one side until the day of liberation, and in the meantime we are co-operating in a defined area, in the cause of liberation. Even in the days when the Communist Party was in its infancy, Congress did not debar them.

It might be said that this is naïve. I have no reason to suppose that the number of ex-Communist Party members in the Resistance Movement is large. If there is any danger of their using Congress for their own ends and infiltrating into "key positions" it can only be the result of apathy among non-Communists. The American reporter's question, with its background of fear and witch hunts, assumes that I am co-operating with Communism. Other things take a change for the better in South Africa, the resistance must be a body of people of diverse outlook and religion (Muslims and Hindus co-operate too) working together for one end. After that, there is no doubt that we shall sort ourselves out into conventional political parties. Resistance movements cannot afford the luxury of McCarthyism, nor can they allow themselves to be divided up into innumerable little homogeneous groups. We are not playing at politics, we are bent on liberation.

For myself, I am in Congress precisely *because* I am a Christian. My Christian belief about human society must find expression here and now, and Congress is the spearhead of the real struggle. Some would have Communists excluded, others would have all non-Communists withdrawn from Congress. My own urge, *because* I am a Christian, is to get into the thick of the struggle with other Christians, taking my Christianity with me and praying that it may be used to influence for good the character of the resistance.

For me there is more to it than that. We Africans are de-personalised by the whites, our humanity and dignity is reduced in their imaginations to a minimum. We are "boys", "girls", "Kaffirs", "good natives" and "bad natives". But we are not, to them, really quite people, scarcely more than units in a labour force and parts of a "Native Problem". Now, I refuse to lend myself to this degraded outlook. The Communist philosophy I reject. But Communists are people, they are among the number of my neighbours, and I will not regard them as less. I believe

138

they are misguided people. That evokes my compassion. I do not find within myself a blind terror of the "Communist Menace".

The strength to combat and rectify their false doctrines, as with the false doctrines of white supremacists, does not lie in my de-personalising them and going apart into an anti-somebody camp. It lies rather in the things I believe in, it lies within me. I am confident enough in the Christian faith to believe that I can serve my neighbour best by remaining in his company. Men doubtful about the inner strength of their own cause will put their faith in exclusiveness, discriminatory laws, apartheid, guns —their fear makes materialists of them, the spirit is weak, and they seek to make the flesh strong. The Christian faith, undiluted, and other creeds which assert justice and humility, whose strength is spiritual rather than material, are strong enough to withstand any onslaught. By that I stand or fall. Were Communism to triumph, it would not be so much because of the zeal of the Communists as the failure of Christians.

After the stimulus and frustration of the Sophiatown rally, I made my way home to the frustration of two years' confinement to the Lower Tugela. It was not, however, as bad as being behind bars. I could move freely about the district which is thirty miles across and includes the town of Stanger.

The main redeeming feature was that there was no ban on visitors. Those who could not visit could send messengers, through whom I could reply. Of necessity I missed a number of Executive meetings. In matters of urgency, however, the Executive met here or there in the Lower Tugela.

I may say in passing that it has been a source of interest to me that if the Government really believes us to be the agitators and inciters which they say we are, they have not banned the organisation entirely. No doubt they will in time.[2] Meantime, do they themselves believe the picture of Congress which they display in all corners? Are they keeping us in existence to shoulder the blame when they have goaded the African too far? Clearly, whatever may be the answer to these questions, it is not in their interests to be without a Black Peril. Perhaps, too, they need the resistance to reach greater maturity before they can plausibly round on it with the violence which they hold in reserve.[3]

The remainder of this year, 1954, was taken up with planning what had come to be known as the Congress of the People.

[2] Note: the A.N.C. was banned on 25th March, 1960.

[3] This was written before Sharpeville and the subsequent State of Emergency.

Professor Matthews's idea had taken root and been endorsed all over the country, not only by the A.N.C. but by the other Congresses. It was agreed that a joint meeting be held of the Executives of all the organisations involved, and the venue was an Indian school at a place called Frasers—in the Lower Tugela so that I might attend.

The Special Branch added a touch of excitement to the proceedings. I was picked up by my people in a car, but we left Groutville by a roundabout way. The result was that we came up on the Special Branch, waiting in a body, from behind. They leapt to their car, and we made a chase of it. When we arrived we found another contingent already waiting at our destination.

The Liberal Party sent observers to this meeting. They grumbled rather that we had got things going and only then invited them in. We found their complaint odd, since all we had done was to define what we, the sponsors, were inviting them to join us in. We pointed out that they had done nothing to respond to the initial invitation sent out to all—we had, in fact, even invited Nationalist organisations.[4]

The Special Branch hung around eavesdropping. Then, early in the afternoon, their top man, Colonel Spengler, arrived from Johannesburg with a search warrant. We went on with the meeting while they went on with the search—much was later made at the Preparatory Examination of the Treason Trial of documents seized here.

The Liberals withdrew, entirely washing their hands of the Congress of the People. The rest of us, at this Frasers meeting, approved certain broad proposals. A date was fixed, when it was clear that the idea had widespread support, and Johannesburg was chosen as the place. An *ad hoc* National Action Committee, already in existence, was approved as a sort of liaison sub-committee of the joint Executives.[5] This Action Committee was to circularise branches of the various organisations, and to contact communities in which there were no branches, in order to ask them to submit contributions to a comprehensive Charter for the South Africa we visualise, to co-ordinate these contributions, and to draw up the Charter. When necessary, the full Executives would meet together, in order to pass judgment on the draft.

---

[4] This should give some idea of how subversive our intentions were.

[5] The organisations involved were: The African National Congress, the South African Indian Congress, the South African Congress of Trade Unions, the South African Coloured People's Organisation, and the Congress of Democrats.

The date chosen for the Congress of the People was 26th June, 1955. I can speak only vaguely of the preparations which went before it, not only because I was excluded by the ban from all but top-level decisions, but because of illness. Early in 1955 my blood-pressure went up into the danger zone, and this culminated in a stroke. Even in this condition I could not be removed to a hospital until my wife was given permission for me to be taken out of Lower Tugela. When it was granted I was taken to McCord's Hospital in Durban. The best part of two months dropped right out of my life. I vaguely recall a visit by the Special Branch who came "just to investigate my condition". I am told that they loitered in the hospital throughout my stay.

My visitors tried to keep my mind, in the lucid intervals of convalescence, on small domestic matters. But this was the time when the Bantu Education system was applied throughout the country. With the help of a colleague, Mr. Jordan Ngubane, and (I regret to say) without the permission of my doctors, I wrote a statement on Bantu Education which was thereafter adopted as an expression of Natal's views.

I was most deeply grateful and moved by the hundreds of letters which I received, and by the number of people who called at McCord's to learn news of me.

After a relapse I made a good recovery, by which time the Congress of the People was about due to occur.

The main disadvantage from which preparations for this suffered was that local branches submitted their material for the Charter at a very late hour—too late, in fact, for the statements to be properly boiled down into one comprehensive statement. It was not even possible for the National Action Committee to circularise the draft Charter fully. The result is that the declaration made in the Freedom Charter is uneven—sometimes it goes into unnecessary detail, at other times it is a little vague. All the same, taken as a whole, it does give insight into the hopes and aspirations of the people who desire South Africa to be one homeland for all its inhabitants.

After tremendous last-minute activity, delegates from all over the country, delegates of every South African race, came together on a sports ground at Kliptown near Johannesburg for a two-day gathering. The people bestowed a great honour on Dr. Dadoo, the Indian leader, on Father Huddleston, and on me. The Xhosa title *Isitwalandwe*[6] was conferred on each of us—though I was perforce far away in Groutville.

---

[6] Applicable to those who have fought courageously in battle.

A small army of police, in and out of uniform, assembled too. Weapons were most prominent, but they behaved with more restraint than usual. The police so arranged it that delegates had to arrive and leave through a screen of policemen who searched and re-searched them. But there were no incidents.

The Congress was fully attended and fully reported. Perhaps it was the first really representative gathering in the Union's history. Over two days it was addressed by different speakers who gave voice to its purpose and to the aspirations of the oppressed peoples of Africa. The Freedom Charter was read out and unanimously adopted.[7] The Special Branch added to its store of confiscated documents—it was here, I think, that they acquired a placard which became a Treason Trial exhibit. It read: "Comrades. Tea 3d. Tea and Sandwich 6d."

Apart from producing the Freedom Charter, the Congress of the People had far-reaching effects. Nothing in the history of the liberatory movement in South Africa quite caught the popular imagination as this did, not even the Defiance Campaign. Even remote rural areas were aware of the significance of what was going on. The noisy opposition in most of the white Press advertised the Congress and the Charter more effectively than our unaided efforts would have done. ("If the white Press objects on this scale," most Africans felt, "it must be a good thing!") So the awakening spread farther. The participation of all race groups in this effort underlined the scale of awakening resistance.

The Charter produced in Kliptown is, line by line, the direct outcome of conditions which obtain—harsh, oppressive and unjust conditions. It is thus a practical and relevant document. It attempted to give a flesh and blood meaning, *in the South African setting*, to such words as *democracy, freedom, liberty*. If the Charter is examined it will be seen that *freedom* means the opening up of the opportunity to all South Africans to live full and abundant lives in terms of country, community and individual. It means the end of legalised bullying, the removal of a sub-human outlook.

The Freedom Charter is open to criticism. It is by no means a perfect document. But its motive must be understood, as must the deep yearning for security and human dignity from which it springs.

The Congress of the People certainly woke up the Government. It angered the oppressor by giving him further notice of our earnestness in the struggle, and it demonstrated that the reckless bannings which followed the Defiance Campaign had by no means made us resolve to be good pro-apartheid natives in the future. The police burst into activity.

I sometimes wonder if life is not one long series of surprises for the Nationalists. Most of them perhaps really *do* think that Africans are so thick-skinned and limited in understanding that they would not notice things like malnutrition, low wages, leaks in the roof, police brutality, or flagrant discrimination, unless an agitator came to point it all out. It takes them gravely aback when we arrive at our conclusions and resolve to do something about them. Deep down, I wonder if they believe us—left to ourselves—capable of more than "*Ja, Baas!*" After the event, they seem sometimes to have the air of people who really had not thought it could happen. They *still* seem to believe, even now, that as soon as their unreal plans are established and applied, the whole African people is going to subside into centuries of subservience.

Police activity in late 1955 was aimed at unearthing some master plan. There were the usual Union-wide raids, but more thorough and persistent than usual. "Man," one of them said impatiently, "where is that plan, where is that plan?"

"What plan?" was the reply. "You've been present at our discussions. We've published our 'plan'. You're already in on the secret."

It would have simplified the lives of the Special Branch at this point if they had believed us. But they went on looking for a secret master plan. Congress has always worked in the open. We prefer it. The only future possibility of secret master plans will come if they drive us underground.[8] So far, our plans and aspirations are public property.

Ever since this time the police have vigilantly gone out of their way to make things difficult for us to meet openly. Busloads of conference delegates have been held up interminably while the police have checked for infringements of the Motor Transportation Act. Sometimes railway carriages containing delegates have been unhooked and left in sidings. We feel encouraged rather than the reverse.

The Congress of the People was an *ad hoc* assembly. Afterwards, it remained for the participating organisations to adopt the Charter. The A.N.C. ratified the Charter in March of the following year.

It was, I may say, necessary that this should happen, since there were principles embodied in the Charter which had not previously been part of Congress policy. I sent a note to the

[8] See note to page 139 sub.

Conference which ratified the Charter urging delegates to discuss very fully such things as, for instance, the principle of nationalisation. I am myself in favour of limited nationalisation—I think it is the only answer to some of the economic problems which we face.

Congress did not unanimously adopt the Charter, though the majority was large. But our extreme right-wing[9] dismissed it *in toto*. Their compromising stand made discussion very difficult.

By now, Dr. Malan had handed white leadership over to Mr. J. G. Strijdom, and the balance of power among the Nationalists had shifted from the Cape to the harsher and angrier Transvaal. It was no new development. It had been obvious for a long time that the Nationalist Party as a whole would go far beyond such men as Malan along the same road. There is logic about totalitarianism which forces its supporters to even greater extremes. They seem permanently unable to reconsider or revise. They press on ruthlessly—along the wrong road. We knew what to expect.

In the winter of 1956 my two-year ban at last came to an end. I was thus able to deliver the presidential address in person. My theme was: "The struggle must go on, bans or no bans:" The Conference took up this theme—indeed, it echoed throughout the liberation movement. It still does, notwithstanding the harsh vigour and cruelty with which we have been repressed since then.

At this Conference, co-operation across the race barrier was well in evidence. Dr. Molota represented the Indian Congress, and Mr. Peter Brown came for the Liberal Party.

After the Conference I waited for two of my Natal office-bearers, Dr. W. Conco and Mr. M. B. Yengwa, to emerge from *their* bans. We decided to give ourselves a shake in the air of freedom. With Dr. Conco's wife and mine—Yengwa was unmarried—we set out on a short unadvertised visit to Swaziland, passing by the Royal House at Nongoma in order to pay our respects, as dutiful Zulu citizens, to our own Paramount. We were accompanied by our mutual friend Mrs. Mary Louise Hooper, an American lady closely associated with the now banned African National Congress.

In Swaziland we were guests of my wife's youngest brother's family, and pleasantly associated with the missionaries at the Nazarene Mission near Bremersdorp. Here, to our great surprise and pleasure, the Swazi Paramount called on us, a short formal visit and an unexpected honour.

I found Swaziland pleasantly free—a welcome contrast to a

[9] The Africanists, now independently led by Mr. Robert Sobukwe.

country plagued with raiding police. There is, of course, a measure of the usual exploitation, dating back to the days of the concession rackets. The development of the territory seems unduly slow. But on the whole, the people of Swaziland, with problems very different from ours, are trying to meet these problems in their own way, and managing to avoid friction.

About one thing I was a little disturbed. I may be wrong, but I seemed to sense that this territory is being left behind by Basutoland and Bechuanaland, partly because some African people are clinging obstinately to a dream of a return of the old Swaziland— a dream incapable of fulfilment now, in any case, and even more so since half the territory is owned by Europeans. There is, perhaps, something a little stagnant in the air, and maybe a slowness in adapting to the challenge of this century. But, if I am right, that is a small price to pay for civil peace; and in time I have no doubt Swaziland will take its place with the rest of southern Africa.

We hurried back over a weekend to our own set of problems.

On 5th December, at 4 a.m., I was arrested in Groutville on a charge of High Treason.

16. *The Treason Trials begin*

The almost casual manner of my arrest seemed quite out of keeping with the magnitude of the charge of High Treason.

I was still in bed when the police knock came, but my wife, according to her industrious custom, was already up. She admitted them and they came through to the bedroom and ordered me out of bed. "Yes," one of them greeted me, "—the day has come!" I do not know what he meant, but one cannot but be aware that the Nationalists encourage their followers to look forward to showdowns, days of reckoning with their opponents. No doubt these will become progressively more *kragdadig*.[1]

Warrants were produced—first the warrant of arrest and then the search warrant. I sat down on the edge of my bed and read them through. The charge of High Treason was unexpected, even though for some months the Minister of Justice and the Chief of Police had separately accused Congress of seditious and traitorous activity. We had, of course, expected the Government to do something. So I was surprised rather than shocked. Police activity had led us all to be ready for some fresh example of *kragdadigheid*.

Two policemen remained with me and two were stationed outside to watch the approaches to the house. Considering my unexpected company, I preferred to waive my early bath—I contented myself with a sponge-down. My wife appeared and asked if there was any point in preparing breakfast. The police said there was. It was just as well—we were not yet on our way.

The police produced a list of things they had power to seize. They asked me to read through it. "Just carry on," I said. They sat themselves down to a two-hour job of sorting papers, slowly and fairly thoroughly.

My eldest daughter decided to enliven proceedings.

"I want to relieve myself," she said to the police.

"Nobody is to leave this house," the man in charge replied.

"Well, will you tell me then what I'm supposed to do?"

So two policemen escorted her down the garden to the lavatory and stood on guard while she was inside. Family morale was

---

[1] Part of Nationalist political jargon. It means "mighty in deed" and it expresses approval of the unrelenting severity of extremist Government policies and utterances.

high. My son came into the room and addressed a policeman by his uncomplimentary Zulu nickname. I thought it time to get back to the business in hand.

The search which followed was extremely thorough, and there was quite enough irrelevant paper by the time we left, enough to prolong the Preparatory Examination which preceded the trial by two days of heavy listening. A policeman crammed some of it tightly into a briefcase which I highly prized—it was a gift from the Johannesburg Youth League.

"Can't you take the papers and leave the briefcase?" I asked.

"Then what do we carry all these documents in?"

"I don't know, but I value that briefcase and I don't see how it can be evidence of treason."

"Part of our instructions is to seize any containers," was the reply. The briefcase was not handed in as evidence. I haven't seen it since.

At the time, of course, I had no way of knowing whether or not I was the only one arrested on this charge, whether I had been selected so that the Government could make an example of me, or whether I was one of many. After going through the awkward, unhappy ceremony of bidding my family farewell, I tried on the way to Durban in the police car to draw out the officer in charge. But either he knew nothing, or else he was keeping quiet.

As soon as we reached Durban, however, I found that I was not alone. M. B. Yengwa, my Provincial Secretary, was already there, and later a further batch arrived from Pietermaritzburg, while a large contingent had already gone ahead. We found that we were all held on the same charge. Soon, unarrested Congress members began to bring us food. A senior member of the Special Branch called in to look us over. We were taken to the Magistrate's Court to be charged and formally remanded. In the afternoon we were flown to the Transvaal in a military plane, and we ended up at the Johannesburg Fort. It was all very flat, a routine sort of thing; yet at the same time everybody seemed aware that there was a difference in the air, as though South Africa and the resistance had passed another point of no return.

But it was not until we had been drafted through various formalities into the cells that we realised just how extensive the arrests were. In the cells we met not just a few friends, but men from every corner of the land—professionals and labourers, priests and laymen, Muslims, Christians, Hindus, infidels, Africans, Indians, Coloureds. And although, according to their fantasy about colour, the authorities did not allow us to glimpse them, we learned in no time that Europeans had been arrested

147

too. Again, as at the Congress of the People, one thing stood out: the resistance has long since ceased to be a matter of face—it is not the dark skin versus the light, but a loose confederation of people of all classes, creeds and colours, lined up against adherents of the Master Race and the injustice which it lives by. Far more significant than the colour-bar in South Africa now is the bar which stands between those who place their faith in rule by force and violence, and those who repudiate the police state.

Not knowing what the outcome of it all would be, we immediately set about organising ourselves for prison life. For me it was my first sight of the inside of a gaol for any reason. Conditions were not acutely difficult—the Prisons Department had anticipated our coming. We were later told that there had been very far-reaching personnel changes just before we were admitted. At all events, we were issued with new equipment—blankets, crockery, cutlery, mats.

Dr. Naicker and I, with the able help of such men as Professor Matthews, naturally took the lead in organising the prisoners—it was rather like a joint Executive of the Congresses. Jealous of the good name of the Congresses, we placed emphasis on order and discipline, even in such details as moving from the cells into the courtyard.

The arrested men were quartered in two large cells, but we could meet during the day. We redistributed the population of these cells and assigned a chaplain to each—we were fortunate in having among us two Anglican priests, Fathers Gawe and Calata. It was necessary to have one in each cell since, although their new congregations were relatively small, we spent most of the twenty-four hours locked in. It was necessary to lock each priest in with his parish.

We shook down very quickly. Obviously, there was no temptation towards idleness. It is extraordinarily difficult in so large a country as South Africa for resistance leaders to meet together, especially since many of us do not belong to the travelling classes. Yet here we all were, met together, and with time on our hands. What distance, other occupations, lack of funds, the police interference had made difficult—frequent meetings—the Government had now insisted on. We could at last confer *sine die*, at any level we liked. Delegates from the remotest areas were never farther than one cell away.

But to prevent too great an absorption with resistance affairs, we saw to it that there was relief. We organised debates, indoor games, lectures, regular worship both Muslim and Christian—and, of course, music. According to Prison Regulations we were supposed to fall silent at 8 p.m. Dr. Naicker and I usually insisted on silence somewhere between 10 and 11 p.m. The guards seemed to recognise tacitly that this regulation was better honoured in the breach than in the observance.

We were heartened by the news that the Bishop of Johannesburg and other good citizens were arranging our defence against the charges. Never low in morale, the arrested men were immeasurably encouraged by this, by visits of defence lawyers, and by the evidence that reached us of the generosity of a host of Johannesburg people. Among other visitors such as the Bishop and the Rev. Canon A. Blaxall, I was delighted to see Dominee du Toit, the man who had led our Christian Council delegation to India almost twenty years before. Such a visit takes more courage than is readily understood.

On the day when we were taken to the Magistrate's Court in closed vans to be formally charged, we had some hint of the stir which the arrests had created. We were carefully insulated, but the evidence that the crowds were not far away was obvious. Even so, this was nothing compared in size with what was to come.

While negotiation over the sum at which bail was to be fixed went on, we spent our days placidly, profitably, and not uncomfortably in the Fort. On one occasion, however, we intervened to stop a near-riot. While in the prison yard one Sunday morning we heard, and then saw, the belting of prisoners by long-term "boss-boy" prisoners in the presence of a white warder. Our own men—the average age, incidentally, was under twenty-eight—wanted to intervene, and we had great difficulty in restraining them. We approved wholeheartedly of the attitude of our Congressmen, but obviously we should set nothing right by contravening prison regulations. When we tried to remonstrate with the warder, who proved to be drunk, he became very angry, but a calmer colleague of his rushed to the scene and the incident subsided. "You mustn't think," said the sober warder apologetically, "that I approve of what he's doing!"

On our last Sunday in the cells Father Calata led our devotions. It was a most moving service, a real spiritual preparation for what lay ahead, which made its mark even on the non-Christians and atheists among us. Afterwards we all stood around in a great circle and sang some of our freedom songs. I led the prisoners in our pledging ourselves to solidarity in the cause of liberation— it proved a touching little impromptu ceremony about which were both formality and dedication. There was no doubt about it, we had not languished in gaol, our morale was very high.

We were warned in advance to be ready for the first day of the Preparatory Examination, and the world knows pretty well how things turned out. It was obvious before we were far from the Fort in our now-familiar closed vans that the people of Johannesburg were out in force. We could do little (but it was enough) to acknowledge their presence. We were driven right into the specially prepared Drill Hall and poured out straight into the wire cage like lions coming into a circus ring. Just before proceedings began the huge crowd outside began *Nkosi Sikelel' iAfrika,* the African National Anthem. It sounded like an angelic choir: to us the sound seemed to come from above. I have never heard this grand hymn so perfectly rendered—to this day the precision and perfection of the singing remain a mystery to me.

The defence team lined up in court, undoubtedly the most massive array of legal ability ever to be concerned in a single South African case, gave us further cause for confidence, and for gratitude to the men and women behind the Treason Trial Defence Fund and those who had contributed to it.

I do not intend to deal here with the affairs of the courtroom—they are a matter of record, in any case. But I will say that it was invariably the Defence team which brought occasional liveliness to essentially dreary proceedings. After a good start, lasting one day, the prosecution was uniformly unimpressive, and the evidence they led was confused, often inaccurate, and appallingly repetitive—they seemed to want to kill us with sheer boredom.

The world knows the story of how the police added their touch of sensation early on—how, without even being given the order to fire, they began wildly shooting and assaulting among the crowd outside. Inside, it sounded as though the place was being stormed. The crowd packing the gallery ran around in a panicky way, policemen rushed out, and as though by common consent proceedings came to a halt. Outside desperate officers ran about trying to bring their subordinates to heel. It is said that a senior policeman appealed to the Bishop of Johannesburg to keep the Africans under control! It would not be the first time that they turned in extremity to one of their opponents to pull their chestnuts out of the fire.

The irresponsible behaviour of so many younger policemen is an alarming symptom. There are times when they are the despair of many of their seniors. The day will come when they will do more serious damage than they did outside the Drill Hall. But it is not a surprising state of affairs when one considers that eighteen-year-old white children have a vote while African professors and clergy (for example) have none.

The police who guarded the Treason Trial accused seemed terrified of us at first, as though they expected us to produce bombs from our pockets. As time went on they began to relax.

In a strange sort of way—strange when one considers the allegations against us and the South African context—some even became quite friendly. So much of the Black Peril disappears for whites who actually *meet* Africans—perhaps that is why the Government wants us out of reach in Reserves and peri-urban "townships". The white sergeant in charge of us came to know each of us fairly well. One day one of the white accused, Advocate Slovo, was sentenced by the magistrate for contempt of court. The accused men spontaneously leapt up and surged forward. I shouted them down and ordered them back to their places. Back they came. Later the sergeant brought me the thanks of his senior officer. The situation could scarcely have been odder, considering that I led a movement charged with plotting to overthrow the State.

On the whole the worst enemy of the accused was sheer utter tedium. Added to that, it is an appalling strain for active adults to sit by the hour, day after day, doing absolutely nothing except lend half an ear to a succession of dull prosecution witnesses. Now and then—these occasions were oases in the desert—things came briefly to life, as when a detective reported one of us as having said that van Riebeck landed at the Cape in command of "a gang of vegetables"; or as when a prosecution witness, the head of the Evaton Basutos, was asked what had become of his predecessor and replied simply, "I killed him."

I was overtaken by a recurrence of my blood pressure troubles and was allowed to be absent for a month. The Bishop of Johannesburg arranged for me to spend the time at St. Benedict's House, Rosettenville—it was a time of real spiritual and physical refreshment.

By this time, of course, all of us were out on bail. Again, it was the Treason Trial Defence Fund which delivered us—much to the relief of the authorities at the Fort, who were able to return to their more customary routine. ("I'll do *anything*," the officer in charge had said to us, "to help you get *out* of here!") The difference which the Fund made to our lives is beyond calculation. Because of the eminence of the lawyers engaged to defend us, the prosecution was put to a very severe test—far more severe, I think, than the Crown had ever contemplated. It cannot be denied that the character of the people who sponsored the Fund gave the world some inkling of the true nature of the trial, and also brought in observers from overseas. It was no routine trial of desperate and violent revolutionaries.

But the succour given by the Fund went far beyond this. Many of the accused were in great financial distress because of the sudden interruption of their lives. The Fund came to the rescue of their dependents. More than this, it made it possible for families to be reunited during adjournments—rail fares were provided—and this was no small comfort. I shudder to think what might have been the fate of parents and families but for this help, and of all of us if we had been obliged to do without a brilliant team of lawyers who fought every inch of the ground.

In order to regulate properly the money collected by the Fund, it was necessary for us to form a liaison committee to lay our condition accurately before the people administering the Fund. Throughout the Preparatory Examination I was chairman of this committee, and I valued immensely the opportunity which this gave me of forming an association with a man who has come to mean more and more to me. I had met the Bishop of Johannesburg before this, but only incidentally—I can remember no more of the earlier meeting than my amusement over his gaiters. But as I now grew to know him more closely I was deeply impressed by his stature as a man of God, by his insight into the true nature of what is happening in South Africa, and by his courage.

I remember that during one meeting of the committee an avowed white Communist said jocularly to the Bishop: "If there were more Christians like you about, people like me might have to think seriously about becoming Christians." The Bishop replied affably, yielding no inch of his belief: "Well, there aren't many Communists like you." It was an education to watch the Bishop in his dealings with men of other persuasions, or none. His primary concern, one could see, was with people, and he met all in the armour of a fearless faith, not proselytising, not shrinking, but always bearing witness—and there was no mistaking what he bears witness to.

It was soon clear that the Treason Trial had provided a new rallying point for the resistance. I must give credit where it is due. I doubt whether we could have devised so effective a method of ensuring cohesion in resistance and of enlarging its embrace as did the Government when it set the Trial in motion. We of the Congresses did not waste the opportunity given. Because of my three years (up to then) under bans, I had formerly not even had the chance to get to know my own A.N.C. officers as well as was desirable. I rectified that, and extended my knowledge into the other Congresses.

But the Congresses were not the boundary by any means. At last I could meet a really representative cross-section of *my*[2] South Africa. There are people as dedicated to justice and human dignity as any in the Congresses who yet belong to no organisa-

[2] I do not claim to own it. I claim to belong to it.

152

tion. The conditions of our lives in Johannesburg gave us the chance to meet such men and women, both eminent and lowly, and to find within us all a common allegiance—and a common refusal to bow to the totalitarian threat. The colour-bar dropped away like the fictitious and beastly thing it is, within the borders of the unexpected world which the Trial had created. These were not chance encounters—part of Johannesburg's generosity was shown in the way in which, recognising the barren quality of our days, a section of its people set themselves to make our lives liveable in the evenings.

We met people well outside of the resistance too. Through the Director of the Institute of Race Relations a number of us met informally with a small party of Potchefstroom Professors in the context of a social gathering. Not altogether at ease in their own camp, they tried to assure us that apartheid really does have a positive side, though it had not yet been favourably presented. Some, they told us, were working for this favourable presentation. It came down to the Bantustan idea—"political rights" in our "own" area, and so on. They suggested that there were differences among the Nationalists. We made it quite clear that this did not affect our view of apartheid, especially since no hint of anything other than bogus-positive has so far been included in various definitions of "positive apartheid". When you come down to schemes for "positive apartheid", it involves giving four-fifths[3] of the land to Africans, and we do not delude ourselves into believing that the whites mean this.

But even if they did, I am against positive apartheid because I'm against apartheid. I am a South African, not four-fifths of a South African. I see no need to admit the failure of people of different races to live together in harmony—whereas Nationalist "positive apartheid" is an advertisement of their pessimism and defeat. They have given up hope of even trying to meet with and live with their neighbour. That hopelessness is suicide. I understand white fears of being "swamped" and surrendering or sharing their privileges. At the same time, I do not for a moment entertain the idea of Africans turning into race oppressors. The Master Race concept is not ours.

Through the good offices of the Institute a few of us had a meeting also with Mr. Harry Oppenheimer, the mining magnate. After a preliminary declaration of his understanding of the

[3] What additional land to our 13 per cent promised us by Nationalist thinkers are the Protectorates which do not belong to the Union Government but are under British rule? How can the Union promise what is not here?

African point of view, he took us to task over what he sees as the excessive nature of our demands and methods—such things as the demand for Universal Adult Suffrage and the methods of public demonstration and boycott. If I sum it up correctly, his plea was that the "extremism" of our demand for recognition made it difficult for him and others like him to persuade "liberal-minded people" of his own group of the justice of our demands.

Our reply to his argument was that however "unpleasant" our demands might seem, they are real demands, and that it was far better that white South Africa should here and now know their nature than be constantly taken by surprise by being admitted to our thoughts instalment by instalment.

Without question, the Treason Trial gave us all—not only the accused, but many more besides—the opportunity to meet and (in some cases) to get to know a far wider variety of people than before. Except that there was a Preparatory Examination in progress, and that many of the accused suffered great hardship, and that we were charged with a capital crime, it might almost be said that the arrests did a great benefit.

Certainly the resistance needed some such experience, and such an opportunity of meeting on a wide scale. This side of things did nothing but good. I do not hesitate to say that out of the mingling of the Government's opponents of all races, both in and out of the ranks of the accused, a new sense of solidarity and a new sense of direction were born.

As is not unusual, the effect of Government action was not the one which they foresaw. One imagines that they expected a successful prosecution (otherwise why the arrests?) and the removal of a large number of their opponents from public affairs. In fact, they produced the very things which they sought to avert —a strengthening of the determination to resist, a new forging of bonds across the colour barrier, countless inter-racial discussions, an influx into the ranks of resisters of formerly un-committed people, and the exchanges of views between people so diverse in outlook as A.N.C. leaders and Potchefstroom Professors.

By the time the Preparatory Examination had drawn to its close, the sense of common purpose among those who reject apartheid was immeasurably deepened. Yet clearly it was just the desire to cripple the common purpose of the resistance which led to the arrests.

17. *The long walk*

I retrace my steps here to mention a situation which arose at just about the time when the Preparatory Examination of the Treason Trial was about to begin, and which helped to focus the attention of the outside world on South Africa.

A subsidised bus company (P.U.T.C.O.) which transports African workers in several of the larger centres throughout the Union, decided to increase fares. The effect of paying the new fare would have been to thrust thousands of African families farther below the bread line than they already were. On the other hand, in relation to the budget of P.U.T.C.O., the increase was probably not exorbitant and it was genuinely needed.

But the African people affected by the proposed change were determined that wherever the money came from it would not come from them. It would not because it *could* not. In Alexandra township, the one-square-mile home of about a hundred thousand Africans on the fringes of Johannesburg, a boycott was organised. The people began to walk. The boycott spread to other areas, including Pretoria.

The thing which startled and dismayed the whites, except for those who were heart and soul with the boycotters, was that Alexandra township applied a *total* boycott. The unanimity with which the people declared their refusal to surrender to exploitation any longer made a tremendous impact. Walking twenty miles and more each day, they chose to suffer rather than be a party to decreasing the amount of food they could give to their children.

The whites were surprised, too, by the fact that the bus boycott persisted. They confidently expected the boycotters to tire, as indeed they did, and to throw in their hand, as they did not. There was the usual talk in the Press of intimidation—as though a few picketers could intimidate a township of a hundred thousand people at bus queues[1] where the police were active to break the boycott. It is quite possible that there were one or two cases of intimidation. A few better-off residents who might have preferred to ride were doubtless deterred by the fact that such action might draw down on them the wrath of the great majority

[1] There were, in fact, no queues. The police assembled at bus stops to protect non-existent "loyal" natives. Loyal to what? Poverty?

of Alexandra people. But this glib white Press talk of intimidation comes ill from people who are not exposed yet to the daily intimidation and terrorism of the police. And the attempt to explain unanimous action by Africans on the grounds that "political gangsters" frighten the mass into such action does not bear examination at all. There are gangsters among Africans, and there are politicians. I do not know of any gangster-politicians. If there are any, they lack the means to coerce the rest of us. Assuming that the whites genuinely believe the intimidation stories which they tell (with evidence), I cannot help wondering if it is because they have become so accustomed to the political coercion of Africans that they expect us to imitate their methods. The intimidation of Africans is their method.

Whatever explanations the white Press may have chosen to give to its readers, the Rand and Pretoria bus boycott was a spontaneous movement of the people. In Alexandra the organisers ranged from conservative stand-holders to political leftists, and they made a common front because they were faced by a common crisis. They made a success of the boycott because the people were determined to boycott.

The determination of the rank-and-file boycotters was certainly put to the test. The Government had a strong interest in breaking the boycott, partly because they need to break all demonstrations of African unity, and partly because the company being boycotted was Government-subsidised—under-subsidised. In an attempt to achieve their aim they used their police force. Systematic police persecution was applied on the route between Alexandra and the heart of Johannesburg. For once the whites had a grandstand view of the viciousness of the police, who interfered with taxis, with walkers, and with cyclists. The pass weapon was used against walkers, taxis were held up for long periods while all drivers and passengers had their names taken, the cyclists were compelled to join walkers when the police deflated their tyres. The white Press went on talking about intimidation—by Africans.

But the manifest harshness of the police who teemed along the route—they should have been elsewhere about the legitimate business of the police force—aroused the sympathy of many whites who saw what was happening. In spite of official threats many of them used their cars to help alleviate the fatigue of the brave workers. It was a heartening performance, and further evidence that the real struggle in South Africa is not Black versus White but Herrenvolk[2] versus the rest.

---

[2] I must not be misunderstood here. By Herrenvolk I do not mean Afrikaners. I mean White Supremacists, whatever language they speak.

Stories such as that of the boycott appear to the general public in outline only as a contest between groups. But behind the headlines what heroism there is! For the strong, a twenty-mile walk on top of the day's work is a sufficient test of endurance. But what of the weak? What of the sick widow with five young children whose only income comes from backbreaking labour, with no trade union hours, and a pittance for payment? The weak walked too, setting out before there was a hint of sunrise and arriving home long after dark, exhausted. For the sake of saving five shillings a month. For those who have not gone soft through living on the sweat of others, South Africa is a heroic country. The patient endurance of the weak is stronger, far stronger, than the toughness of the bully with the gun. The bully knows it in his heart too. His pitiful reaction is to bully harder while the sun still seems to shine.

The boycott was essentially a movement of the common people. The African National Congress had no part in organising it. There were, of course, Congress members living in the township, and as residents they took part in the boycott. It might be tempting to some to claim credit for so successful an effort. In this case, however, Congress can go no further than to claim that it helped to create a climate of resistance in which such action could take place. In honesty, we cannot go further than that—in any case, the Treason arrests had put our leadership temporarily out of action. The boycott was a local declaration, it was organised by local people, and local people bore the burden of it. In other centres where sympathy boycotters were launched, Congress did play some part. But people of Pretoria, the Rand, and the other affected areas must take full credit for the boycott. They certainly deserve it.

Nevertheless, the Minister of Transport, B. J. Schoeman, had scarcely set foot on South African soil, after his return from a trip overseas, before he made bold to say that Congress had organised the boycott. At the airport, having said that we had engineered the whole thing, he declared flatly that he was going to break it. As it turned out, he failed, in spite of enthusiastic co-operation from the police.

Congress leaders deliberately held aloof from the boycott (except to refute Mr. Schoeman's allegation) until well after other bodies had come in—the worried Chambers of Commerce and Industry, for instance. We came in at a late stage for a specific reason.

From the early days of the boycott, behind-the-scenes negotiations were carried on. The Bishop of Johannesburg was drawn into the negotiations before they had gone far for the good reason that he was one of the few whites whom the boycotters trusted. His sympathy with the boycott was no secret. He understood the reasons for it, and the people knew he understood. At the same time, his knowledge of such matters went back to days[3] before he was in South Africa, so that his practical advice came out of experience. At his home and in Alexandra township he was often up well after midnight—he put himself wholeheartedly at the disposal of those who sought his help. His aim was simply to seek an honourable conclusion to the boycott.

A stage was reached when an honourable conclusion became a possibility, as a result of a set of proposals made by the Chamber of Commerce—the fatigue of workers was not doing production any good. To put it briefly, the Chamber of Commerce appeared willing to do what the adamant Government refused to do, which was to subsidise the company indirectly rather than place a new burden on poor folk. It was here that Congress leadership came in.

The difficulty was that the boycott was such an unqualified success that many people wanted to extend it whether or not the boycotters' demands were met. To us it seemed that if the declared objective could be attained, the boycott should cease. We were very much aware of the hardship of rank-and-file boycotters, and aware, too, that if opinion became divided the whole boycott might fizzle out and the Government intention ultimately triumph. For these reasons we threw the weight of our argument in on the side of terminating the boycott if the initial demands of the people were met. There is an end to endurance. That is a reality which wise leadership must take into account.

In the event, the demands were met completely, the Minister of Transport's promise to break the boycott was not fulfilled, and the boycott was called off. We did, however, have to endure some stiff criticism from the diehards.

The tortuousness which can accompany such affairs in South Africa was shown in the dishonourable behaviour of some African "leaders". A few self-styled African leaders and a certain white missionary entered into discussions, while the boycott was in progress, with figures in the world of commerce and with other "liberal" elements. The Press did us a favour here—it revealed their names. They had absolutely no authority from the boycotters to "represent" them. They had not even consulted the organisers of the boycott. Yet they were carrying on negotiations, and even arriving at solutions, in the name of the boy-

---

[3] When Rector of Liverpool he helped in negotiations to end a dockers' strike.

cotters. One can imagine the confusion to the cause if the Press suddenly announced: "Native Leaders Call Off Boycott." This might well have happened but for the fact that, once their names were revealed, they were repudiated to a man by the boy-cotters. They represented nobody but themselves. Whether this little group was carried away by a sense of its own importance, or whether they were cynically lending themselves to the betrayal of the boycotters, I do not pretend to know. Happily, once their identity was known, they retired from the scene abruptly.

They retired from the scene, the boycott came to its proper ending, and the accused spent most of 1957 meeting daily in the Drill Hall while proceedings droned on. At the University of the Witwatersrand a multi-racial conference was held, but we could not attend it. Oliver Tambo and I went to a dinner for delegates, but even then our defence lawyers rather wondered whether that was legal or not. This multi-racial conference, providing so major an opportunity of meeting across our multifarious race barriers, made a strong impact. It was in part, no doubt, brought about by the peculiar circumstances arising out of the Treason arrests. Certainly, after the arrests, race relations seriously deteriorated through the country as a whole; though within a narrower circle there was such good will as had not previously found expression. Again, Bishop Reeves was one of the leading organisers.

On 26th June a fairly successful one-day stay-at-home of workers was held. Much later, we were all committed for trial on the charge of High Treason. Subsequently sixty-five of us were discharged. To this day nobody can see any method governing the choice of those who were released and those who were to undergo the ordeal of trial. As far as I was concerned, although I had been discharged, my organisation was still on trial. At the time of writing, over four years since it began, it still is. For over four years nearly a hundred people have watched the trial drag on—a trial about them. They cannot see the end. But for the Treason Trial Defence Fund, who among them would not be broken and forgotten people?

If, in the Drill Hall during 1957, dreariness and boredom seemed to envelop us, this was certainly not true of the country at large. South Africa was filled with a new excitement, and there was ample evidence, in the boycott and elsewhere, that resistance was beginning to assume a mass character. A significant fact of the bus boycott itself was that here was a demonstration for which there had been no prior planning. Moreover, it was conceived and executed on the spot. This may not seem particularly significant, but it was. For too long the tendency, inherited from calmer days, was to "ask the leaders" if anything was contemplated. To branches of Congress which have applied to the top leadership, I have usually retorted: "There is not more wisdom here than in your own area. Tackle your local problems yourself. Don't call for help until you find they're beyond you." It was refreshing to see the boycott throwing up sound leaders who met the demands of the situation on their own initiative.

Another significant feature of the boycott was the co-operation, uneasy though it may have been, between groups of very different outlook—the "conservatives" and the "radicals" sinking their differences to meet a common threat.

The boycott brought home more of the realities to a wider number of people. One of these realities is the theoretical nature of the sympathy we get from some whites. For a while, when the issue of bus fares and therefore wages was at its height, many whites were loud in their demand for higher wages. Here and there, to shut our mouths and salve their consciences, petty increases were made. As the voices raised at the height of the campaign subsided, so was the question of African wages shelved. Some whites thought no doubt that it had been dealt with. Their newspapers always quote percentages or *total* increases. They seldom work out for their readers that 10 per cent of thirty shillings a week is three shillings. They seldom divide the total increase by the number of mouths receiving it. The whites at once feel better, Africans are left in much the same position; and any discontented African voice is at once accused of "ingratitude"! For twenty-seven years and more, expert statistics have been thrown at the whites. In relation to the cost of living our lot does not improve. Employers are secure in their knowledge that the Government approves of their desire to keep African wages low.

Beyond the boycott areas, too, resistance was growing and hardening. Attempts by Dr. Verwoerd's Native Affairs Department to find acceptance for the Bantu Authorities Act were not meeting with the expected success. These attempts were leading to opposition and, in fact, to turmoil in rural areas which was destined to cost life. Already the Government had been given notice, in a massive demonstration in Pretoria, that African women had no desire to share with their men the disability of passes. Now in 1957 the Reference Book Units in rural areas began to run into trouble. Lives were lost in police shootings in the Western Transvaal, in Lichtenburg and in Zeerust. As usual, African lives.

I think that what was becoming daily clearer to us at that

time was that neither from the Government, nor from the white general public, was any alleviation to be expected. Somewhere we ceased hoping for a white voluntary change of heart. The boycott showed that we fool ourselves if we think that employers will come to respect any moral principles in their dealing with us. Events in rural areas showed that the Government is relentless and remorseless in its determination to ram every one of its reprehensible measures down our throats at whatever cost. Perhaps, foolishly, we have never quite abandoned hope for the whites. But I think that very little *reasoned* hope survived the year 1957.

I must make one qualification. At the same time as it became clearer and clearer that the great majority of whites are unlikely to change their ways, and that many sympathisers sympathise in theory only, it also seemed that a small section of the whites was at last becoming genuinely approachable. So while resistance stiffened and the majority of whites continued along the road as decreed by supremacists, it is also true that the area of meeting and understanding between Africans and non-Herrenvolk whites increased appreciably. White South Africans, it seems to me, make their choice. The few who exert themselves make a choice which is like opening a door into a new world. Once they have dissociated themselves from the white herd and chosen common humanity, each succeeding step follows. And, unless they are to go back on their initial choice, they find themselves weekly more identified with the resistance to barbarism and the mangling of people.

The year 1957, then, was by no means a year of tedium except within the Drill Hall where the Preparatory Examination wound on: on the contrary, it was a year which saw further cleavage between South Africans who stand for two opposed ways of life and types of Government. It was this year too, probably, which made the outside world aware of trends in the Union. The march of events caught their attention, and I doubt whether that attention will quickly falter since there seems to me little likelihood of quiet years ahead. World attention is something which we of the resistance need and desire. Our rulers, on the other hand, desire and need that the rest of the world shall turn a blind eye to their behaviour and accept their *bona fides* without question, continuing mechanically and politely to invest money in South Africa and to buy South African goods, produced with our miserably paid toil.

The beginning of 1958, with some of us out of the Treason Trial, saw white South Africa facing towards another election. In a press interview I declared my conviction that it was a mistake for us to be indifferent to this event. True, there are no African voters. But our past and present, and the whole of South Africa's immediate future, are determined by these white voters. An election seemed to me an appropriate occasion for the electioneers' football to exhibit a life of its own. I do not think that any African utterance or action would influence the outcome. It may be true that African political liveliness sends potential United Party voters into the ranks of the Nationalists, but then upholding the United Party is no part of our purpose. What I had in mind was that, at a time when the whites' parties were as usual wooing their voters with competing plans for our harsher oppression, the African voice should be heard. I see no clever strategy in leaving them to attribute fictitious attitudes to us when in fact we have *real* attitudes of our own. Further, it has always been my aim to ensure that if the whites are ignorant of the realities, the fault does not lie with us.

As the result of my press interview, it was agreed by all the Congresses that the resistance should not remain indifferent to the elections. For various reasons we did not plan anything on the scale of the Defiance Campaign or the Congress of the People. A large conference of workers was held in Johannesburg, and this meeting decided to demonstrate by means of a stay-at-home. The brief campaign was to be conducted under two slogans —the first was "Away with the Nationalists!"; the second was "A Pound a Day".[4] It was the latter, with its bearing on our poverty, which caught the imagination. The former was not intended to express any preference for the United Party. Merely, there seemed no point in wasting our breath on them since the part they now play feebly echoes that of the Nationalists.

Our intended action provoked the Government into preventive measures. At the end of February, Dr. Verwoerd drew up a proclamation for the Governor-General to sign. At that time, when he was still Minister for Native Affairs, he had his eye both on the coming election and on the mounting resentment against his Department in rural areas, notably in Zeerust and Sekhukhuniland. His proclamation gave him power to ban the African National Congress anywhere under his jurisdiction, which in practice meant in any rural area. He immediately applied the ban to three areas. Thereafter he called the attention of the electorate to his action, and publicly invited other Cabinet Ministers—many of them his seniors—to follow his example.

[4] i.e. for unskilled workers.

This the Minister of Justice did, banning meetings of more than nine Africans in cities and towns.

The lead-up to our proposed election activity certainly aroused the white Press, and white politicians of nearly every brand. After all the noise, the scope of our action was an anti-climax. We ourselves do not measure our strength exclusively by our ability to organise, though I do not pretend that organisation is not essential. But at all events the stay-at-home must generally be counted a failure.

The reasons behind this failure were not hard to see. One was that organisation of the stay-at-home fell between two stools. It was undertaken largely by local workers' groups which followed Congress general policy. The result was that the call was made with too many voices, and the great mass of the people, too often misled by dubious statements publicised in the white Press, were in doubt about whence the call came. Durban was typical. Directives were not clear, nor was the authority behind them. Only when Dr. Naicker and I stepped in and issued a circular of instructions to be followed did my people say, "*Now* we have heard the voice of Luthuli and Dr. Naicker."

To add to the confusion of too many voices, Congress itself, as distinct from local workers' groups, did in fact speak with a divided voice. What happened was this. There was a long-standing clash within Congress between the organisations as a whole and a group known as the Africanists. This need not have been a major difficulty, since Congress has never claimed to represent only one resistance point of view. But divergence had been growing. The Africanists did not thrash out their contentions in Congress conferences in reasoned debate, and they did not submit their views to the majority vote. Most unfortunately, they chose this time to attack Congress policy not from within its ranks (as they were entitled to do) but as though from without. This effectively confused our people further, at the last moment. The white Press made the most of it.

Nevertheless, whether the stay-at-home failed or not (it was by no means a total flop), the public excitement which preceded the election certainly succeeded in making the electorate aware of some of our demands—some whites were near hysteria. I recognise the failure in organisation, but the total impact of the campaign was considerable, even if not precisely what we intended.

The election itself duly ran its course. The Nationalists offered apartheid and more apartheid, not bothering much to veil their threats. The United Party distinguished itself more than ever in the role of political buffoon with a cry of "Discrimination with

163

Justice!" The Nationalists, one need hardly say, increased their lead.

Some time later the United Party held a post-mortem. As a result, it split. There was in the party a minority which had had enough of the game of abandoning all principles and trying to persuade the electorate that it can oppress more effectively than the Nationalists. The contentious issue was significantly, land for Africans. The "English Nationalists", led by a Mr. Douglas Mitchell from Natal, were insistent that the empty Government promise to buy more land for us should be opposed. Mitchell's strategy was to get the United Party to declare itself uncompromisingly against enlargement of the reserves. His group alleged that the Government's Bantustan policy would lead to the sovereign independence of African areas—an idea repugnant to them. At the same time, another idea repugnant to this group is that of extending to Africans any right in an undivided South Africa. The party officially adopted his view. No doubt it hoped in its pathetic way to capture more votes, to recommend itself by this anti-African stand to the whites.

But the "left" wing of the United Party could stomach no more. They resigned to form the Progressive Party. We wait to see what course the Progressives will follow. At present it would seem that there is hope, if only because they have made a stand over a moral issue. But just how they will succeed in keeping their seats in Parliament remains to be seen.

18. *We regroup*

It was not only the played-out United Party which suffered from dissension. The African resistance was in some trouble too. The clash between Congress as a whole and its "Africanist" membership was becoming difficult to contain, and it was beginning to do injury to the movement. The number of Africanists was small, but they were vocal.

The history of this difference in approach to our resistance problems is a complex one, going back to the years after World War II. Broadly, Congress policy is in favour of uniting all resisters to white supremacy, regardless of race, while the Africanists prefer to follow a solitary course, disregarding Indian, white, and Coloured opponents of apartheid. For them the resistance is an Africans-only movement, and they repudiate the broad South Africanism of the A.N.C.

In argument the Africanists base their approach on the claim that the 1949 programme of Action[1] did not envisage anything but an Africans-only resistance. It is true, as some Congress members maintain, that the Programme of Action simply reflected conditions as they were at that time, when there was no co-ordinated resistance. But for myself, I am ready to grant the logic of the Africanist argument. I maintain, however, that since this is no longer 1949, we have gone some way beyond the Programme of Action. It would seem to me unnecessarily doctrinaire to cling to an outlook which may have been appropriate then. The Programme of Action was an adaptation to prevailing circumstances. Since then further adaptations have been necessary to meet changing circumstances.

The emergence of co-operation between people of different race is one of the most hopeful advances of the last twelve years, not merely because it increases the impact of resistance, but because it is the beginning of a non-racial South Africa. I believe that radically exclusive resistance is the wrong reply to a radically exclusive oppression. It is *morally* the wrong reply, and it is also a demonstration of the wrong method if we think of the ideal it sets before our children. Tactically, the drawing in of our horns and the concentration of our forces may have some advantages,

[1] This involved extra-parliamentary pressures: civil disobedience, non-co-operation, demonstrations, and strike action.

but in the long run it will obstruct the way to a South Africa which embraces all her citizens.

During the time of the bus boycott and the election demonstrations, a great deal of publicity was given to the open Africanist opposition to Congress policy. They did not merely hold off, they attacked. With its usual tendency to make the most of African disagreement, the white Press played this up for all it was worth, and so did that section of the non-white Press which dances to the tune piped by white money.

Reluctantly, for the sake of avoiding the confusion which weakens resistance, Congress found itself compelled to act against the Africanists. As a last resort the A.N.C. Working Committee took the matter up and expelled two men. They were not expelled because they held minority views. They were expelled because they had made it their business to impede and hamper the policy officially adopted by Congress after full discussion and voting.

The split created acute difficulty in parts of the Transvaal, where there had already been discontent over alleged mismanagement of internal affairs by the Provincial Executive. In the end the National Executive took temporary control of Provincial affairs in order to put the Provincial organisation properly on its feet again.

During this period of National Executive control, a Provincial Conference was called, in order that we might openly go into grievances and causes of discontent. It developed into an unhappy clash. The Africanists were vocal and not amenable to reason, and abuse was hurled freely, this way and that. They made desperate attempts to wreck the Conference. (Among other things I was characterised as an agent of Moscow!)

To put it briefly, the Africanists withdrew after refusing adamantly to meet the credentials committee. Later they sent in their joint resignation to the conference on the grounds that Congress had acted "in a hooligan manner".

At the time of writing it is difficult to judge the possible effect of the split. The Africanists have formed themselves into the Pan-African Congress, and it is becoming clear that they are operating as a rival body to the A.N.C. The rivalry carries the seeds of possible tragedy for the resistance. At any time such a rivalry would be a pity in the South African context. At present it is without doubt worse than a pity, in view of the degree to which the adherents of white supremacy have united themselves against African advancement.

I refrain from criticism of the Africanists, except for a few particulars. It is still my hope that the breach may be healed,

166

although at present tempers are still a little high. It would not matter to me which side the initiative came from, and as to the causes—well, all of us Africans in the Union live under strain, and bitter things have been said by both sides.

I cannot say that I am clear about what the Pan-Africanist Congress stands for, especially as its statements to date have been contradictory and vacillating. If their slogan "Africa for the Africans" means "Africa for the Aboriginals", then their appeal is obviously explosive. The white Nationalists daily make such a counsel of despair more acceptable, since they daily frustrate the achieving of a South Africa along non-racial lines, and a rabid form of African Nationalism is the easy answer to rabid white Nationalism.

But if I am misled here and "Africa for the Africans" does not mean "and the devil take all the others", then P.A.C. policy is not greatly divergent from ours, and the goal may not be dissimilar.

They do, however, claim divergence of method. I do not know what the P.A.C. method is, but they have no hesitation in declaring that the A.N.C. tinkers and fiddles—here a boycott, there a demonstration, elsewhere a defiance campaign. Their claim is that while we occupy ourselves with details, they will turn off the tap whence comes the flood of oppression. I do not know what this means, stripped of metaphor. My reply, though, is that in order to get at the tap a good deal of wading through dirty water is necessary. Furthermore, what single blow does one deal this particular tap which will stop the flow? I suspect that when it emerges from theory, the P.A.C. may well find itself committed, like us, not to a single master-stroke, but to a series of partial successes. You have to wade.

The P.A.C. may be strong in a few centres, but it has not made a visible dent in Congress membership, even in the Transvaal. In one or two centres, in the Transvaal and the Cape Peninsula, it appears that they have gathered in numbers of formerly uncommitted citizens. I look forward to the day when we may be able to rejoin forces. There will be time enough for contest after Freedom. Meantime it would be no small thing if the P.A.C. could go their way without spending energy trying to discredit Congress. It would also make for a saner future if they refrained from representing African leadership farther north as intent on elbowing out whites. There is some distortion here. Africa as a whole is sick of colonial "partnership", with whites as perpetual "senior partner". This is not the same as being sick of whites, and we do South Africa no service if we let ourselves be tarred with the supremacist brush.

167

The Africanist breakaway, whether its effect will prove major or minor, good or ill, is a reminder (should it be needed) that the road to our goal is long and hard. In moments of optimism we of the oppressed peoples are aware of our strength. The situation in South Africa will never be static again before freedom is won, and there is no doubt about the outcome of the struggle. But in sober moments one is aware also of the weak spots in the resistance—and it has never seemed to me the path of wisdom to blind myself to these.

Disunity and lack of co-ordination retard our forward march. But it is possible that there are sources of weaknesses which lie deeper than these.

I shall never forget the effect on me of a visit to farming areas in the days when I was seeking election to the Native Representative Council. I travelled with Dr. Edgar Brookes, who represented the same area in the white Parliament. Our business took us among Africans who lived on white farms. These people were victims of the farm labour system. Many of the people we encountered were depressed and oppressed to the point of hopelessness. Some of them perhaps had even acquired a sort of slave-mentality, a sense that their lot was incurable and was best accepted and borne until death relieved them of their load. They were without any hope at all of mercy from the white overlord. They seemed to themselves to have been born with their shackles, and they expected to die in them.

This outlook is not confined altogether to serfs on white farms. One finds its counterpart in some African rural areas, though the cause is different. Here it is most noticeable among the men. What has happened is that the traditional rural pursuits of men have been whittled down. Guardians of great herds of cattle have, with the theft of our land, become keepers of a couple of bony cows. Many of the men thus affected have lapsed into something near to apathy. There is not much one can do with a handful of beasts on a few acres of family commonage. Life presents little challenge and little change. The men are hard to rouse—and I do not refer only to politics.

Tribal life itself presents little challenge. It is simple. In many respects it is backward. People subjected to it become quickly satisfied with little. It is no wonder that the oppressor is going to fantastic lengths in a futile effort to preserve it. He counts on the attitude it engenders. He knows full well that the average rural migrant labourer will be glad of a ten-shilling rise in pay once in ten years, and will fail to see that he *still* cannot feed his children. The impact of modern technology would revolutionise tribal life and the outlook that goes with it. If the whites can prevent it, modern technology will be kept carefully at bay.

Another real weakness is that many Africans are still ignorant of the workings of a political system. They are even ignorant of what goes on in South Africa, apart from their local affairs. The white system, with its use of delay, camouflage, fine-sounding phrases, rule by promises, is still capable of outwitting some of us, and I do not hold out the hope that this will change all of a sudden. It is something we of the resistance have to contend with, not ignore. Nor should those whose concern is with the lively towns overlook the effects of these things there. Yet another source of weakness: some of the better-off by native standards accept economic apartheid schemes that seem to make them relatively more affluent than others. But these in reality make them no more than better slaves. Affluence does not change one's political status.

Along with this sort of depression, or capacity to be deceived or bought off by hollow promises, there is to be found an unexpected and widespread misapplication of Christian trust. "Ah, Chief," people say to me sadly, "God will give us freedom when He is ready." It is a point of view expressed as often by heathens as by Christians—more often, perhaps. Personal responsibility is abandoned, and God, some god or other, is invoked to justify it. The product is a kind of resigned fatalism, a daydream about what God may do in the future, while the present slips by. It is not altogether healthy, and of course it cannot be reconciled with the Christian principle of work *and* pray.

The whites bank on this sort of thing. Indeed, they encourage it. Active religion, actually applied to the problems of human lives and society, usually offends them.

It is clear to me—I mention it in passing—that the Church will find a much-neglected field of endeavour here. I do not say that resignation and inertness about the present is an outcome of bad Christianity. It may just as well be the result of leaving the spirits of the ancestors to work things out. But I do say that the Church should work to see that Christians do not think and act like this. And that can only be done by *demonstrating* the relevance of Christianity in the South African context. We cannot do this if we expend all our energies on polygamy and finance.

And while I am on this subject, there are heathenisms among us besides the unproductive stoicism which I mention. There are modern heathenisms introduced from a world that was old when we were young. In South Africa the majority of the whites have gone far along the road to the worship of material prosperity.

They cling to it with religious fervour, and I sometimes suspect that this is because they have no *living* alternative. Materialism is rampant. The mysterious, the profound, and the supernatural are elbowed aside. And contempt for true religion is taken a stage further by white South Africa's growing state-worship, comparable already to that of the Nazis. It is a sad heritage that we should acquire if we modelled ourselves on the whites. It is part of the Church's duty to see that we do not acquire such a heritage.

Great, then, though the potential strength of the resistance to oppression is, it must be borne in mind that the movement is confronted with problems. When the outside world sees us fail here and there in specific attempts to resist, it must be aware of our weakness as well as our strength. And it must know, too, just how much has to be overcome. But when the white rulers resort to wholesale indiscriminate violence and concentration camp methods—as they surely will do—it will be the sign that their end *as a master-race* is beginning. Our strength is greater than our weakness, and they are year by year forced to fall back on undisguised brutality. That they do this is an admission that our weaknesses are retarding us less and less.

Among us Africans, the weight of the resistance has been greatly increased in the last few years by the emergence of our women. It may even be true that, had the women hung back, resistance would still have been faltering and uncertain. But they have been roused not simply by Congress, but by the Nationalists' flow of apartheid laws, particularly those which affect the family. But it would take more than the Nationalists to lull them back into passivity again.

Women concern themselves, by and large, with fundamentals. It is the fundamentals at which the Nationalists have struck. Their Abolition of Passes Act imposed the pass system on them. The intensification of measures which shatter families has made it harder than ever before to keep families together, or to be sure of earning anything with which to feed children. Allied to this is the fact that in recent years white wages have soared while African wages have hardly changed. All these things are the concern of women, and the involvement of African women in the struggle in the last ten or fifteen years has made them a formidable enemy of the oppressor. The things they live for— the security of their homes and families, and the well-being of their children—have been savagely assaulted. For them in many ways the struggle is a matter of life and death, quite literally.

Women in African society have never been a subservient group. They have played to the full the part allotted to them by their nature—and some have gone well beyond that. One African woman of the last century led an army across the Orange Free State, and her name became a name of terror. Another, in the Transkei, had the authority to persuade her people to abandon their work and wait for the end of the world. When it did not come, the consequent starvation did terrible damage. More recently, the Swazis were ruled by a queen. And among the Zulus, both before and since the coming of the whites, some Zulu women have played a decisive political role.

My point here is simply this: our women have never been treated by us as inferiors. It is the whites, misunderstanding the laws and customs by which we formerly governed ourselves, who have done this. Having no ready-made laws in their own society to meet the needs of ours, *they* have overstressed that *our* women are legally minors, throughout their lives. This does not reflect the situation as seen through traditional African eyes, and it has done great injury to the position occupied by African women.[2]

For a long time they bore the legal reduction in status inflicted on them by obtuse European laws quite meekly, but by no means negatively. They have not ceased to be African women. The events of the last few years have shown that up clearly. By a happy coincidence, the Nationalist assault on the fundamentals held dear by women brought into the struggle their numbers, their liveliness, and their practicality.

It was the Government threat to subject women to the provisions of the pass system which set them moving. This brought them into Congress in large numbers round about the time of the Defiance Campaign. Their opposition gathered strength and led in 1956 to a massive demonstration in Pretoria, the administrative capital. Women from every corner of the Union took part, some of them travelling a thousand miles to be there. It is worthy of note, too, that this was an all-race demonstration. "Strijdom," they sang, "you have struck a rock!"

The Government (Mr. Strijdom was Prime Minister) as usual buried its head in the sand. The demonstration made a great impact and gave strong impetus both to Congress and to the Women's League. Increasingly, our women have played a major part in conferences and demonstrations—in the Defiance Campaign of 1952, in opposing Bantu Education since 1954, and in protests against the Pass Laws since 1956. Furthermore, women of all races have had far less hesitation than men in making common cause about things basic to them.

Except for the huge Pretoria demonstration, action by women

[2] In the context of modern civilisation, the status of African women needs elevation to equal that of men legally.

against the passes had been mainly local or provincial in character. In places it has been very effective indeed, and sometimes it has been quite spontaneous. In the western and southern Transvaal it was rural women who led the way by the staunchness and determination of their opposition. The Government intention was clearly to get the passes issued among the more "backward" women of the farms and country, and only then, when the majority of women already had them, impose them in the towns. But the rural women were not as easily deceived as Dr. Verwoerd's Department had hoped. Because of the unyielding courage of our women, authorities were only able to issue passes to them by guile or brute force, and at the cost of lives.

In the middle of 1957 a deputation of Zulu women went to see the Zulu Paramount about this. He had shortly before stated in the Press his acceptance of the Bantu Authorities Act. At the same time he had urged that those who wished to comment on this or any other public matter should see him personally rather than write in the Press. The women accepted the invitation. The delegation, which included my wife and the wife of the late Dr. Dube, was widely representative of Natal.

They were cordially received. In conversation the wife of the Paramount divulged that she had taken a pass, having (as she claimed) no option. She said, too, that she was unaware of the disfavour with which Zulu women regarded the passes.

The Paramount saw the women. He agreed to convey their views to the authorities. The matter ended there, as far as the Paramount was concerned. There was no reply. The resistance went on.

The next year, 1958, was a year of widespread demonstrations by African women all over the Union. Indeed, the agitation was so intense that it outstripped the ability of the Congress Women's League to organise it. Towards the end of October the activity of the women led to the mass demonstrations in Johannesburg. The police mobilised all their available local transport to deal with the situation. Over 2000 women were arrested and held. Characteristically, the thing which really perturbed the white Press was: DOMESTIC SERVANTS NOT AT WORK. The dislocation of African home life which resulted from the arrest of 2000 women, most of them mothers, can perhaps be imagined by readers not subject to the white South African way of looking at things.

In December the Annual Conference of Congress, meeting in Durban, voted through a resolution about passes which was to keep us busy during 1959. Our decision was to intensify the campaign against all passes by all non-violent means in our power, emphasising particularly our opposition to passes for our women. A feature of this Conference was the large numbers of women who came from the most remote country regions, dressed in blankets and bangles and beads. Among men, political awareness presupposes a certain sophistication. Among women, awareness of the fundamentals presupposes no such thing.

With 1959 the pressure exerted by the women did not abate. Natal particularly saw much activity which, while most of it was in keeping with the Congress spirit, was spontaneous rather than organised.

I have already referred to the beer hall disturbances at Cato Manor, and their cause, and I shall not dwell on them here. It was the poor purse and concern for the empty stomachs of children which spoke. It was the white municipal authorities who emerged blameworthy. Before this time the Corporation had undertaken the clearance of slums—and much of Cato Manor came into this category. But (these are the things the white Press does not advertise) they had gone forward with demolition *before* they had provided alternative accommodation. Moreover, they had so adjusted rentals in kwaMashu[3] that any increase in wages meant an increase in rental which more than wiped out the gain. On top of this, economic rentals were being charged in what had openly been described as a sub-economic scheme.

Long before the beer hall upheavals, the women of the area had tried to make contact with the authorities. From Cato Manor they sent a deputation to the Mayor of Durban. After they had slept in the open for two successive nights, they eventually saw him—by planting themselves firmly on the City Hall steps. He did try to do something, if it was too little and too late. Cato Manor burst into anger before any but minor temporary alleviations had been offered. The destruction of beer halls spread to other townships and into Durban itself.

At first, in this affair, the police behaved with restraint and reasonableness. As is often the case, it was only after higher officials of the Native Affairs Department and the police had visited the area that brutality and mass arrests followed.

The demonstrations spread. It is difficult to explain quite why they spread where they did, except that poverty among Africans is not confined to any one place. In one centre after another,

[3] A new township capable of accommodating only a fraction of the homeless people.

women marched on beer halls, on dipping tanks[4] and to the offices of Native Commissioners. Influx Control (the artificial control of the labour force), the starvation in Reserves, beer halls, (said to be in the interests of the tribe), all featured, as did passes and new increases in taxation.

As the series of demonstrations developed, the women showed greater militancy. In one or two areas there was minor violence but, as far as I have been able to ascertain, this was not caused by the demonstrators. There is always a small minority of hooligans, and there are often *agents provocateurs*, who take advantage of such situations. In Pietermaritzburg, for instance, country women marched into town and picketed the beer hall. The police arrived in force. After a couple of hours of tense watchfulness on both sides, they charged with batons. Passers-by, even old Indian women in saris, were included in the beatings which they administered. That evening, in Sobantu Village, lying next door to the city, all the Bantu Education Schools went up in flames. The police contented themselves with throwing a cordon around the Dutch Reformed Church and then killing two men who (it turned out) were about peaceful errands and were nowhere near the scene of the burnings. The actual destruction appears to have been the work of irresponsible youths. (Even so, think of the bravery of the boy who rushed into a blazing building —in order to rescue his headmaster's typewriter!)

After the visit of the high officials, Native Commissioners were forbidden to receive deputations. Petitioning groups of women were told to go home and explain their grievances to their husbands, who were then expected to carry them to the local chief.

Congress, which had not organised this chain reaction, came in after the large-scale arrests in order to arrange the defence and supply the needs of arrested women, and in order to try to keep in hand a situation which was leaderless in many places. The women went on demanding replies to their original submissions to Native Commissioners.

The police came in at this juncture with riot tactics. Camperdown, a rural area near Pietermaritzburg, was typical. Holding white flags, and carrying neither sticks nor stones, the women approached the Native Commissioner with their demands. The

---

[4] Tribal Africans have always been suspicious of the dipping of cattle. Their dislike for dipping tanks increased when the Nationalist Government required stock-owners to fill them without being paid. This had been the duty of a paid African. In the absence of men, most of whom would be in the urban areas, women were forced to fill dipping tanks, deputising for their menfolk. This they objected to.

police met them. Almost at the same moment the order to disperse and the order for a baton charge were given. The women were beaten. At Ixopo, where there was some very efficient organisation, the women met this threat with a tactic of their own. When the order to disperse was given, they fell down on their knees and began to pray! The police hung around helplessly.

One thing is clear. Our army of "legal minors" is on the march, and the gap between city women and their country sisters is rapidly being closed. The question which we men who lead the movement and who see the suffering of our women ask ourselves is this: just how long can our women be expected to keep within bounds their indignation?

19. *A huge deceit*

In the later half of 1958, Johannes Gerhardus Strijdom died, and Hendrik Frensch Verwoerd took his place at the head of South African affairs. It was as we had expected. The whites will not of their own accord relent or turn back. From General Botha to Dr. Verwoerd, each new Prime Minister has deliberately placed a heavier burden on African backs.

Of the men who have ruled South Africa, no one has taken to himself such power as Dr. Verwoerd, and no one has been the guiding mind behind so much negative and oppressive legislation. If any one man is remembered as the author of our calamity, it will be he.

I could not here possibly deal with the flow of apartheid legislation which has either come directly from him or has been inspired by him. One or two examples will serve to show the effect of his laws, and the intentions behind them. They will serve to show his driving desire to conform flesh-and-blood people to the theory on which he bases his actions.

Dr. Verwoerd did not invent the Pass Laws. They are rooted in colonial days, and the battle over them has ebbed and flowed. But Dr. Verwoerd was the architect of the Abolition of Passes and Co-ordination of Documents Act. At a time when some relief from the Pass System was long overdue, Dr. Verwoerd imposed it afresh in a far more drastic form than had ever been thought of before. He went further. He applied this system for the first time to African women. It is not only some aspects of our public lives which Dr. Verwoerd seeks to control—it is in the whole life of every African, from the moment he enters a Bantu Education school to the day of his death.

The Pass System lies at the heart of his ambition. By it he is able to control freedom of movement, the sale of labour on the better markets (and hence wages), place of residence, the supply of forced labour to white farmers. Without a pass, an African man is worse than emasculated. Without a pass we have no right to work, to travel, to walk up a street, even to be alone at home. The only privilege that remains is to go to gaol. The economic effects of the system are convenient for whites, and quite disastrous for Africans. The moral effects are disastrous all round.

The Group Areas Act is not Dr. Verwoerd's; it was devised by Dr. Donges. Though Verwoerdian in spirit, Dr. Verwoerd found it too cumbersome, and in any case it was directed mainly against Asiatics and Coloureds. Dr. Verwoerd (then still Minister for Native Affairs) needed something as drastic, but quicker. He guided through Parliament the Native Resettlement Act, an amended form of the Urban Areas Act. These dovetail perfectly with the Pass Laws, reinforced by certain provisions of the 1913 Land Act for which Dr. Verwoerd cannot be blamed. Whites are hardly affected, but for Africans our country has been made into a vast series of displaced persons' camps. Individuals are shuttled around. They are taken suddenly out of urban areas and dumped in Reserves where the chiefs do not know them and the ancestral lands have long since gone. Whole towns of thousands of people—the example of Sophiatown is well known—are lifted up and thrown down elsewhere, minus freehold rights. Individuals are "endorsed out" of one area because there is no work. In a neighbouring town they are told, "Well, you can't work here, you have to live where you work, you have to work where you live!" Individuals, townships, villages, whole tribes, are picked up and put down elsewhere—thirty miles a day to work means nothing. It has reached fantastic proportions—and this callousness is not temporary: every year sees it extended.

Many years ago, around about 1913, when first the significance of being landless pawns began to dawn, we sang a folk song:

> *Sikho siphi tina maAfrika,*
> *Sikho siphi tina maAfrika,*
> *Siyo zula, sizule, sizule,*
> *Size sishonephina?*
> *Sakubona sakubaletha maAfrika,*
> *Siyo zula, sizule, sizule,*
> *iNgisi ngala, iBunu ngala,*
> *iJalimani ngala, iJalimani ngala,*
> *Siyo zula, sizule, sizule,*
> *Size sishonephina?*
> *Sakubona sakubaletha maAfrika.*[1]

[1] *Where are we Africans?*
(We seem to be nowhere),
We shall wander, and wander, and wander.
How far shall we go?
Behold, people of Africa, what a burden we bear!
We shall wander, and wander, and wander.
The Englishman this side, the Afrikaner this side,
The German this side, the German this side,
We shall wander, and wander, and wander.
How far shall we go?
Behold, people of Africa, what a burden we bear!

This song came out of the early, raw years of our dispossession. Yet how much more apposite it is now, when our dispossession is driven further by every law in the white man's armoury!

And not only our African dispossession. The Group Areas Act has been used to uproot and render homeless Asiatics and Coloured people. On top of this the Coloured people have another threat constantly hanging over them. They get classified. The result is often appalling, as for instance in the event of one partner to a marriage being classified as white and another as Coloured. The dissolution of human partnerships does not deter the Boards which classify, nor does the subsequent fate of the children of such unions concern them. Nothing is so precious that this apartheid plough cannot be induced to plough it under.

Out of the whole range of apartheid legislation there is one particular Act which I wish to deal with here, not because it is necessarily worse than others, but because it has been widely publicised by the Nationalists. If only because it is a major part of their propaganda, it needs to be inspected closely. It is called the Promotion of Bantu Self-Government Act. It purports to solve South Africa's troubles by creating territorial apartheid—that is, Bantustans. An examination of the scheme, which this Act is designed to put into effect, tears away the coverings from the whole sham of apartheid.

Dr. Verwoerd told the white Parliament—and thereby the world at large—that the Bantustan plan was intended to do for Africans in South Africa what the British Government is doing in Basutoland. I do not know whether anybody accepted this assertion or trust. If so, that man is not acquainted with the provisions of the Act. The Bantustan Act no more promotes African self-government than the Documents Act abolished passes, or the Fort Hare Act extends university education.

The Bantustan Act divides South Africa neatly, horizontally. At the top there is an upper-crust white parliament. Beneath the white crust there is created an authoritarian state governed by one man (the Minister of Bantu Administration and Development), aided by such men as the Minister of Justice and the Minister of Bantu Education. This man is in effect no longer answerable even to the white parliament. He is the absolute controller henceforward of all African affairs. Not even white representatives, as heretofore, will represent Africans in parliament. The Bantustans virtually become the estate of the Minister of Bantu administration. There is provision for no inspection of his realm, with its ten million Africans. Only he (and his officers) may grant even ingress into his realm, whether to M.P.,

178

trader, archbishop, or African.[2] The Act seals us off utterly.

Inside this closed world there is no hint, not the remotest suggestion, of democratic rule. There is provision only for the march back to tribalism—but in a far more dictatorial form than Shaka dreamed of. The modes of government proposed are a caricature. They are neither democratic nor African. The Act makes our chiefs, quite straightforwardly and simply, into minor puppets and agents of the Big Dictator. They are answerable to him and to him only, never to their people. The whites have made a mockery of the type of rule we knew. Their attempt to substitute dictatorship for what they have efficiently destroyed does not deceive us.

Even in the composition of local councils, the people have no say. The members are nominated by the Government, and by Government-approved chiefs. And the chiefs' nominees must have Government approval. I remind my reader that this system is known as Bantu Self-Government. It is government by stooge. Ever since Union in 1910, systems have been set up whereby there has been at least some flimsy election and representation. Now there is nothing. The tiny fires, such as they were, have been put out.

In earlier days of Nationalist rule the Government made the mistake of consulting Africans about this scheme. *Without exception* it was rejected. The Government changed its tactics, approaching chiefs singly rather than in open meetings. We still do not consent. Individual chiefs here and there have submitted to the new type of rule—but rarely, if ever, have these men sought the opinion of their subjects.

Then there is the question of land. I stand, with many others, for an undivided South Africa. Even so, I could believe in the misguided sincerity of those who embrace territorial segregation if they suggested some fair division. But all that the Bantustan Act envisages is the old, old 13 per cent of the land for 70 per cent of the people. And that on the fundamental assumption that the land belong to the Government.[3]

The Act brings the final halt to all African expansion. The disastrous consequences of the 1913 and 1936 Land Acts are

[2] In some reserves like the Transkei even an African may not enter without a permit. In all reserves a stranger must be reported to the Chief or the Chief's representative of the area by the head of the family he is visiting.

[3] For the present, they ignore the unpleasant fact that tens of thousands of square miles of the proposed Bantustans consist of the Protectorates, under the control of the British Government. Their desire to extend "Bantu Self-Government" to these is urgent.

treated as though they do not exist. Nothing is to be done about them.

The Bantustan planners—there is, of course, not one African among them—offer a solution to the desperate poverty of the Reserves. They propose to establish "border industries". White industrialists are invited to place factories on the edges of the destitute Reserves. The bait is cheap labour. Nothing but cruelly underpaid labour could counteract the economic effect of putting factories out of reach of railheads and sources of power. We are told that these factories will enrich the Reserve population. We shall never have had it so good.

We are even told what proportion of the populace will be employed in border industries, solely as unskilled workers. Quite arbitrarily, it is arranged that 40 per cent of the Reserve people will remain farmers, while 60 per cent will become industrial workers. The industrialists' response to the Government invitation so far is a few clothing factories and a few peanut factories. But already 60 per cent of us are theoretically industrial workers. Border industries cannot conceivably employ 60 per cent of the Reserve people. Economics will not obey racial blueprints.

As for the internal industries which have been mentioned, we can forget them. The niggardly token vote (£500,000) given to the Bantu Development Corporation makes it unmistakably clear that what is envisaged is a few grants to African shop-keepers, and a few cottage industries. Outside capital is not allowed in—that, obviously, might result in a measure of competition with the "border industries".

So the position, simply stated, is that fifty-nine out of sixty of the new theoretical workers start off by joining the ranks of the unemployed. Meanwhile, the cities have reached saturation. The authorities are busy trying to send city workers back to the Reserves to swell the ranks of the unemployed. At the same time the provisions of the Land Husbandry Act are squeezing people off the land in the Reserves and impelling them towards the cities. The vast circular tour of people with empty bellies is already under way. I am not predicting. I am commenting on a situation which is worsening daily, now, today. This is the Bantustan solution to poverty in the Reserves. One can see how useful, in time, will be the Minister's right to prevent any visitors from coming in to see how we are thriving.

The whole scheme is one vast exploitation stunt. It creates a new class of workless workers, and in the same breath we are told that the Government will henceforth absolve itself from financing African services from the central treasury. "Do it yourself!" we are told. Do what? And for whom?

180

Then look at the 40 per cent peasant group. They are to get holdings of eight to ten acres, with commonage for the grazing of drastically reduced herds. One allotment will go to the head of each family classified as peasant.[4] On his death, the eldest son may inherit the allotment. The rest of the family is allowed to join the workless workers.

The average yield of such an allotment will be about sixty pounds per year, according to a Nationalist expert (Dr. Tomlinson), and the maximum may be £120. This will not produce contented and civilised families. If the whites do not desire to produce contented and civilised families then they have no vestige of a right to rule. It is admitted that South Africa has enough for all, but covetousness and squandering by whites reduce Africans to this.

The Nationalists highlight the opportunities in the Bantustans for African traders and professionals (doctors and lawyers). To what can they aspire? They are invited in as though they were vultures to prey on the poverty-stricken peasants and workless workers. And their children, if they do not become moneyed idlers, will find their place among the workless workers. It is an ignoble invitation. I have not noticed any appreciable eagerness among those to whom it is addressed.

In the end Bantustans become destitute reservoirs of cheap labour, to be kept in order to discipline city workers who might dare to demand higher wages. There will be work enough for good doctors. To us Bantustan means the home of disease and miserable poverty, the place where we shall be swept into heaps in order to rot, the dumping ground of "undesirable elements", delinquents, criminals created especially in towns and cities by the system. And the place where old people and sick people are sent when the cities have taken what they had to give by way of strength, youth and labour. And still, to the day of death, whether in cities or farms or Reserves, we are tenants on the white man's land. That is our share of South Africa. Our home is in the white man's garbage can.

The living conditions promise to be appalling beyond anything we have seen yet. In the Reserves closer settlements are aimed at, in order to free the land for the "peasants". Taking into account the poverty of the people, the houses will have to be mud huts, thatch, wattle and daub. They are bad enough scattered around. One can imagine what they will be like huddled together. At

---

[4] This will be especially hard on the polygamists who are developing along the old tribal lines.

present the Reserves fall far below our earlier standards.[5] I would go so far as to say that in general they are sub-human in comparison with what we once knew. The land to which we have been relegated is sometimes just aloes and stones, aloes and stones. The people are shabbily clad, animals are feeble and bony. We have rural slums enough and to spare now. I shudder to think what the Bantustan future will hold.

"We have carried the native too long," the Government cries, and the electorate echoes its voice. "The native spending power is a million a day!" they declare. But when you divide a million pounds by ten million people, you get two shillings per person a day. That is the average. The Reserves have the lowest standard. I wonder if their spending power is sixpence per person per day? I doubt it. On top of that, there is no emergency margin, we are spending all our wages, and this is not a welfare state, not for Africans. Our charge is that because we live like this the whites live in comparative luxury.[6]

The political aim of the Bantustan, of course, is to wipe Africans off the South African political map. A hierarchy of Government pawns will appear to rule, and the world is told that this is our traditional way. Already—and this is an exclusive Nationalist contribution—we are riddled with spies, in the Civil Service, in the teaching profession, in the police force, and in the Reserves.

The Minister for Foreign Affairs did, it is true, tell the world that this route leads to eventual independence, and Dr. Verwoerd backed this statement up. At the same time, the Secretary of Native Affairs, Dr. Eiselen, assured the home consumer that, while Bantustans will go far in local government, they will never achieve autonomy. As far as the Act itself goes, there is nothing, either in the preamble or the text, which hints at Bantu Self-Government, and everything is arranged to ensure our being at the complete mercy of one Minister, with no appeal to Parliament or to the courts. The hope here, I need hardly say, is that the grip will tighten so drastically that we shall cease even to whisper of independence or liberation. A few years of Bantustan will do away with the question. It is an academic one, and it scarcely matters that Ministers contradict one another.[7] The

[5] I advise tourists to beware the guided tour by selected routes, with exhibitions of the noble savage at home.
[6] Whites in South Africa rank fourth in the world's standard of living when 60 per cent of the Africans live below the bread line. Most of the rest are just above it.
[7] Already Nationalists widely accept that what their Ministers say in public is meant for outside consumption. What their local M.P.s say in private is the *real* party line.

intention is to do away with our appetite for self-government, and the Bantustan Act is essential for this purpose. Does any Nationalist doubt that?

It is a huge deceit. I am not a man given to threats. But when my people see the magnitude of this bluff, as indeed they are seeing it, the docile people with whom the Government is now dealing will change beyond recognition. The lie is too big. You cannot fool all the people all the time.

A further problem which the Bantustan scheme does nothing about is the six million landless and rightless people who work in the cities and on white farms. No pretence is made that they will have even the "rights" accorded to the dwellers in Bantustans. Even if the Bantustans are gardens of Eden (as we are asked to believe), what African could rejoice while 60 per cent of his brethren remain beyond the borders of bondage? I shall try to draw a parallel. It is as though the workers of Cardiff were told: "You have no voice. You do not vote. You elect nobody to represent you in Parliament. But never fear, we shall look after your best interests. We shall send a man along to you from a Welsh farm. We shall ensure that he is a Welshman—be proud of that. If there is anything which worries you, tell it to him. Then he will pass it along the correct channels, any of which may get blocked up. If eventually your need or grievance reaches the Minister for Welsh Affairs (who is not preoccupied by being answerable to Parliament), he will deal with it. In this way, workers of Cardiff, you are governing yourselves!"

This only partly represents the situation. No English parallel gives any hint of the rapidity with which the disappearance of the rule of law is affecting us. What of the man who makes the wrong sort of complaint? Is it to be the labour camp, the "rehabilitation centre", for him? The Bantustan Act puts us utterly at the uncurbed mercy of a Government which works away tirelessly at this sort of "law". It throws overboard the last moral and legal restraints.

No British parallel gives any indication of the babel which the large urban centres are to be. In each centre there will be, literally, dozens of "tribal ambassadors" as the Minister calls them. There is no machinery for them to consult the people. They will be headmen from the country, with little comprehension of the strivings and needs and complexity of the cities. With an opportunity for these go-betweens to be bribed, to report back to the remote tribal chief just what they choose to report, or what they are paid to report. And what redress is there for city people— even supposing they could really *consult* their tribal ambassadors

—if the go-between fails them? None at all. All that is provided for is an unending series of bottlenecks.

There is no hope in the Bantustan Act for the city workers. They will no doubt continue to have ties of sentiment with chiefs. But for bread (there is no butter) they will have to rely on themselves, as they have always done, and as workers even in affluent countries like the U.S.A. have to do.

There is no hope in the Bantustan Act for any African. There is not intended to be any. It is the white man's solution, at ruthless cost to the African, of the white man's problems. Its only disadvantage from the white man's point of view is that it will not work. Considered as an economic proposition, it is insanity and murder. As a way to create orderly government, it is a pipedream. It will create nothing but chaos, and it will, because of the frustration and unrest which will follow from it, be the direct cause of numerous police shootings.[8] The only type of rule which is consonant with this Act is brutalised rule by force. It would be some small comfort to us if the "civilised" world refrained from supplying the arms and ammunition for this tragic venture.

For Africans the Promotion of Bantu Self-Government Act is the end of a long road of subjection and tyranny. For the whites it is the abandonment of any pretence of the rule of law, the beginning of the long-drawn-out, agonising end.

[8] As in Pondoland, a "Bantustan", since this was written.

20. *Which route to freedom?*

It is not possible to predict how far away the end may be. If we are to rely solely upon the effort we are able to make at home, the end will come, but it might not come soon. White supremacy is equipping itself for a last-ditch stand. The longer it persists, the more does it resort to outrage and reckless violence. I do not delude myself into thinking that it will stop short of concentration camps, terrorism, legalised murder by army and police forces.

But white South Africa is at last becoming aware, with surprise and embarrassment, that it does not hold all the keys to its own future. It has tried to be isolationist, but it finds itself on a rapidly awakening continent and in a world which watches it closely. What is happening elsewhere affects us here. The indignation of other countries can have a practical bearing on the course events follow in South Africa. It is for this reason that we Africans have watched the growth of this indignation with rising hope. It is rather similar to the way in which we cheer overseas rugby teams. We are not anti-South Africa. We are anti-white-supremacist.

We do not invite other countries to make war on the whites. We do not enter into dark conspiracies with foreign powers. But we are acutely aware that the disapproval and ostracism of other countries will have the effect, if properly directed, of shortening the day of bloodshed and bondage.

Some of them show a natural reluctance to be practical about their disapproval. They seem to rely on a quiet word in a diplomat's ear. It is ineffective. Moreover, it belongs to a type of international Relationship which the present South African Government does not recognise, though it takes advantage of it when possible. They are too far out of touch with the realities to pay heed to courteous hints.

The present situation, if I may put it in a parable, seems to me something like this. My next-door neighbour and I may like each other or we may not. At all events, we shall, if we are normal people, pay attention to the social conventions. We shall mind our own business unless invited to do otherwise. We shall not interfere with each other's wife or children or property. We shall avoid abusive language and greet each other when we meet.

But a day might conceivably come when this relationship breaks down. I might happen to glance across to his lands and see him savagely whipping a member of his household or attacking a defenceless child with a lethal weapon. I might learn that he has done his brother to death.

I could shrug and go my way. I could say, "Well, after all, he's the head of the household, it's no business of mine. I don't want him interfering here, so I'd better keep myself to myself." Or I suppose I could go round to the door and leave a little note suggesting that it might be wise if he were to make a few changes in his behaviour, and then leave him to think it all over.

But I doubt if I would be morally justified in taking any course except doing my utmost to prevent his doing further damage. My aim would not be to kill or injure him. It would be to stop him. I should find myself impelled to do that, by lawful and recognised means, and preferably by means which did him no personal hurt.

I recognise that there may be some difficulty in deciding when a "master-race" falls into this category, and I recognise that international relations are not carried on according to an accepted system of ethics. But if anyone doubts that South Africa does fall into this category, let him count up the cost of white supremacy in African lives. The total should leave him in no doubt. And I do not see why citizens of democratic countries should be content to allow their governments to ignore ethical standards.

I shall not argue that the economic ostracism of South Africa is desirable from every point of view. But I have little doubt that it represents our only chance of a relatively *peaceful* transition from the present unacceptable type of rule to a system of government which gives us all our rightful voice. The alternative to it is to let things run their course, while white South Africa earns its bread on the international market by the sweat of African brows. At home the situation will get further out of hand, and when all African leaders have been put away, violence, rioting and counter-rioting will become the order of the day. It can only deteriorate into disorder and ultimate disaster.

The economic boycott of South Africa will entail undoubted hardship for Africans. We do not doubt that. But if it is a method which shortens the day of bloodshed, the suffering to us will be a price we are willing to pay. In any case, we suffer already, our children are often undernourished, and on a small scale (so far) we die at the whim of a policeman.

The free world outside need not intervene physically, and it need not stand by impotently. There is much to be saved from possible shipwreck. And I cannot think that if this country becomes, for a time, the write-off that Nationalist rule threatens to make it, this would be in the interests of the democracies.

The type of rule which might emerge from a long period of worsening civil disorder cannot be predicted; but it is not yet too late to bring a true democracy to pass in South Africa. I do not believe that it will ever come *willingly* from the whites. Even so, it could be made to come *peacefully*.

It is a tragedy that the great majority of South African whites are determined to permit no peaceful evolution. They have for so long refused to adapt themselves and insisted that all adaptation shall come from us, that they seem incapable now of anything but rigidity. It is this attitude which is likely to make difficult, if not impossible, bargaining and compromise. Each new challenge leads to a further hardening of heart.

Such obduracy is doubly criminal in view of the persistent good will of Africans. The whites cannot or will not see that it is there. The trouble is that they credit us with their own ambitions. They mislead themselves by believing that we too have master-race aspirations. And since they see things in those terms, they terrify themselves into an attitude which knows only two alternatives—dominate or perish. For us, we do not desire to dominate but to share as between brethren, basing our hierarchy on ability, not colour. That is our offer. And we shall not consent to perish. Let them never cherish that foolhardy illusion, for all their guns and Saracens.

In our eagerness to hasten peaceful, non-violent political evolution here, we watch the outside world closely, particularly those parts of it whose trade with South Africa involves them with the fruit of African labour. Our liberatory movement has received great impetus from successful liberation in other countries after World War II, such as India and Ghana.

The way in which India at U.N.O. has taken up the cudgels on behalf of the oppressed South African majority, and dragged the whole scandal of apartheid into the open, has heartened us immeasurably, and in Africa small Ghana shines out. We have noted with satisfaction too the concern displayed by the World Council of Churches over issues affecting our freedom, and the transactions of Anglican Bishops at Lambeth have put heart and hope into more than their own people. There is no doubt in my mind that white South Africa wriggles with increasing discomfort under these things, try as they will to brazen it out.

But it is the growing world boycott, and the withdrawal—the very wise withdrawal—of foreign capital from the Union which jolts them worst.

The Accra Conference of December 1958 made an immense impact not only on us but on the whites. South Africa's rulers hardened their hearts further, but among a number of uncommitted whites some awareness displayed itself. For us this meeting of independent African states was the fulfilment of a long-cherished hope, even though we could not take our place in it. As far back as the time of my entry into Congress, we actively revived our interest in the Pan-African ideal.

Conditions in South Africa prevented us from sending delegates to Accra. We had to rely on a "delegation" of people who were by chance already out of the country and who did not ever return to report back. Nevertheless, we had informed reports.

We attached great importance to the establishing of a secretariat to give permanence to the meeting of African leaders. To the All Africa People's Convention we look for direction and guidance. For us, and other parts of Africa, freedom is still not around the corner. We are up against régimes which cannot be shamed before the conscience of mankind.

We lost no time after the Accra Conference in giving effect here to the decision to observe 15th March as Africa Day. All over the country we organised meetings for March 1959. Africa Day became a new big event on our calendar, and the meetings were well attended in all the larger centres. It has lately become a feature of such meetings that there are as many people unable to gain access as there are inside the places of meeting.

After I had addressed a huge gathering in Durban, I found myself travelling towards the railway station over the heads of the crowd. In the enthusiasm of the moment, the traffic regulations and the prohibitions against outdoor meetings were forgotten. I managed to persuade people to put me down so that I could leave for Ladysmith.

The Ladysmith meeting was held in a cinema, with loudspeakers outside to cope with the overflow. This had the effect of making it audible in the police station—though the Special Police were as usual in attendance inside the hall. According to inside information, the reactions among the white police in the station ranged from indifference among the older men to fury among the younger. Particularly did the youngsters have to be restrained when I referred to the Berlin Convention, which agreed upon the dismemberment of Africa, as an act not far removed from hooligan robbery, and added that we are gratified to see that some European powers are, however hesitatingly or haltingly, beginning to see the evil of their ways and make amends.

This address, inadvertently channelled to the police station, was followed up before long by an entirely deliberate approach on my part to white audiences. I had already begun this on a small scale during the second half of 1958 when I addressed a meeting in Johannesburg of the Congress of Democrats, and when I opened the Transvaal Conference of the Liberal Party. Although I recognised that this activity would draw the criticism of right-wing Africans, particularly of members of the Pan-African Congress, I had no hesitation about it.

A proportion of our difficulty in South Africa arises from the fact that the white fifth has almost no idea how the other four-fifths live. The recent intensification of apartheid, reinforced by such measures as the Group Areas Act, has made this ignorance acutely dangerous. I have never felt that my obligation to fellow South Africans ends with Congress activity, so that when the opportunity to shed a little light among the whites occurs, I take it with both hands.

I felt encouraged by the response of the Europeans whom I was able to speak to. I think they came with more than curiosity in their minds. They seemed to have a real sense of purpose, and a real desire to face and to discuss the issues. Their ignorance was often disturbing—but I must make this partial extenuation for them: it is more and more a Government-enforced ignorance.

One meeting led to another. During the early months of 1959 I was asked to address a predominantly Afrikaner all-white study group in Pretoria, where I was spending a good deal of time at the Treason Trial, now as an observer. In my audience, on this occasion, there was an unexpected mixture of Afrikaner theologians and professors and foreign diplomats, and to my surprise some of the Afrikaners had come from as far afield as Potchefstroom, about two hundred miles away.

The police arrived too late to prevent the disturbance with which the meeting began. A well-organised group of Afrikaner men entered, and before anybody was aware of what was developing, they assaulted the chairman and secretary—and the guest speaker. The secretary (a woman) was flung into the auditorium, and I found myself being systematically kicked under the platform table. Our assailants revealed at their trial that they acted as they did because they considered it grossly improper for an African to address a white gathering.[1]

I was touched by the shame and concern shown by many of the people present. When at last the police had arrived and removed the offenders, and the place had been set to rights, I was asked if I could go on. I had no reluctance, though my jaw was painfully swollen and I was well battered.

It was a good and encouraging meeting. The audience clearly

---

[1] Some of the men brought to trial were found guilty and duly sentenced.

wished to hear from an African what account we give of ourselves. A small number of Afrikaners who have begun to think are beginning to ask whether Dr. Verwoerd and Mr. de Wet Nel really do speak with the authentic voice of the African.

Not long after the Pretoria meeting I left to fulfil a series of engagements at the Cape. Some of my time was taken up with speaking to predominantly white meetings, but I managed to fit in some profitable Congress work as well.

Arrangements for this visit were on a large scale. I was met at the railway station and escorted to an open square packed with people whom I greeted in the lovely setting of Table Mountain. I remember commenting on the sad fact that the inspiration which General Smuts sought on that mountain had failed to benefit some of us.

In the afternoon there was a racially mixed gathering at the Drill Hall. There were more people outside than in. After this I was able to meet with the local branches of Congress, and then with Indian and Coloured people.

I was whisked away from Capetown to Rondebosch, where a meeting which had been meant to cater mainly for whites turned out to be multi-racial. Again, there were more people outside than in, and I remember well the gesture Africans made in huddling up to make room for whites. It is not the only time I have observed it, and I know the courtesy it springs from. A further meeting was fitted in in Rondesbosch—the Black Sash[2] wanted me.

The Black Sash meeting was a private one with an audience limited to about a hundred white people. The nature of this meeting gave me a chance to touch on some of the things which are best not dealt with in mass meetings, but which (I believe) lie in the minds of many whites—such things as the white fear of being "swamped", of "losing their identity", and of miscegenation. These fears are grounded in the emotions, and hence they are not easy to bring into the open. I sympathise with people who are afflicted by them, but I cannot agree that it is wise or sane to base one's outlook on a knot of fear. In any case, they are largely fictitious. Cornishmen have not been swamped by living in the United Kingdom. And the picture of ten million Africans yearning for miscegenation is a white invention. We do not particularly want it. At the same time we are not prepared, like the whites, to legislate against it. It is a matter of individual choice. We are not prepared to make living individuals miserable in order to "ensure the happiness" of a hypotheti-

[2] An organisation of white women opposed to the Government.

cal posterity. We are not prepared to be prosecuted and hounded either, for the preservation of skins of *any* shade.

During this time I had the privilege of meeting the Archbishop of Capetown, Dr. de Blank, and former Chief Justice Centlivres. On the same day I was taken by Senator Rubin to visit Parliament. The Extension of University Education Bill was under discussion—the Rape of Fort Hare was in progress.

After my glimpse of the white Parliament in action I was standing in a corridor with Senator Rubin and a reporter. A young Afrikaner passed us. Impulsively he turned back, and to my astonishment gripped my hand. "You know," he said, "I come from the Orange Free State.[3] I'm *ashamed* of what's being said in there, I'm *ashamed* of what they're doing!" Then he was gone before I could reply.

Outside the Black Sash kept a silent vigil, holding a torch which they extinguished when the Bill was passed. I was invited to inspect them in an informal way. They stood there in the rain—whites at last demonstrating unmistakably against a corrupt law which does not affect them directly. If only it had started years ago!

Capetown, my own people of the A.N.C., and many others of all races, gave me a rousing send-off.

But it could not go on. The Government cannot afford to permit this sort of thing. It creates good will and mutual understanding, and Bantustans and apartheid do not thrive on those. The Black Peril must be kept alive.

On 25th May the Special Branch called on me at my home, tendering a familiar document. They gave me a muzzle from the Minister of Justice. This time I was silenced and confined to Groutville for five years.

I had seven days' grace before the banning order took effect. I was due to go to Johannesburg, and when I got in touch with Congress there we agreed that I should take advantage of this time.

At Durban railway station a large crowd of Congress members saw me off. I could not speak to them or join them. All the way up the line people assembled to see me on my way. Women brought us food and sang Congress songs while the train stood. At one station only one man braved the cold and the curfew in the depths of the bitter winter night. I was asleep. He gave a pound to the men who were with me—"for the Chief to buy tea on the way". This moved me very deeply. By the time we reached the Transvaal the police had grown wise to what was happening, and they tried to keep people away.

[3] A Nationalist stronghold.

Near the end of the journey two top men of the Special Branch joined me. "Look here, Chief," they told me, "we don't want trouble. We know there'll be a crowd in Jo'burg. We're warning you that your ban isn't like the last. You're debarred from gatherings—that means you and one other. We thought we'd warn you."

"Thank you, gentlemen," I said. "I appreciate your concern. I've just come to breathe from afar the meetings your authorities have debarred me from."

Nearer to Johannesburg reporters climbed on. The white ones could not meet me in my compartment on a colour-bar train. So we conversed across the balconies where the train changed its colour.

I was met at Germiston by Oliver Tambo. It was decided that I should get off there and go to Johannesburg next day. Congress could not meet me—most people were still at work in the factories and kitchens of white Germiston. But the Africans in the streets, A.N.C. or not, mobbed the car, and then whites surged in too. All the way to Tambo's home we had a guard of honour of Special Branch cars. They kept their vigil through the night, but in spite of this I managed to slip away to take my five-year leave of a dear friend, the Bishop of Johannesburg.

In Johannesburg next day Congress met me at the station in force, augmented by sympathetic or curious whites. Across busy central Johannesburg, Congress volunteers ran beside the car all the way to our destination.

The great Congress meeting planned for 31st May was banned. The meeting of protest against this banning, called for 1st June, was duly banned too. Some quick thinking by the lawyers among us enabled us to take advantage of a legality and hold an indoor meeting in the Gandhi Hall. I could not be there. I was in a private house, and outside it was the Special Branch.

An address of mine was read out to the Gandhi Hall gathering. The Special Branch called on me to ask for a copy. I had none. "What are your plans?" they asked.

"I leave tomorrow, by plane."

"You mean you'll be here tonight?"

"I'm leaving tomorrow by plane. You'll find me here in the morning."

Later two more of them came to check up on this information. Next day I flew down in style with an escort of three.

To my surprise and joy a large array of Congress volunteers, men and women, met me at the D. F. Malan airport, standing in disciplined rows. Again I could do no more than view them at a distance. Elsewhere in Durban I inspected from a distance another company of volunteers. It was desperately frustrating, and deeply moving, the wide gulf and beyond it the devotion to which I could not respond.

A procession of cars, like a funeral cortège, took me the fifty miles to Groutville. More joined us along the road, people of all races, and more cars came to meet us from Stanger.

The road runs through Groutville. At the edge of the turf we stopped. There was nothing to be said. I parted from my loyal friends, who returned the Congress salute. Leaving the group by the roadside, I walked to my home, a short distance, alone.

(This and the following chapter have been written since the Sharpeville shootings and the State of Emergency.)

At the beginning of June 1959, then, I was back in Groutville, with the prospect before me of five years of isolation and frustration. It was a bleak outlook.

But the struggle must go on—bans or no bans. The Congress leaders lost little time in adapting themselves to the new situation, and I found myself busier at home in Groutville than I had been away from home.

One of our primary concerns at this time was the Potato Boycott. Since we reject violence as a method, we are always in search of telling and relevant ways of struggling against our degradation—ways that are peaceful but at the same time impossible for the whites to ignore.

Before this time we had boycotted "Nationalist" products on the market with a measure of success. But it is not an easy matter to identify this or that product as "Nationalist". Some are obviously made in factories owned by the more extreme of our oppressors, but with others it is not easy to avoid injury to the wrong man's pocket, and we have never been callously indiscriminate in our attitudes.

When it came to the common potato, we were on ground where not many of the wrong people would suffer. Particularly in the Eastern Transvaal, but elsewhere also, the conditions under which African labourers work is nothing short of horrifying. The Eastern Transvaal does not include any large African native reserves. In consequence, there is a shortage of labour. Never at a loss to come to the help of the white farmer in labour difficulties, the Government has found a solution. This is the system of Farm Gaols. It depends upon an unholy alliance between the police and the white farmers, and it is at its worst in the Eastern Transvaal. It also depends on the Pass Laws. Pass offenders—half a million men a year—are drafted out of gaols into the safekeeping of farmers. Both gaolers and farmers are delighted with the arrangement. The system helps to keep down the gaol population, and it provides the farms with an unending flow of completely rightless beasts of burden.

On the affected farms, African men—some are no more than boys—dig potatoes with their bare fingers. "Boss-boys" and overseers stand over them with whips, which they do not hesitate to use. The "convicts"—their crime is purely statutory—live in hovels, filthy little huts or filthy great barracks, under guard. Their diet is unmentionable, a good deal worse than prison fare for Africans—why keep them alive when there are more where they came from? "Inspection" amounts to a call on the white farmer, and a little chat over coffee on the stoep. Murders, the result of prolonged beatings and semi-starvation, or of sudden fits of anger, are committed. Some come to light.

I do not say these conditions prevail on every farm where there are farm prisons and convict labour. I say that the system exists, and I say that it is not only isolated farmers of bestial morality who take advantage of it. And I say that the system exists because the Government approves of it.[1] It is their system.

It was against this system—against the Pass Laws which draft men on to farms, often with no notice to their families, against Farm Gaols, and against those farmers whose avarice flourishes on this iniquity—that the Potato Boycott was directed. We made our call Union-wide, and our original intention was to boycott all potatoes for one month.

Its success was instantaneous—and consider here that potatoes are the staple diet of many Africans. It was certainly the hardest-hitting of all our boycotts. I think it caught the imagination of the people because it dragged into the light of day specific and appalling human suffering and misery.

So high was our indignation, so complete was the boycott, that it went on for three months instead of one. Farmers, merchants and the Government joined hands to break this boy-cott, but without avail. And even after three months, when I called off the boycott, the A.N.C. Executive was sharply criticised by many of our own people and by some of our white allies. But we called off the boycott because of the extreme hardship endured by those of us who live on potatoes, and those shop-keepers among us—I include Indians—who buy and sell them. True, the boycott might have continued successfully for another month or two. But we had made our point (the glut on the market was impressive), we had never intended an indefinite boycott, and there is a limit to endurance of this sort. Further,

[1] The Hon. C. R. Swart, Governor-General of the Union, made it his custom, while he was Minister of Justice, to open Farm Gaols officially. He was loud in their praise. They relieved the country of the expense of accommodating offenders, they helped farmers—and they rehabilitated criminals!

we felt ourselves bound by the proposal we had originally put to the people.

The enthusiasm of our people for the boycott did not go to waste. In Natal a good deal of it was taken up by the demonstrations against the municipal beer-hall system, the dipping tanks, and the Pass Laws, with which I have already dealt.[2] A feature of these events, which arose mainly from the action of women, was that, as recently in Zeerust and Sekhukhuniland and currently in Pondoland, the struggle was carried into country areas. Town and city workers will remain our spearhead, but the shaft of the spear, still imperfectly fashioned, is the country, where two-thirds of our people live.

At the end of 1959, and early in 1960, we were much concerned in the course of the boycott of South African goods by other countries. The motion before the Accra Conference of 1959, which set the ball rolling, came from the A.N.C., and it heartened us to see that it made sense to liberatory forces outside our own country. It heartened us because it made it plain, in practice, that from Malaya to Scandinavia, from Tanganyika to the British Isles, there are people in earnest about being their brother's keeper. I make it clear that we mean to cling to methods such as this, to non-violence, and we mean increasingly to use these weapons even against such tyrants as South Africa's present Government. This is not only a question of morality. As long as our patience can be made to hold out, we shall not jeopardise the South Africa of tomorrow by precipitating violence today.

The Government belittled the effect of the external boycott, but that did not deceive us. Industry and Commerce rushed to take counsel with each other, and the result was the formation of the South African Foundation. Its declared object was to preserve the good name of South Africa abroad. It is, however, an all-white affair, and the names of its sponsors made one thing plain: it is there, looking rather sheepishly after Sharpeville, in order to take care of the business interests of white business moguls. The boycott of South African goods certainly made some white South Africans feel the pinch. But it must be confessed that it was a humble affair in this regard compared with the Nationalist Government's own Sharpeville.

A comic sidelight was thrown on to this boycott by a visit of a former champion of the West against Nazism and Fascism—a man, moreover, with a good war record. Viscount Montgomery of Alamein spent his time in South Africa shunning all recognised African, Indian and Coloured leaders, and consorting with men

[2] See pages 58, 59, and 170-75.

on the fringes of the Government, and well within the fringes of big business. He returned to Great Britain and asked the world to give Dr. Verwoerd a chance. We still wonder who paid his fare. His host, another English warrior of the last war, took a lead in establishing the South African Foundation.

Africa's Year of Liberation, 1960, did not begin happily for us. In Cato Manor police pass and liquor raids intensified until they were taking place without fail at least three times a week. The residents of this shocking slum saw in this degree of police attention a reprisal for their beer-hall demonstrations of 1959. And police raiding was linked with the enforced removal of residents to the new location of kwaMashu, a measure most bitterly resented.

This resentment needs a word of explanation—after all, Cato Manor *is* a slum, and the residents there have reason to know that better than anybody. It began as an "Emergency Camp" after the 1949 Afro-Indian riots in Durban, and it has remained an emergency camp ever since, squalid, the breeding ground of diseases both physical and social, and a place with no future.

The people of Cato Manor loathe the squalor and the lack of amenities—let there be no doubt about that. They want effective sanitation and weatherproof walls as much as the next man. All the same, under the Durban Municipality they have enjoyed one or two meagre liberties of which removal deprives them. In kwaMashu their own children will become "lodgers" at the age of eighteen, and once they are lodgers they will cause their parents' rents to go up, or they will be removed to "single quarters" where family life does not exist. In kwaMashu, residents will be unable to have as guests for a single night their closest relatives, unless the Location Superintendent gives his consent. In kwaMashu they will be far more irrevocably pulled into the Government's machinery for "dealing with urban natives".

In this context occurred the brutal, unpremeditated killing of nine policemen cut off by chance during a routine raid. Once these poorly armed men had been left exposed by the rest of their party, and once a trivial but passionate incident had aroused the fury of the populace, it is doubtful whether anything or anybody could have saved the situation. Tragically, it lay along the road our rulers tread.

The Coalbrook mine disaster, with its appalling death toll, did not lighten the darkness of our 1960 skies; and then came Sharpeville, Langa, Nyanga.

It chanced that I was in Pretoria at this time. My evidence was required in the Treason Trial as it entered its fourth year, and my ban had been temporarily waived to allow me to give it. The burden of my evidence was the burden of this book. It was a description of what the Congress movement has stood for, of the reasons for our actions, the method we have embraced, the goals which we mean to achieve, and the South Africa we envisage.

Meanwhile, the A.N.C. was preparing itself for yet another non-violent assault upon the Pass Laws. Our preparations were neither in their infancy nor yet fully mature, and it was our intention, for reasons which I have explained earlier, not to launch the new campaign until our people were thoroughly briefed and completely ready to participate and endure.

But the Pan-African Congress[3] had also in mind a programme of agitation against the passes. Their method was to go to police stations, leaving their passes at home, and court arrest. Taking the country as a whole, they were organised only in a few centres. When it came to the point the police—in places[4] where they did not lose their heads—met the challenge by arresting a handful of leaders and ignoring their followers. The followers were thus placed in a position where they were still in possession of their passes, and their protest against them was being overlooked.

Fully conversant with the A.N.C. view that the people were not yet ready for the launching of an anti-pass campaign, Pan-Africanist leader Robert Sobukwe called on all Africans to follow him in leaving his pass at home and declaring this fact to the police. His call cut across A.N.C. plans for an orderly, carefully mounted campaign with a deliberately timed climax. Except in a small number of centres in the Transvaal and the Cape, the response to Sobukwe's appeal was mild. There was no sign that the campaign would snowball—and unless this had happened it could not have succeeded, since there was no country-wide organisation behind it.

But at Sharpeville the police perpetrated their murderous shootings. At Langa, Philip Kgosana turned back 30,000 demonstrators and thus avoided bloodshed, and at Nyanga the whole demonstration degenerated into prolonged riot and arson. Suddenly everything was in a different perspective. The guns of Sharpeville echoed across the world, and nowhere except among totalitarians was there any doubt about the true nature of what had occurred. The Government had placed beyond question the implacable, wanton brutality of their régime.

In the new situation created by the gunmen of Sharpeville,

---

[3] For the genesis of this movement, see page 165.
[4] Such as Evaton.

the A.N.C. at once went into action. From Pretoria, to which my banned state confined me, I called for a national day of mourning on 28th March for the victims and their families. On this day I asked people to stay at home and treat it as a day of prayer. The response was good, and in some centres it was magnificent.[5] Moreover, it was multi-racial, and went far beyond our usual allies. Many churches were open for prayer throughout the land, and students of all races participated in the mourning.

But passive mourning and active prayer seemed to the A.N.C. leadership to be not enough. The Pass system had claimed more victims, death and gaol being its allies. Congress called for the burning of passes. We did not desire to leave our shackles at home. We desired to be rid of them. I burned my Reference Book, others burned theirs, and the bonfires began to grow in number.

The Government replied promptly to the threat by declaring unlawful the two pass-carrying Congresses, and by proclaiming a State of Emergency. Units of the army were called out to reinforce the police. Arrests began on a large scale, and went on until 20,000 South Africans of all colours had been drafted into detention. A few evaded the police net and sat out the Emergency in more hospitable places, and a handful appears to have left for the duration.[6]

My own arrest took place, like many others, in the small hours of the morning. I was staying in the home of white Pretoria friends, the Brinks—a home distinguished by a complete absence of any hint of colour-bar. My host entered my bedroom with the police in order to arouse me. He himself was already under arrest. I had to drag myself from sleep—no easy matter, since in these days I sat up late studying documents and preparing myself nightly for the next day's ordeal in the witness-box. The police lost no time in placing me under arrest. They could not, however, produce any warrant, and in fact the arrests were illegal since at that time the Emergency had not been gazetted.

After the house had been searched, we were taken out to the police car. Dr. Lang was picked up, but at the home of Fr. Mark Nye, an Anglican priest in charge of a mission which gave hospitality to the Treason Trial accused, the police drew a blank. He had heard he was "wanted" and had already surrendered himself. We met up with Fr. Nye at the Pretoria Central Police Station,

[5] Many Pan-Africanists were among those who respected this day.
[6] I do not, in general, approve of this latter type of exodus, though it has strengthened our representation abroad. On a larger scale it could be demoralising at home. Only the Vice-President of A.N.C., Mr. Oliver Tambo, left with our prior agreement, and his departure had been intended before the crisis—we wanted a roving ambassador.

where we were shocked and horrified to find Miss Hannah Stanton also under arrest.

The morning was bitterly cold, especially for a man like me accustomed to the warm coastal belt. We longed in vain for a hot drink. Our reception was none too cordial. I was wearing conventional emblems of mourning for the Sharpeville victims— a black tie and black crêpe. The white head warder ordered me in harsh tones to divest myself of them, adding that the wearing of decorations and the exchange of signs would not be tolerated. He made his point with somewhat unnecessary emphasis— nobody showed any reluctance to obey him. Later, when his crisis was over, this officer relaxed towards us and proved quite friendly.

More harshness awaited me. As we were being marched to our cells in the dim light of early morning, I was obliged to slow down to negotiate a flight of steps. I was instantly slapped hard across the face from behind. I stooped to gather my hat, and I was hit again. I was not afterwards able to identify my assailant with certainty—the light was poor—but I know him to have been a white policeman. At a subsequent inquiry other detainees testified to having seen this assault, and it emerged that others too had been struck. I was angered; but not surprised. Among Africans the South African police have long been notorious for this sort of thing.

At first it looked as though my days as a detainee might be fairly "normal", even though the nights were spent in gaol. I was still giving evidence in the Treason Trial and expected for some time to appear regularly in court and meet the other accused and our defence lawyers. Two things altered this. In view of the banning of the Congresses, and the Emergency, our Defence Team withdrew, and from that time until near the end of the State of Emergency the defence was conducted by two of the accused, Duma Nokwe and Nelson Mandela. These two men, though not old in years, were among the foremost leaders of the A.N.C.

Secondly, my health declined. I was subject to an acute recurrence of high blood pressure, apparently the result of the protracted daily strain of giving evidence. I was removed to the prison hospital where I remained throughout my detention. Nevertheless, I was able to continue to give evidence, though under difficulties, and the Bench gave me every consideration and indulgence. As long as it was necessary they allowed the court hours to be determined by what my doctors felt I could stand up to. I deeply regretted being the cause of thus lengthening the ordeal of the accused. I was greatly comforted in these days of stress by the solicitude of the defence attorney, Michael Parkington, and the diligent care and humane manner of Dr. M. de Villiers, who attended me. The latter, especially, greatly eased the tension of those days, as far as Prison Regulations allowed.

Vigilant steps were taken to seal me off from other prisoners. (I believe this was true of some other detainees too.) Even African warders were under instructions not to speak to me. Especially as long as my illness kept me confined to bed for most of the day, I led a solitary life. Nevertheless, I do not remember my cell as a place of boredom. It became, in fact, a place of sanctuary, a place where I could make up for the neglect of religious meditation occasioned by the hurly-burly of public life. There was time, there was quietness, there was comparative solitude. I used it. Frail man that I am, I pray humbly that I may never forget the opportunity God gave me to rededicate myself, to consider the problems of our resistance to bondage, and above all to be quiet in His Presence. My whitewashed cell became my chapel, my place of retreat.

I was further nurtured in this regard by regular visits from the Rev. Mr. Junod, chaplain to condemned men in the Pretoria Central Prison,[7] and an ardent champion of Penal Reform in South Africa; and by two visits from a retired minister of the Dutch Reformed Church, Ds. Reynecke, whom I had known in our days on the Christian Council.

For the first three months of detention I saw nothing of the other detainees. Then, at the end of June, I was told that nothing in the regulations debarred me from being with them when they were in the prison yard for exercise. I used the opportunity at once, but only in a limited way, since my health prevented frequent visits. I made a point of being with them on Sundays at times of worship, and on occasions, after Mr. Junod had gone overseas, I conducted the services myself. Other prisoners did the same, and our communal worship was marked by a high level of seriousness—and by magnificent singing.

My liberty to associate with the other detainees lasted for no more than five weeks. Then, one afternoon, they demonstrated against the unexplained curtailment of their exercise time by refusing to march back into the lock-up. At this point the hospital detainees (there were two of us) asked to be taken back to our own cells. I had not long returned when I was taken to the officer in command, who accused me of having stirred up trouble among the detainees. He added that according to his officer in

[7] He has since been dismissed by the Government.

charge the detainees had been unruly ever since I was allowed among them. I hotly refuted this. The colonel said he would accept my word—but all the same, I was not again allowed these visits.

The most precious visits were those of my wife, who twice made the 1,000-mile journey to see me. The least welcome visitors were the three security police who called on me to charge me formally on three main counts—one, burning my reference book; two, disobeying a law by way of protest; and three, 102 counts of inciting others to do the same. This case eventually came before the court in June. With repeated adjournments it dragged on until the end of the Emergency at the end of August, when I was found guilty on the first two counts and not guilty on the remaining 102. For burning my pass I was sentenced to six months without option of a fine, suspended for three years because of my health. For disobeying a law by way of protest I was sentenced to a year or £100. I intended to make a statement before the imposing of sentence, but in the event I did not do this.[8]

Thanks to the magnificent defence my lawyers provided in this trial, and thanks to the generosity of friends who paid my fine, I was soon a free man again—free to go home to Groutville and live under the terms of my ban. My relief was marred by knowledge of the damage done to the lives of so great a number of detainees, and by the continued imprisonment of many of my fellow-fighters for freedom, who languish in gaols throughout the land.

I carry away from my trial one moving memory—not of the court or the prosecution or even of the brilliant defence, but of the spectators. The area of the court accommodating them was always thronged, and I heard later that many people had to be turned away. Apartheid prevailed in the seating arrangements, of course; but the spectators were a multi-racial company all the same. There, in embryo, was a portrayal of my new South Africa, a company of men and women of goodwill, learning to begin work on the building of a structure both permanent and real. Indeed, they have already begun.

Before I embarked on the first stage of my journey home I went back to the gaol which had been my home for five months, to bid farewell to the hospital staff and my warders, and to collect my belongings.

From there I was taken by white ladies of the Black Sash to the Anglican St. Benedict's Retreat House in Johannesburg. My inquisitiveness got the better of me. In response to my im-

[8] See Appendix C.

portuning, my Black Sash friends revealed how my fine had been paid. They had paid it. The Defence and Aid Fund, which came magnificently to the rescue of the detainees,[9] was to reimburse them. Later I learned that Canon Collins of Christian Action had wired £100 from England to the Defence and Aid Fund. What an encouraging chain-reaction of kindness!

I travelled to Natal by train in the company of a veteran of the Resistance, Dr. Conco, a Treason Trial defendant who had arranged his trip to be at my disposal as friend, medical adviser and equerry. (Lest the term "equerry" should seem to stem from self-importance, I must explain that the idea that I am no longer a chief does not seem to have cut much ice among Africans. My people *still* refuse to let me travel alone!) My heart bleeds for Dr. Conco and men like him—a ruined medical practice, five years of anxiety and misery, constant absence from home, devastating impoverishment—and yet what courage!

We were besieged on the train. News that I was aboard got round. A white ticket collector helped to spread the tidings. As I moved along the crowded corridor he called out: "Make way, move out of the way. Don't you know this is Chief Luthuli? Don't you know your own leader? Stand out of the way!" Many called on Dr. Conco and me in our compartment, both Africans and Indians, some out of curiosity, some to express pleasure and allegiance, and at least one to report back to the Special Branch. We had left Johannesburg just after nine o'clock in the morning. It was midnight before we were free to retire.

In Durban I was joined by my wife who had, in spite of a severe fever, risen in the dark in Groutville and come in to Durban to meet me. It cost her a week in bed. There was also at the Durban Station to meet me my friend Dr. Taylor and two of my daughters, Dr. Albertina and Staff Nurse Hilda. At the close of the day we went back to Groutville and another warm welcome.

[9] This Fund was inspired by Bishop Reeves, financed from several countries, and administered by a committee under South African ex-Labour Parliamentarian, Alex. Hepple.

If friendships make a man rich, then I am rich indeed. I grieve over the ban which, until May 1964, cuts me off from my many friends in all parts of South Africa. But I grieve more deeply for the men and women—their number is not known—whose desire for sanity in South Africa, whose insistence on no more than our human dignity, has led to banishment, deportation and gaol, while their families suffer poverty and acute distress. I have no illusions. Their number will grow.

But the struggle goes on, bans, banishments, deportations, gaol or not. We do not struggle with guns and violence, and the Supremacist's array of weapons is powerless against the spirit. The struggle goes on as much in gaol as out of it, and every time cruel men injure or kill defenceless ones they lose ground. The Supremacist illusion is that this is a battle of numbers, a battle of race, a battle of modern armaments against primitives. It is not. It is right against wrong, good against evil, the espousal of what is twisted, distorted and maimed against the yearning for health. They rejoice in what hurts the weak man's mind and soul. They embrace what hurts their own soul.

Since the State of Emergency ended in August 1960 the struggle has gone into further phases. The Promotion of Bantu Self-Government Act[1] had borne bitter fruit in Pondoland. For months now a local State of Emergency has been in force there. Were it needed, Pondoland would afford clear demonstration that our rejection of the whole apartheid ethos is not the product of Congress extremists. Even the Minister for Bantu Administration, Mr. de Wet Nel, looked for an alternative explanation of the Pondoland unrest. He said it was the result of the activities in that area of white Communists. He suggested that they had been landed on the coast from submarines. When asked in Parliament why he did not arrest them, he replied that they ran into the hills when they saw the police coming.

Pondoland is sealed off by the Emergency regulations obtaining there. Precise factual information is hard to come by. However, certain things do emerge. In Pondoland, the largest of the Bantustans, there have been deaths[2] as the result of police shoot-

---

[1] See pages 178ff.
[2] Certainly not fewer than thirty.

ings, and accurate numbers of the casualties have not been released. Why? Is it a slow-motion Sharpeville? Besides this, people have been spirited out of the area on a large scale by Government forces. Their whereabouts are unknown except to the authorities. There are reports of men herded into barbed-wire enclosures without covering while they wait to have their papers examined, sometimes for two or three days. Pro-Government Chiefs carry out their duties, as defined by the Government, behind the protection of heavily armed bodyguards—Mr. de Wet Nel speaks of these as "civic guards". And in Pondoland, army and police force for the first time work together in close co-ordination.

This last is a new feature in South African life. Since the Emergency of 1960, a thorough reorganisation has taken place in the relation between police force and army. The army has a new role—not the defence of our borders, but "internal security". It is clear that when we press our claims to the rights of citizenship and human dignity, this newly organised force will be turned on us as a last resort. Pondoland is witnessing the experimental stages of the new alliance.

But the situation in Pondoland is no new thing. It is the latest in a series which includes Zeerust, Sekhukhuniland, Natal, and now the ward on the Zulu Paramount. New techniques are being elaborated, a new stage has been reached. And now as never before the Government is responsible for the civil violence that takes place, since they have banned the one politically experienced organisation in Pondoland whose influence has always been fully deployed against violence.

If Pondoland causes us anguish, there are other things which hearten us. The Nationalist Government's own success in driving overseas capital away from South Africa tells in our favour. We do not want South Africa to be poor; but we do not desire any continuance of the system whereby our labour and foreign capital keep the present state of affairs indefinitely in existence.

Nor do we desire the isolation of our country. But the progressive isolation of the men who live by the apartheid creed is desirable, if only because they are sick with a loathsome disease. The outcome of the Commonwealth Prime Ministers' Conference gladdens us, primarily because of the stand made there for the things we believe in. Had there been an attempt to accommodate Dr. Verwoerd's wild dream, the end of the Commonwealth would have been in sight because of a basic betrayal of the things the Commonwealth stands for. Now it is strong in a world shaken by the myths of Hitler, Mussolini, and other despots. I do not doubt but that we shall return when South Africa is differently ordered.

Even the withdrawal of the Dutch Reformed Church from the World Council does not dismay me. I deplore the divisions of Christendom. But I think the withdrawal is logical, for I do not see how any Church which does not openly oppose and denounce apartheid can have much in common with the rest of Christendom. Yet even the Dutch Reformed Church may one day find itself, without contradiction, back within the World Council. The voices in its own ranks which today it derides and shouts down, are the voices of its own prophets.

The task is not finished. South Africa is not yet a home for all her sons and daughters. Such a home we wish to ensure. From the beginning our history has been one of ascending unities, the breaking of tribal, racial and credal barriers. The past cannot hope to have a life sustained by itself, wrenched from the whole. There remains before us the building of a new land, a home for men who are black, white, brown, from the ruins of the old narrow groups, a synthesis of the rich cultural strains which we have inherited. There remains to be achieved our integration with the rest of our continent. Somewhere ahead there beckons a civilisation, a culture, which will take its place in the parade of God's history beside other great human syntheses, Chinese, Egyptian, Jewish, European. It will not necessarily be all black; but it will be African.

The task is immense. Dr. Verwoerd, a man of my generation, will not even see that it is there, he will not set his hand to the plough. Some of my own people will sell their birthright for a mess of pottage, and feed thereafter out of the Nationalist garbage can. The present and the immediate future are pregnant with anguish and suffering for men of all races in South Africa.

It could be avoided. We could not achieve the new South Africa overnight, but we could begin to build it. We have suffered enough. We have suffered rape, plunder and demolition, selfishness, avarice and oppression. We seek no vengeance. More than other continents, perhaps, and as much as any other nation on this continent, we need the ways of peace, the ways of industry, the ways of concord.

Will the outstretched hand be taken? I fear not, not by the devisers of apartheid. It is a black hand. The minds of Dr. Verwoerd and his company are already preoccupied with their last bunker, with the picture they will make as they go down—martyrs to what? Why must they continue to destroy, when so much lies ready for the hand that will create?

The struggle must go on—the struggle to make the opportunity for the building to begin. The struggle will go on. I speak humbly and without levity when I say that, God giving me strength and courage enough, I shall die, if need be, for this cause. But I do not want to die until I have seen the building begun.

Mayibuye iAfrika! Come, Africa, come!

THE ROAD TO FREEDOM IS VIA
THE CROSS

*A Public Statement made by Albert Luthuli immediately
after he was dismissed from his position as Chief by the
Government in November, 1952. It was issued jointly by the
African National Congress and the Natal Indian Congress*

I have been dismissed from the Chieftainship of the Abase-
Makolweni Tribe in the Groutville Mission Reserve. I presume
that this has been done by the Governor-General in his capacity
as Supreme Chief of the "Native" people of the Union of South
Africa save those of the Cape Province. I was democratically
elected to this position in 1935 by the people of Groutville
Mission Reserve and was duly approved and appointed by the
Governor-General.

PATH OF MODERATION

Previous to being a chief I was a schoolteacher for about seventeen years. In these past thirty years or so I have striven with
tremendous zeal and patience to work for the progress and welfare of my people and for their harmonious relations with other
sections of our multi-racial society in the Union of South Africa.
In this effort I always pursued what liberal-minded people rightly
regarded as the path of moderation. Over this great length of
time I have, year by year, gladly spent hours of my time with
such organisations as the Church and its various agencies such
as the Christian Council of South Africa, the Joint Council of
Europeans and Africans, and the now defunct Native Representative Council.

In so far as gaining citizenship rights and opportunities for
the unfettered development of the African people, who will deny
that thirty years of my life have been spent knocking in vain,
patiently, moderately and modestly at a closed and barred door?

What have been the fruits of my many years of moderation?
Has there been any reciprocal tolerance or moderation from the
Government, be it Nationalist or United Party? No! On the

contrary, the past thirty years have seen the greatest number of laws restricting our rights and progress until today we have reached a stage where we have almost no rights at all: no adequate land for our occupation, our only asset, cattle, dwindling, no security of homes, no decent and remunerative employment, more restrictions to freedom of movement through passes, curfew regulations, influx control measures; in short, we have witnessed in these years an intensification of our subjection to ensure and protect white supremacy.

A NEW SPIRIT

It is with this background and with a full sense of responsibility that, under the auspices of the African National Congress (Natal), I have joined my people in the new spirit which moves them today, the spirit that revolts openly and boldly against injustice and expresses itself in a determined and non-violent manner. Because of my association with the African National Congress in this new spirit which has found an effective and legitimate way of expression in the non-violent Passive Resistance Campaign, I was given a two-week limit ultimatum by the Secretary for Native Affairs calling upon me to choose between the African National Congress and the chieftainship of the Groutville Mission Reserve. He alleged that my association with Congress in its non-violent Passive Resistance Campaign was an act of disloyalty to the State. I did not, and do not, agree with this view. Viewing non-Violent Passive Resistance as a non-revolutionary and, therefore, a most legitimate and humane political pressure technique for a people denied all effective forms of constitutional striving, I saw no real conflict in my dual leadership of my people: leader of this tribe as chief, and political leader in Congress.

SERVANT OF PEOPLE

I saw no cause to resign from either. This stand of mine which resulted in my being sacked from the chieftainship might seem foolish and disappointing to some liberal and moderate Europeans and non-Europeans with whom I have worked these many years and with whom I still hope to work. This is no parting of the ways but "a launching farther into the deep". I invite them to join us in our unequivocal pronouncement of all legitimate African aspirations and in our firm stand against injustice and oppression.

I do not wish to challenge my dismissal, but I would like to suggest that in the interest of the institution of chieftainship in these modern times of democracy the Government should define more precisely and make more widely known the status, functions and privileges of chiefs. '

My view has been, and still is, that a chief is primarily a servant of his people. He is the voice of his people. He is the voice of his people in local affairs. Unlike a Native Commissioner, he is part and parcel of the Tribe, and not a local agent of the Government. Within the bounds of loyalty it is conceivable that he may vote and press the claims of his people even if they should be unpalatable to the Government of the day. He may use all legitimate modern techniques to get these demands satisfied. It is inconceivable how chiefs could effectively serve the wider and common interest of their own tribe without co-operating with other leaders of the people, both the natural leaders (chiefs) and leaders elected democratically by the people themselves.

MUST FIGHT FEARLESSLY

It was to allow for these wider associations intended to promote the common national interests of the people as against purely local interests that the Government in making rules governing chiefs did not debar them from joining political associations so long as those associations had not been declared "by the Minister to be subversive of or prejudicial to constituted Government". The African National Congress, its non-Violent Passive Resistance Campaign, may be of nuisance value to the Government, but it is not subversive since it does not seek to overthrow the form and machinery of the state but only urges for the inclusion of all sections of the community in a partnership in the Government of the country on the basis of equality.

Laws and conditions that tend to debase human personality—a God-given force—be they brought about by the State or other individuals, must be relentlessly opposed in the spirit of defiance shown by St. Peter when he said to the rulers of his day: "Shall we obey God or man?" No one can deny that in so far as non-Whites are concerned in the Union of South Africa, laws and conditions that debase human personality abound. Any chief worthy of his position must fight fearlessly against such debasing conditions and laws. If the Government should resort to dismissing such chiefs, it may find itself dismissing many chiefs or causing people to dismiss from their hearts chiefs who are indifferent to the needs of the people through fear of dismissal by the Government. Surely the Government cannot place chiefs in such an uncomfortable and invidious position.

EVEN DEATH

As for myself, with a full sense of responsibility and a clear conviction, I decided to remain in the struggle for extending democratic rights and responsibilities to all sections of the South African community. I have embraced the non-Violent Passive Resistance technique in fighting for freedom because I am convinced it is the only non-revolutionary, legitimate and humane way that could be used by people denied, as we are, effective constitutional means to further aspirations.

The wisdom or foolishness of this decision I place in the hands of the Almighty.

What the future has in store for me I do not know. It might be ridicule, imprisonment, concentration camp, flogging, banishment, and even death. I only pray to the Almighty to strengthen my resolve so that none of those grim possibilities may deter me from striving, for the sake of the good name of our beloved country, the Union of South Africa, to make it a true democracy and a true union in form and spirit of all the communities in the land.

My only painful concern at times is that of the welfare of my family, but I try even in this regard, in a spirit of trust and surrender to God's will as I see it, to say: "God will provide."

It is inevitable that in working for Freedom some individuals and some families must take the lead and suffer: The Road to Freedom is via the CROSS.

MAYIBUYE!

AFRIKA! AFRIKA! AFRIKA!

THE FREEDOM CHARTER

*Adopted at the Congress of the People at Kliptown, Johannes-
burg, on June 25 and 26, 1955*

We, the People of South Africa, declare for all our country and
the world to know:

that South Africa belongs to all who live in it, black and
white, and that no government can justly claim authority
unless it is based on the will of all the people;

that our people have been robbed of their birthright to land,
liberty and peace by a form of government founded on injustice and inequality;

that our country will never be prosperous or free until all our
people live in brotherhood, enjoying equal rights and opportunities;

that only a democratic state, based on the will of all the
people, can secure to all their birthright without distinction of
colour, race, sex, or belief;

And therefore we, the People of South Africa, black and white
together—equals, countrymen and brothers—adopt this Freedom
Charter. And we pledge ourselves to strive together, sparing
neither strength nor courage, until the democratic changes here
set out have been won.

THE PEOPLE SHALL GOVERN!

Every man and woman shall have the right to vote for and to
stand as a candidate for all bodies which make laws;

All people shall be entitled to take part in the administration
of the country;

The rights of the people shall be the same, regardless of race,
colour or sex;

All bodies of minority rule, advisory boards, councils and
authorities shall be replaced by democratic organs of self-
government.

212

ALL NATIONAL GROUPS SHALL HAVE EQUAL RIGHTS!

There shall be equal status in the bodies of state, in the courts and in the schools for all national groups and races.

All people shall have equal right to use their own languages and to develop their own folk culture and customs;

All national groups shall be protected by law against insults to their race and national pride;

The preaching and practice of national, race or colour discrimination and contempt shall be a punishable crime;

All apartheid laws and practices shall be set aside.

THE PEOPLE SHALL SHARE IN THE COUNTRY'S WEALTH!

The national wealth of our country, the heritage of all South Africans, shall be restored to the people;

The mineral wealth beneath the soil, the banks and monopoly industry shall be transferred to the ownership of the people as a whole;

All other industry and trade shall be controlled to assist the well-being of the people;

All people shall have equal rights to trade where they choose, to manufacture and to enter all trades, crafts and professions.

THE LAND SHALL BE SHARED AMONG THOSE WHO WORK IT!

Restriction of land ownership on a racial basis shall be ended, and all the land redivided amongst those who work it, to banish famine and land hunger;

The State shall help the peasants with implements, seed, tractors and dams to save the soil and assist the tillers;

Freedom of movement shall be guaranteed to all who work on the land;

All shall have the right to occupy land wherever they choose;

People shall not be robbed of their cattle, and forced labour and farm prisons shall be abolished.

ALL SHALL BE EQUAL BEFORE THE LAW!

No one shall be imprisoned, deported or restricted without a fair trial;

No one shall be condemned by the order of any Government official;

The courts shall be representative of all the people:

Imprisonment shall be only for serious crimes against the people, and shall aim at re-education, not vengeance;

The police force and army shall be open to all on an equal basis and shall be the helpers and protectors of the people;

All laws which discriminate on grounds of race, colour or belief shall be repealed.

ALL SHALL ENJOY EQUAL HUMAN RIGHTS!

The law shall guarantee to all their right to speak, to organise, to meet together, to publish, to preach, to worship, and to educate their children;

The privacy of the house from police raids shall be protected by law;

All shall be free to travel without restriction from countryside to town, from province to province, and from South Africa abroad;

Pass laws, permits and all other laws restricting these freedoms shall be abolished.

THERE SHALL BE WORK AND SECURITY!

All who work shall be free to form trade unions, to elect their officers, and to make wage agreements with their employers;

The State shall recognise the right and duty of all to work, and to draw full unemployment benefits;

Men and women of all races shall receive equal pay for equal work;

There shall be a forty-hour working week, a national minimum wage, paid annual leave, and sick leave for all workers, and maternity leave on full pay for all working mothers;

Miners, domestic workers, farm workers and civil servants shall have the same right as all others who work;

Child labour, compound labour, the tot system and contract labour shall be abolished.

THE DOORS OF LEARNING AND OF CULTURE SHALL BE OPENED!

The Government shall discover, develop and encourage national talent for the enhancement of our cultural life;

All the cultural treasures of mankind shall be open to all, by free exchange of books, ideas and contact with other lands;

The aim of education shall be to teach the youth to love their people and their culture, to honour human brotherhood, liberty and peace;

Education shall be free, compulsory, universal and equal for all children;

Higher education and technical training shall be opened to all by means of state allowances and scholarships awarded on the basis of merit;

Adult illiteracy shall be ended by a mass state education plan;

Teachers shall have all the rights of other citizens;

The colour-bar in cultural life, in sport and in education shall be abolished.

THERE SHALL BE HOUSES, SECURITY AND COMFORT!

All people shall have the right to live where they choose, to be decently housed, and to bring up their families in comfort and security;

Unused housing space shall be made available to the people;

Rent and prices shall be lowered, food plentiful, and no one shall go hungry;

A preventive health scheme shall be run by the State;

Free medical care and hospitalisation shall be provided for all, with special care for mothers and young children;

Slums shall be demolished and new suburbs built, where all have transport, roads, lighting, playing-fields, crèches and social centres;

The aged, the orphans, the disabled and the sick shall be cared for by the State;

Rest, leisure and recreation shall be the right of all;

Fenced locations and ghettoes shall be abolished and laws which break up families shall be repealed.

THERE SHALL BE PEACE AND FRIENDSHIP!

South Africa shall be a fully independent state, which respects the rights and sovereignty of all nations;

South Africa shall strive to maintain world peace and the settlement of all international disputes by negotiation—not war;

Peace and friendship amongst all our people shall be secured by upholding the equal rights, opportunities and status of all;

The people of the protectorates—Basutoland, Bechuanaland and Swaziland—shall be free to decide for themselves their own future;

The rights of all the peoples of Africa to independence and self-government shall be recognised and shall be the basis of close co-operation.

Let all who love their people and their country now say, as we say here: "THESE FREEDOMS WE WILL FIGHT FOR, SIDE BY SIDE, THROUGHOUT OUR LIVES, UNTIL WE HAVE WON OUR LIBERTY."

LUTHULI'S UNDELIVERED STATE-MENT AT THE TIME OF HIS TRIAL FOR BURNING HIS PASS

This statement was to have been made to the court before the passing of sentence, after which I had been found guilty of burning my pass, guilty of disobeying a law by way of protest, and not guilty of incitement. At the time I voluntarily accepted the advice of my lawyers, and because of the very poor state of my health I did not make it. I am still not sure whether I made the right decision. I place it on record here and leave the reader to decide. Whether he applauds or derides, he will know what I feel.

I stand before you, your Worship, charged with the destruction of my Reference Book (or Pass) and because of that with the crime of inciting my people to do the same. I have pleaded legally not guilty to all the charges.

What I did, I did because I, together with the overwhelming majority of my people, condemn the pass system as the cause of much evil and suffering among us. We charge that it is nothing less than an instrument of studied degradation and humiliation of us as a people, a badge of slavery, a weapon used by the authorities to keep us in a position of inferiority.

It cannot be very easy for you, sir, to understand the very deep hatred all Africans feel for a pass. I say this not as a mark of disrespect to your person, sir, but because only a direct experience and contact with a pass and all that it means can make one really understand and appreciate the justice of our charge against the evil thing, the pass. We are deeply conscious of, and grateful for, the fact that there is a growing number of fellow white South Africans who appreciate our situation and feel deeply about it; but they, too, can never really fully understand the depth of our suffering. Can anyone who has not gone through it possibly imagine what has happened when they read in the Press of a routine police announcement that there has been a pass raid in a location? The fear of the loud, rude bang on the door in the middle of the night, the bitter humiliation of an undignified search, the shame of husband and wife being huddled out of bed in front of their children by the police and taken off to the police cell.

If there is a law in any country in the whole wide world which makes it a crime in many instances for husband and wife to live together, which separates eighteen-year-olds from their parents, I have yet to learn of it. But the pass does so in the Union of South Africa.

Each year half a million of my people are arrested under the pass laws. Government Annual Reports tell of this tragic story. But statistics can tell only half the tale. The physical act of arrest and detention with the consequence of a broken home, a lost job, a loss of earnings, is only part of this grim picture. The deep humiliation felt by a black man, whether he be a labourer, an advocate, a nurse, a teacher or a professor, or even a minister of religion, when, over and over again, he hears the shout, "Kaffir, where is your pass?—*Kaffir, waar's jo paas?*" fills in the rest of this grim picture.

Our feelings about the pass laws are not new or something born in recent years. The whole history of the African people since Union is studded with our complaints, petitions, mass demonstrations, pass burnings, etc.

In all these campaigns, sir, over the years, other sections of the South African population have gradually come to see the justice of our claim that the Pass Laws are oppressive in the extreme. One way or another, large and varied sections of the population have come to understand that the well-being of South Africa, no less than the cause of humanity and justice, demands the abolition of the drastic curtailment of these laws. I will refer you, sir, only to such well-known facts as these: that in the war years the late Mr. Deneys Reitz, then Minister of Native Affairs, spoke publicly of the need to repeal these laws, and in fact, for a time, virtually suspended the system of summary arrest on which these laws are based; then in 1948 the Fagan Commission, presided over by a man who as Minister of Native Affairs had administered these laws, and as judge had punished those who broke them, recommended a drastic revision and curtailment; that in more recent years these views have been echoed by churches, by the South African Institute of Race Relations, by at least two recognised political parties in the country, the Liberal Party and the Progressive Party, and by many hundreds of people and organisations of different kinds. In fact, sir, most public commissions appointed since 1912 by successful governments have been, to say the least, highly critical of it. World opinion generally has been critical too, and some sections of it, at times, outspokenly condemnatory. It has been a cause of regret and even bitterness amongst our people that in spite of such widespread condemnation, internal and external, of the inhumanity of these laws, the present Government has not only not seen it fit to curtail or abolish them, but has extended and intensified their operation, cancelled all exemptions from these laws and, to add insult to injury, extended them, for the first time in the history of our country, to our womenfolk. All this is done in terms of the "Abolition of Passes and the Co-ordination of Documents Act". We are asked to be grateful for this. Grateful for what? For stitching neatly into a single book various pieces of paper formerly needed to comply with the law. If this is not contempt for our National feelings, sir, it must be cruel mockery.

Each year since the so-called "Abolition of Passes Act" came into effect more of our people have been arrested for pass law offences. We do not have to read the Government Blue Books or Statistics to know this. Almost every African family knows this to their cost from their family experience.

It has long been clear to us in the Liberatory Movement that this Government action, to enforce and extend these laws, would increase tension between the African people and the Government and further strain white-black relations to the injury of the true interests and welfare of our country.

I do not want to comment much on the tragic events that occurred on 21st March of this year at Sharpeville, save to say merely this. All versions of this shocking event agree that the crowd which collected at the Police Station in Sharpeville did so because of—and only because of—the Pass Laws. All that is in dispute is whether people come to hear an official statement on the future of the Pass Laws or to demonstrate against these laws. Whichever version may be true, the end was an event which shocked and horrified every decent South African, black and white, and outraged the world. A large number of my people lost their lives, and a much larger number were wounded. If ever the cup of bitterness against the Pass Laws ran over, it was then. It was with deep feelings of disgust for the Pass Laws that many people, black and white throughout the country, responded magnificently to the A.N.C. call to observe a National day of mourning to mourn these late victims of the Pass Laws and for Africans to burn their passes.

In such an atmosphere it is understandable that hundreds, perhaps thousands, of Africans, to show their mourning, voluntarily destroyed the symbol of bondage and burnt their passes; spontaneously, without urging, sir, many, many did so.

For me, sir, the situation demanded a momentous decision. I felt it my inescapable duty to give meaning to the Congress call to observe in a peaceful way the Day of Mourning and to bear witness in a practical way to our abhorrence for a pass. I saw no other effective peaceful way than to burn my own pass. This I did.

There comes a time, sir, when a leader must give as practical a demonstration of his convictions and willingness to live up to the demands of the cause, as he expects of his people. I felt that was the hour in our history, and in my life, for this demonstration. I am not sorry nor ashamed of what I did. I could not have done less than I did and still live with my conscience. I would rightly lose the confidence of my people, and earn the disrespect of right-thinking people in my country and in the world, and the disdain of posterity.

In all humility, I say that I acted as was my duty in response to the highest moral law in the best interest of the people of South Africa, because I am convinced that the urgent need of our country, for the maintenance of peace and harmony amongst the various races, black and white, is the immediate and whole-sale abolition of the pass. It is my firm belief that it is the duty of all right-thinking people, black and white, who have the true interest of our country at heart, to strive for this without flinching.

A. LUTHULI

Also available in Fount Paperbacks

BOOKS BY C. S. LEWIS

Christian Reflections

'This collection . . . deserves the warmest of Christian welcomes on this happy reappearance . . . a devastating counter-attack on the "new morality" and a magnificent restatement of the essence of the Gospel and the faith.'

Church Times

The Four Loves

'He has never written better. Nearly every page scintillates with observations which are illuminating, provocative and original.'

Church Times

Prayer: Letters to Malcolm

'A book full of wisdom, of bitter honesty and of deep charity. It nowhere tells us "how to pray" but . . . stimulates afresh that hunger and thirst for God without which we should never pray at all.'

J. B. Phillips

The Pilgrim's Regress

'A welcome reappearance in paperback. Bunyanesque in form, as the title suggests, this reissue may well pick up a new generation of readers . . .'

Methodist Recorder

Also available in Fount Paperbacks

Audacity to Believe
SHEILA CASSIDY

'A story of extraordinarily unpretentious courage in the horror of Chile after Allende's overthrow. It is easy to read, totally sincere and sometimes moving. Sheila Cassidy is totally disarming.'

Frank O'Reilly
The Furrow

Prayer for Pilgrims
SHEILA CASSIDY

'. . . a direct and practical book about prayer . . . has the freshness of someone who writes of what she has personally discovered . . . many people . . . will be grateful for this book and helped by it.'

Neville Ward
Church Times

The General Next to God
RICHARD COLLIER

'An absorbing, sympathetic record of the man (General Booth) and his family and the movement they created.'

Michael Foot
Evening Standard

Also available in Fount Paperbacks

Mother Teresa: Her People and Her Work
DESMOND DOIG

'Desmond Doig has written a beautiful book and his writing and the pictures capture Mother Teresa and her people and her work exactly. He understands it. I want to cry, with anger, with passion, with compassion, with sadness at the waste of human life and energy. But no, that is not enough, it is a waste of energy, we must do something to help her.'

Financial Times

Something Beautiful for God
MALCOLM MUGGERIDGE

'For me, Mother Teresa of Calcutta embodies Christian love in action. Her face shines with the love of Christ on which her whole life is centred. *Something Beautiful for God* is about her and the religious order she has instituted.'

Malcolm Muggeridge

A Gift for God
MOTHER TERESA

'This selection of Mother Teresa's sayings, prayers, meditations, letters and addresses on themes of love and compassion . . . touches profound spiritual themes . . . Its size belies its power to inspire and uplift.'

Church of England Newspaper

The Love of Christ
MOTHER TERESA

A further collection of Mother Teresa's writings and sayings, including hitherto unpublished extracts from her retreat addresses to her community of nuns.

'Do not read this book . . . if you do not want . . . to be shaken in conscience and shamed into loving God and other people more.'

Iain Mackenzie, Church Times

Fount Paperbacks

Fount is one of the leading paperback publishers of religious books and below are some of its recent titles.

- ☐ THE WAY OF THE CROSS Richard Holloway £1.95
- ☐ LIKE WIND ON THE GRASSES Rita Snowden £1.95
- ☐ AN INTRODUCTION TO MARITAL
     PROBLEMS Jack Dominian £2.50
- ☐ I AM WITH YOU John Woolley £2.95
- ☐ NOW AND FOR EVER Anne Townsend £1.95
- ☐ THE PERFECTION OF LOVE Tony Castle £2.95
- ☐ A PROPHETIC PEOPLE Clifford Hill £2.95
- ☐ THOMAS MORE Richard Marius £7.95
- ☐ WALKING IN THE LIGHT David Winter £1.95
- ☐ HALF WAY Jim Thompson £2.50
- ☐ THE HEART OF THE BIBLE George Appleton £4.95
- ☐ I BELIEVE Trevor Huddleston £1.75
- ☐ PRESENT CONCERNS C. S. Lewis £1.95
- ☐ PSALMS OF PRAISE Frances Hogan £2.50
- ☐ MOTHER TERESA: CONTEMPLATIVE IN THE
     HEART OF THE WORLD Angelo Devananda £2.50
- ☐ IN THE HURRICANE Adrian Hastings £2.50

All Fount paperbacks are available at your bookshop or newsagent, or they can be ordered by post from Fount Paperbacks, Cash Sales Department, G.P.O. Box 29, Douglas, Isle of Man. Please send purchase price plus 22p per book, maximum postage £3. Customers outside the UK send purchase price, plus 22p per book. Cheque, postal order or money order. No currency.

NAME (Block letters) _____

ADDRESS_____

_____

_____